Handbook of Gardening for New Zealand, With Chapters on Poultry and Bee-keeping

S. B. SEYMOUR
SURGEON DENTIST

215, COLOMBO STREET

(New Buildings near corner of Gloucester Street)

——:o:——

ESTABLISHED   -   -   -   -   1869

——:o:——

SCALE OF CHARGES:

Extraction, 2/6 per tooth; Fillings, 5/- per tooth

A REDUCTION MADE WHERE A NUMBER REQUIRE ATTENDING TO

——:o:——

ARTIFICIAL TEETH

The charges for ARTIFICIAL TEETH are made with a view to STRICT ECONOMY, regulated by such circumstances as cases present, or such materials as patients prefer.   Particulars given on application.

CONSULTATION FREE

NITROUS OXIDE (Laughing Gas) administered when required

ATTENDANCE   -   -   -   9 a.m. to 6 p.m.

215, COLOMBO STREET, CHRISTCHURCH

HANDBOOK

OF

GARDENING FOR NEW ZEALAND

WITH CHAPTERS ON

Poultry & Bee-keeping

By M. MURPHY, F.L.S.

Secretary Canterbury Agricultural and Pastoral Association, and Editor
of " New Zealand Country Journal," &c., &c.

———•●•———

"MORAL OF THE GARDEN.—Nothing teaches patience like a garden. All have to wait for the fruit of the earth. You may go round and watch the opening bud from day to day, but it takes its own time, and you cannot urge it on faster than it will. If forced, it is only torn to pieces. All the best results of a garden, like those of life, are slowly but regularly progressive. Each year does a work that nothing but a year can do. 'Learn to labour and to wait' is one of the best lessons of a garden. All that is good takes time, and comes only by growth."

SECOND EDITION. REVISED AND ENLARGED.

CHRISTCHURCH, N.Z.:

WHITCOMBE & TOMBS, LIMITED.

PREFACE TO THE FIRST EDITION.

In compiling this little work on "Gardening in New Zealand" an attempt has been made to collect the greatest amount of useful information which *could* be condensed within its limits, at the same time rendering such information as full and practicable as possible, so that the most inexperienced may with its assistance carry on the various operations of the several departments of the garden with every prospect of success. I do not claim much originality for the work, except in so far as my own experience, extending over many years in the Old Country and in the Colonies, enables me to determine the difference between the Home seasons and those of this country. Although we are at the antipodes of England, it does not follow that the seasons are exactly opposite. In New Zealand the growing season extends over a period of nine months, while in England it may be said not to exceed seven months.

Up to the present time no attempt has been made to produce a comprehensive manual of Gardening suitable to our requirements. It is true that calendars abound, and weekly instructions, but these fragmentary efforts (good so far as they go) do not enter sufficiently into details to be of much service to those persons who know little of the subject, but who, nevertheless, take pleasure in the growth of flowers, fruit, and vegetables. Much of the information embraced in the chapters of this work has been gleaned from the best authorities on the subjects treated of. I desire particularly to acknowledge my obligations in this matter to the editors of those excellent works entitled "Manuals for the Many," and Thomson's "Gardener's Assistant," Miss Omerod's

"Injurious Insects," Louden's "Encyclopædia," and others of like character. The extract matter has been thoroughly sifted, and only those portions have been chosen which from my own observations have convinced me of their suitability for New Zealand. It has not been found convenient to place within quotation marks the passages selected from the above works, because they have been altered and modified in important particulars to suit New Zealand seasons, but where the language of these authors has been found applicable, I have not hesitated to use it freely. I desire also to acknowledge my obligations to Mr. Thos. Turner, of Christchurch, a gardener of many years' experience, who has rendered me much valuable assistance in reading and correcting the proofs of this work.

The premier position in the arrangement of the matter has been allotted to the Vegetable Garden. It is, unfortunately, a notable fact that vegetable growing is much neglected by the large majority of small farmers. Cheap bread and cheap meat, with an abundance of potatoes, seem to satisfy most of those engaged in rural pursuits. It is an accepted theory that a diet consisting mainly of animal food is not conducive to good health, particularly in the case of children. Radishes, mustard and ·cress, lettuce, and spinach are all easily grown, and as purifiers of the blood cannot be surpassed in the early Spring. The latter vegetable is so highly esteemed by the French for such purposes, that it is called by them the "Broom of the Stomach." All that is required in the culture of vegetables is deep tillage, plenty of manure, and secure fencing, coupled with a practical knowledge of the subject. One quarter of an acre, well managed, would provide a large family all the year round with an ample supply of wholesome vegetables,

PREFACE TO THE SECOND EDITION.

THE first edition of this Manual of Gardening having sold
out, and a favourable reception having been accorded it by
the public of New Zealand, the author has been encouraged
to present a second edition, which has been carefully revised
and enlarged. Suggestions kindly offered by experts and
others have been acted upon where practicable. A large
addition has been made to the directions for selecting,
planting, and for the general management of fruit trees.
Wherever instructions in other sections of the work were
not considered sufficiently explicit the defect has been
remedied. Instructions for Fern Growing have been enlarged
upon by request. A chapter on Orange Culture has been
added ; also one on miscellaneous subjects, which embraces
a large amount of useful information, including a chapter on
Fowl Keeping.

Persons residing north of Napier, or in Australia, who
may wish to consult the pages of this Manual, will do
well to remember that the seasons in the parts referred
to are quite one month in advance of the South Island
of New Zealand, and allowances must accordingly be
made.

CONTENTS

—o—

GARDEN CALENDAR—1

VEGETABLE GARDEN—27

THE ORCHARD AND THE FRUIT GARDEN—43

FLOWER GARDEN—73

FLORISTS' FLOWERS—87

GRAFTING—146

HE GREENHOUSE—150

ORCHIDS—159

NEW ZEALAND PLANTS—162

THE FERNERY—166

ORANGE CULTURE—172

MISCELLANEOUS—174

INSECT PESTS AND DISEASES OF PLANTS—182

GARDEN CALENDAR

In the preface to this work the value of vegetables as an article of diet has been pointed out. It is, therefore, of the first importance that every homestead should have a piece of ground devoted to this purpose, which should be free from trees of any kind. Vegetables should not be grown between the rows of fruit trees, after the latter has attained to three years' growth, for the following reasons:—Vegetables to be of the best quality require a free circulation of sun and air, they also require that the soil should be manured and deeply dug for each crop. This treatment, while absolutely necessary for the successful growth of vegetables, is detrimental to the well-being of fruit trees, which require that an active growth of surface roots should be encouraged. This is impossible when the spade has to be

B

used. Many promising young fruit trees are destroyed in this way. In cropping a garden some attempt should be made to carry out a system of rotation, by which is meant that cabbages should not follow immediately after plants of the same order—the crops should be varied as much as is practicable. Having selected a piece of land, the first thing will be to trench it two or three feet deep, according as the nature of the soil will admit. Proceed in the following manner :—Open a trench across one end (the lowest if there is a fall) three feet wide, remove the top spit say for nine inches deep, and wheel or cart the soil to the end of the plot where it is proposed to finish the work ; loosen well the remainder of the soil, adding an abundance of manure. This done, mark off another trench the same width as the last ; throw the surface soil into the first trench, level off, manure and loosen the bottom soil as before, taking care not to throw much of the underneath soil on to the surface. Continue in this manner until the end of the plot is reached ; finish off the last trench with the surface taken from the first opening. This kind of trenching is known as Bastard trenching, and is the best for most soils. Trenching should be done as early in Autumn as possible in order that the soil may get the benefit of the Winter frosts. Trenching the ground, however, will be labour thrown away if the subsoil is naturally wet ; where water prevails thorough drainage must first be resorted to.

The following is a general calendar of work to be done in the Vegetable, Flower, and Fruit Gardens throughout the year, commencing with July. Detailed instructions will be found under the separate headings of Vegetable, Fruit, and Flower Gardens.

* JULY (corresponds with January in Britain).

It is customary to recommend the sowing of a large variety of garden seeds in July. Our own experience is that except in the North Island, or in dry and well-sheltered localities, it will be better to defer the sowing of most vegetable seeds till the middle or end of August. The

---

* Amateurs residing in the North Island, who may use this little manual as a guide, will bear in mind that the seasons, North of Napier, are a month in advance of the South Island.

principal work for July will be the trenching—in dry weather —of the ground for the reception of seeds in August and September. Continue the planting of all kinds of fruit trees, unless the soil be saturated with water, in which case it will be better to defer planting till August. Continue the pruning of all kinds of fruit trees, following the instructions given under the head of "Pruning." If fowls are kept, it will be well to let them have the run of the garden for a few hours of each day during this month. They will do good service in clearing the ground of worms, woodlice, and a host of other pests. When planting and sowing commence they must be confined to their run.

AUGUST.

Kitchen Garden.—Although August is the first month of Spring, Spring work does not really commence till towards the end of the month. In dry warm situations, two or three sowings of peas and broad beans should be made. A few potatoes of the very earliest sorts may be tried on the north side of a hedge or fence. Cabbage plants may be planted out now, and small sowings of the whole of the tribe should be made in sheltered situations; they will however in most localities require protection from the birds. Celery may be sown in a frame or under a handlight. Leeks and onions should be sown on the ground prepared in the Autumn; sow in drills twelve inches apart and very shallow, so that the seed will be nicely covered, and no more; after covering up, tread the whole of the bed gently but firmly with your feet, then rake lightly, and the job is finished. A good breadth of parsnips should now be sown in rich light soil, in drills eighteen inches apart, the plants to be thinned out to nine inches. All kinds of salads may be sown in such quantities as are likely to be required. These operations can only be carried out with advantage in dry situations. Jerusalem artichokes may now be planted in rows three feet apart, and two feet apart in the rows, six inches deep. Asparagus beds, if not already attended to, should be top-dressed with well-rotted manure.

Flower Garden.—Advantage should be taken of dry open weather for making necessary alterations in the form of the garden. This is a good time to remove the old exhausted soil from flower beds, to be replaced with fresh material, pruning and transplanting shrubs should now be completed. Some of the hardiest annuals may be sown in warmer parts of the garden towards the end of the month. Herbaceous plants may be divided with advantage, and the mixed flower borders may be much improved by careful digging over and forking in a liberal supply of old manure or fresh soil. Lawns may be formed by sowing or turfing, and old ones should be carefully mown as required, and any bad places turfed over.

Bulbs.—Crown imperials, lilies, hyacinths, ixias, narcissus, gladioli, and tulips may still be planted, always selecting a time when the ground is dry; a little sand put about the bulbs will be of service. Anemones and ranunculuses may also be planted, they thrive best in a rich sandy loam. Pinks, pansies, and carnations may be transplanted and the soil renewed with a rich compost of well-decomposed manure. In districts not subject to late Spring frosts roses may now be pruned, otherwise defer the work till next month; a plentiful supply of rich rotten manure should be applied to the beds, if not already done; a sprinkling of bone dust as well will be an improvement.

Gravel Walks.—When the gravel is soft and spongy, get two sieves—one that would not let a horse bean through, and the other somewhat larger. Gravel thus cleared of the large and small stones should be laid on, and rolled in every time the wet comes, until the surface is as solid as a rock.

SEPTEMBER.

September should be the busiest month in the kitchen garden. As seed time and seed sowing are now upon us and in general operation, and believing as we do, that many of the failures attributed to seeds may be more justly attributed to some drawback as regards the preparation of the seed bed, the sowing, covering, &c., the following useful hints on the subject will be found not undeserving of perusal:— Seeds, to germinate, require light, heat, air, and moisture. They should be sown when the ground is mellow and fine, and, if possible, before a gentle rain; and the soil should be

rolled or gently pressed upon the seed after sowing. The
best of seeds often fail from improper management. When
sown too early, while the ground is wet, they are apt to rot.
When sown too shallow, in a dry time, there may not be
sufficient moisture to sprout them, or they may be destroyed
by dry and hot weather after they have germinated, or insects
may destroy the plants as soon as they appear above ground.
The first effect of air, heat, and moisture is to change the
starchy matter of the seed into a sugary pulp, the proper
food of the embryo. If at this time the seed be withered
by exposure to heat without sufficient covering it will perish ;
or if planted in a fresh dug soil and the above change in the
nature of the seed takes place, but the earth if not pressed
upon it, the seed dries up and the embryo perishes. Others,
again, are buried too deeply, and though the seed swells,
yet sufficient warmth and air are not obtained to give it life.
The first thing in sowing is a suitable preparation of the soil,
so that the young roots may easily penetrate it. It must be
made more or less fine for different seeds. The size of a
seed is a nearly safe guide as to the depth at which it should
be sown : beans, of all kinds, at two inches ; peas, an inch
and a half ; carrots, parsnips, turnips, onions, radishes,
lettuce, cabbage, and such seeds require to be sown shallow,
almost close to the surface. The seed must be firmly fixed
in the soil and pressed by the earth on every part, in order
to retain moisture sufficient to encourage vegetation, yet not
so firmly buried as to be deprived of air, or to have their
ascending shoots impeded by too much soil above. The
earth should be pressed upon them with a roller, or by treading with the feet in case of large seeds, or by smoothing the
surface with the back of the spade, or by walking over them
on a board for the smaller kinds. In all cases seeds should
be sown in fresh-dug soil, that they might have the benefit
of the moisture within ; but they should never be put in
when the soil is really wet, as the ground will bake, and the
seeds perish. And never sow broadcast if it is desirable to
save time, expense, and trouble. When sown in drills or
rows, weeds can be more easily destroyed and the ground
kept open and loose. · Almost all kinds of vegetable seeds
may be sown this month, with a prospect of success. See
that the soil is thoroughly well prepared and well manured
with old well-mellowed dung.

Peas and broad beans should be largely sown now.

Broccoli, and all varieties of the cabbage tribe, should also be sown for general crops to be transplanted when strong enough. In sowing all kinds of the cabbage tribe, it will be found best to sow them in drills, in an open situation, and rather thinly; as, when sown in the ordinary Old-Country method of thickly-sown beds, they are liable to be drawn up by the heat of our climate, and seldom attain the same perfection as when grown thinly.

Potatoes.—The early varieties should be planted in the driest part of the garden. Early potatoes should always be planted in drills from four to six inches deep.

Turnips may also be sown in drills, in any dry, warm situation.

Celery, for the main crop, may be sown towards the end of the month, in fine mould, in a sheltered place; it should be kept growing freely, as a check is very injurious to it.

Beet may now be sown in drills eighteen inches apart, in ground manured last autumn. Dwarf red and Dell's superb are good varieties. All kinds of salads should now be sown in small quantities, and sowings of most of them may be repeated every fortnight from now to the end of February. The main crop of onions should be got in early in September. They require a rich mellow soil on a dry subsoil. Any manure used for onions, carrots, and parsnips should be well rotted, and ought to have been dug in in the Autumn. Crops of carrots and parsnips may also be sown during this month in deep dry soils, well prepared, in drills fifteen to eighteen inches apart.

Fruit Garden.—Newly-planted fruit trees should have a mulch of rotted manure over their roots. Grafting is generally performed this month, with scions previously gathered and heeled in, in order that the stock may be somewhat in advance at the time of the scions being inserted.

Vines.—During the present month young vines may be planted, provided the new borders have sufficiently settled down and are in a suitable condition to receive them; if not, planting may be deferred somewhat. Recently-started vines may be frequently syringed with soft, tepid water, continued till the flowers are going to expand, and then discontinued. A moist atmosphere should be maintained by sprinkling the floor, etc. Close betimes in the afternoon, when the house is naturally warm from sun heat. As soon as the embryo bunches show sufficiently for selection, be prompt to remove those that do not promise well or that are superfluous, and stop at the second joint above the bunch selected to remain. Thinning is a most important process in grape growing, and should be commenced as soon as the berries are the size of small peas, or rather before. Attend assiduously to stopping, thinning and tying-in the shoots. The last is an operation requiring care, as unless done gradually and cautiously the shoots are apt to snap off.

Melons.—Plants which have been stopped and ridged out in frames should be encouraged by a nice bottom heat of from 80 to 85, and an atmosphere of 75 or 10 degrees over, when from sun heat, closing early on fine, sunny days with brisk heat and abundant moisture. Whenever the little white roots show through the sides of the ridges or hillocks, add gradually fresh soil, making it very firm ; for all through a firm bed must be afforded the melon for its growth. As soon as the laterals resulting from the first stopping have made seven or eight leaves, they too should be stopped. When further advanced, and the fruits show, and those selected to remain fixed upon, the shoots should be pinched at the joint above the fruit. The sashes should be covered carefully at night with mats, and the bottom heat be kept up by fresh linings.

Cucumbers.—Unlike the melon, cucumbers should not be exposed to strong light or sunshine ; exposure to either is calculated to make the fruit bitter ; consequently the plants should be carefully shaded during mid-day. The cucumber, too, likes a richer and more open soil, and luxuriates in warmth and moisture. Unless in the case of seed saving, impregnation is not necessary with the cucumber, though very much so in the case of the melon. Cover at night and keep up the bottom heat by linings, as directed in the case of the melon. This treatment is only necessary when it is required to have very early cuttings.

Flower Garden.—Bedding plants should now be hardened off preparatory to planting out next month. Dahlias may be propagated by division of the roots at the crown, and planted out at once. They may also be propagated by cuttings. This is done by placing the roots in gentle heat ; as soon as the shoots have attained a length of a couple of inches they are slipped off with a sharp knife, placed singly in small pots, and plunged in heat ; and after ten or twelve days they may be removed to a cold frame for hardening off, to be planted out as soon as all danger from frost is past. Hardy annuals may now be sown. Finish pruning roses, and point up the surface of the beds with a broad-tined fork. Do not be tempted by the occasional warm days, which occur during this month, to commence bedding out tender plants. The middle of next month or the beginning of November will be quite time enough. This is a good time for sowing seeds of Californian and other pines.

OCTOBER.

Continue planting potatoes, and successive crops.

Onions sown in the Autumn should now be transplanted into rows about one foot apart and four inches between the plants. The work should be done with a dibble in moist warm weather, and the soil should be prepared as for the Spring sowing of this vegetable. Leeks give excellent crops in this climate if sown in drills in October and planted out thinly in rich soil during the Autumn. Tomatoes may be sown in October, in a hot-bed or cold frame, and planted out in November, in light rich soil, in rows, and trained to trellis work. Tomatoes are much improved by pinching the points of the young shoots as soon as the flowers are visible. The lateral, or side shoots should be thinned also. Vegetable marrows, gourds, etc., may be sown by the end of this month in warm situations. Renew or make fresh plantations of pot-herbs, such as sage, thyme, chamomile, marjoram, parsley, etc. Plant cuttings of rosemary, lavender, thyme, etc., and make the herb garden clean and tidy. All the walks in the garden should be put in proper order. All vacant ground should be dug and cropped as soon as possible. Weeds should be destroyed as soon as they appear. This can only be done by the persistent use of the push-hoe. The constant moving of the ground between the growing crops has a beneficial effect on them.

Vinery.—Temperature, early vinery, 75° to 80° by day; night 65° to 70°. Thin the berries, as directed last month, before they are the size of small peas. In thinning, do not cut the shank, but point the scissors just between the berry and the petiole, leaving the broad end, or seal, attached to the latter. The operator should be very careful not to touch the berries with the fingers or his hair, as this removes the fine, powdery flue or bloom, so beautiful in well grown grapes, which is never after restored, and which is calculated to preserve the berries from many injuries, particularly water, which cannot remain on them as long as this fine, powdery substance is preserved. Late vines will now be pushing. Temperature in the late vinery, day, 70°; night, 60°. Attend to former directions in stopping the laterals, removing secondary shoots, and tying-in. Do not syringe the vines when in flower; but shake the trellis daily to disperse the pollen. Maintain a moist, warm atmosphere. Pot vines should be kept near the glass, and be liberally supplied with liquid manure.

Fruit Garden.—Finish grafting, and promptly renew the clay applied to previous grafts, if it crack or fall off. Mulch newly planted trees with well-decomposed manure, both to nourish them and to prevent the ground from drying and cracking, treading the soil firmly at the same time about the stems. Remove the runners of strawberries, fork lightly between the rows, and dress with soot in showery weather. Look closely after slugs, which will now be numerous and destructive. A light dusting of fresh-slacked lime once a week will destroy all slugs.

Pits and Frames.—Give air on all favourable opportunities to the half-hardy plants in pits and frames, in order to harden them gradually to a full exposure of the open air when planted out during this month.

Flower Garden.—Prepare for summer bedding by forking and intimately incorporating fresh compost with the soil of the beds; but do not make the beds too rich, especially for scarlet geraniums. Mow, sweep, and roll lawns and walks as required. Plant hardy annuals, biennials, and perennials ; protect such as have been wintered in frames till they are properly established. Sow another crop of annuals—hardy · kinds in the open ground. This is also a good time to put in a small sowing in a frame, of primula, cineraria, calceolaria, and cyclamen. Divide and propagate all perennials. Prune roses intended for late flowering. Auriculas, in order to bloom them to perfection, for show purposes, should be protected from the noon-day sun by a semi-transparent covering; allow them the full benefit of the morning and evening sun. Early-struck dahlias may be removed to a cold frame, to harden them off.

NOVEMBER.

Kitchen Garden.—The principal work of the month will be the thinning, cleaning, and planting out of the crops already sown. Stir the soil frequently with the push-hoe, and destroy all weeds as soon as they appear. Cress, lettuce, and all other saladings, should be sown in small quantities weekly or fortnightly. Beans should be sown now, both the French and common kinds Peas should be sown in considerable quantities, say twice during the month. Cauliflowers and broccoli may be sown for the later crops, and the earlier sown crops of these vegetables should be planted out on well-manured ground. Spring-sown cabbage should be transplanted for Autumn supply. Sow early sorts of cabbages for Winter use, also curled kale, savoys, and brussels sprouts, any of which may be planted now. An occasional dusting with fresh-slacked lime will destroy slugs and help to keep off small birds. Ridge cucumbers, vegetable marrows and pumpkins may now be sown out of doors. Cutting asparagus should not be continued longer than is absolutely necessary, as it is very important that the plants should have sufficient time to make good growth and allow the buds for the ensuing season's supply to become matured. Abundant supplies of liquid manure may be given, and in exposed situations it. is advisable to secure the stems to stakes a few feet distance apart, and connected by tarred string. Seakale must be kept from seeding by breaking off .

the flower stems ; and if the crowns are very much crowded, thin them so as to leave two or three to each strong root. Liquid manure will assist the growth ; similar remarks applying to rhubarb. Celery may still be sown, and the plants raised in September should be planted out about the end of the month in trenches of richly-manured soil and watered copiously during dry weather. Potatoes may still be planted, and those previously put in should be well stirred between the rows with a push-hoe. Tomatoes may now be planted out in rows, and trained to a trellis in a sunny situation. Turnips and radishes should be sown at short intervals throughout this and the next month. Birds are very troublesome during this month, and should be kept off the seed beds by wire netting or otherwise. The chaffinches, green linnets and blackbirds are usually the most troublesome in seed time, and in the fruit garden.

Flower Garden.—This department should now be putting on its Summer appearance. The later kinds of Spring flowers, and those of early Summer, should now be in full bloom. Hardy annuals may still be sown for Autumn flowering. Annuals sown in September should now be thinned, and the thinnings transplanted during showery weather. Herbaceous perennials may now be propagated by cuttings of the young shoots, and those kinds which root naturally may be divided and removed to any part of the garden requiring furnishing. Dahlias should be planted out without delay. A rich deep soil and open situation, but sheltered, should be chosen for them. Plant out pelargoniums, verbenas, petunias, heliotropes, and other half-hardy and tender budding plants in beds on the lawn, or in groups in the borders. All lawns and grass verges should be closely mown and rolled once a week, and all the walks and borders in the garden should be kept in the highest state of neatness.

DECEMBER.

Kitchen Garden.—Another sowing of broad beans may be made this month for a last crop. Peas, for Autumn crops, should be sown at short intervals up to the end of the month they must be kept growing freely, or they will be a failure. Cauliflowers, cabbages, brussels sprouts, broccoli, &c., should be planted out as soon as they are strong enough, in rows two feet apart, and two feet from plant to plant. Seeds of these should also be sown for successional crops. All sorts of salads should be sown frequently in small quantities. Potatoes may still be planted, but the crop is not to be relied on. Those previously planted should be kept clear of weeds, and earthed up as required. Turnips may be sown now, selecting showery weather if possible. A successional crop of kidney beans or scarlet runners should be sown about the middle of the month. The moment a plot or portion of ground becomes vacant, dig it forthwith for a successional crop. Attend to thinning and keeping free of weeds young seed crops. Keep the push-hoe constantly going amongst growing crops. Sow kidney beans, peas, cabbages, lettuces, radishes, spinach, &c., in succession; and salading every ten days or so; and turnips and beet for late crops. Plant out cabbages for succession, cauliflowers for a full crop, early celery in trenches, onions on rich prepared ground, early varieties of potatoes for late crops. Protect and shade tomatoes or other plants turned out from pits and frames, until they are well established, and rooting freely. Water seed beds in dry weather always at night, dust with soot or lime, to destroy insects. Cucumbers for pickling may still be sown; they thrive best in rich, deep, moist soil. Put out capsicum with some fine rich compost for their roots to revel in. Keep the shoots of tomatoes well tied, if grown against a trellis; remove useless laterals, thin out the clusters, selecting for removal such fruits as are small and unpromising These may be pickled in jars. Liberal doses of liquid manure will greatly help the production of fine large fruit. Now is the best time to put layer strawberry runners into pots for early forcing.

Vines.—Where the crop is approaching maturity keep the atmosphere rather dry than otherwise, give air freely, and leave on a little at night. In the case of later houses, the atmosphere should be kept moist, by frequently damping the floor and other exposed surfaces. Remove secondary shoots, sling and tie out the shoulders of large bunches, and if necessary thin the berries further. The size of the berries and symmetry of the bunches depend largely on proper and timely thinning. In the case of grapes intended to hang late, thinning should be all the more pronounced. The strength of the vine should be the standard by which to judge the weight of crop it will be able to mature, without deterioration of the quality of the fruit or injury to the future bearing of the vine. It is, therefore, safer to allow one bunch only to remain on a shoot than two or three, even though the vine be strong and vigorous. The borders, both inside and outside the house, should have a good soaking of liquid manure while the berries are swelling, and just as they commence to colour. Before soaking the border, point the surface over very lightly and somewhat roughly. It will then drink in the moisture regularly and deeply, instead of, as is too often the case, allowing it to pass over the surface with scarcely a drop finding its way to the roots. After soaking the border, a light mulching over to prevent evaporation will be of great advantage. Should the slightest trace of mildew appear, dust the affected parts immediately with flour of sulphur, and for a few days keep the atmosphere rather dry and the temperature somewhat higher. Where due preparation has been made for planting, the present is about the best time for planting out young vines struck from eyes early in the year. With plenty of heat, moisture, and a genial atmosphere they will develop into fine canes, reaching the ridge of the house before the end of the season. The growth of newly-planted vines should be stimulated by affording them plenty of heat and moisture and closing early in the afternoon, with abundance of sun heat. In the case of early forced vineries, as soon as the crop is cut it is important that they should have abundance of air, and a free circulation of it. Care, too, should be taken to syringe the foliage frequently, both to keep red spider in check and the former clean and vigorous until they have fulfilled their functions.

Cucumbers in Frames.—Cucumbers require much more shade and moisture than melons; the heat, too, should be well kept up, as they are sure to resent any check resulting from any deficiency of it. Plants which are in full bearing will be greatly invigorated by having a soaking of liquid manure and a rich top-dressing afterwards. Syringe

or water overhead from a rose every fine afternoon, and close
with plenty of sun heat; the growths, in whatever stage,
should be kept regularly disposed, and never allowed
to get crowded or confused.

Flower Garden.—Fill vacancies as they occur with
annuals or bedding plants reserved for the purpose. All
newly-planted trees and shrubs should be freely watered.
All kinds of hardy annuals may be transplanted during
cloudy weather, and well watered in. Another sowing
may be made in the early part of this month of primula,
cineraria, and cyclamen in boxes or pans. Dahlias, and
similar tall growers, should be supported with strong stakes,
and their superfluous branches removed. The flower
borders must be carefully attended to, and all weeds destroyed as soon as they appear. The oftener these borders
are hoed, the better they will look, and the plants will thrive
better. All decaying branches should be at once removed.
Clean and top-dress auriculas grown for show purposes in
pots, and give them shady, sheltered, but airy quarters.
Border auriculas, primulas, and polyanthus may be divided
and replanted in well-prepared, deep, rich soil. Increase
carnations, picotees, and pinks by cuttings, pipings, and
layers, and choice double wallflowers by slips, or cuttings.
Roses will now require a good deal of attention. Wash
the bushes well with a vigorous syringing of soft water,
and occasionally, if fly appear, with quassia water (about
a lb. of chips to four gallons of water), or with Gishurst's compound, two ounces to the gallon of water. A
wine glass of McDougal's sheep dip, in six quarts of water,
is also a useful dressing. A good soaking of liquid manure
at the roots, and a mulch over after, if not objected to, will
be of much service in helping the swelling blooms and in-
vigorating the plants. Suckers should not be tolerated;
trace them to their origin and cut clean away with a sharp
knife. Buds may now be put in if the bark rise freely.
Look over and ease after a week or ten days the bandages
of any which have taken. Put in cuttings of China roses.
Plant out stocks and asters (the latter particularly require a
deep, rich soil, if fine blooms are desired). Thin out all
superfluous shoots of dahlias, when sufficiently advanced.

Stake tall growing plants as they advance. Ordinary bedding plants will now be making strong growth. Clip box edgings, weed and roll walks, mow lawns and grass plots, and save seeds of choice annual and other plants as they ripen.

JANUARY.

Kitchen Garden.—Clear off all crops as they become matured, and prepare the ground for others; hoe between growing crops; and gather seeds and herbs as they arrive at maturity. Make a sowing of early cabbages towards the end of the month for planting out in Autumn and Spring; sow kidney beans for late use; sow lettuces thinly, to stand without transplanting, and onions to draw young; also early sorts of peas to come in late; spinach and turnips for a full crop. Sow radishes and small salading once in ten days; plant out celery, broccoli, cauliflowers, lettuces, endive, borecole, and early and late cabbages for full crops. Choose showery weather for planting. Earth up celery— encasing them in three-inch tile pipes is said to be a clean method of blanching, raise and dry onions, shalots and garlic, and store; cut herbs when in flower, and dry in the shade; stop tomatoes, and do not allow the leaves to shade the fruit; take up early potatoes and dry and green them in the sun for future planting; top beans; keep scarlet runners staked; and thin late-sown onions, carrots, turnips, and beet. Some of the most vigorous shoots of the cucumbers and vegetable marrows will require pegging down, or bits of brick or stone put on them to keep them down and cause them to root. In dry weather, water abundantly, so as to keep them in vigorous health, and prevent mildew, watering should always be done after sunset in warm weather.

Vinery.—Day temperature, 80° to 85°; night, 70°. Remove secondary shoots; stop laterals on late vines; tie out and thin the berries, as directed last month; keep up a steady moist heat, with free air, but do not syringe. Towards the end of the month or sooner, if the crop be removed from the early vines, admit abundance of air day and night, to harden the wood.

Hardy Fruit Garden.—Tie and secure the shoots of grafts; cut down the strongest to three or four eyes;

they will throw out laterals that will ripen in the Autumn.
Continue watering newly-planted trees if the weather be dry
—a thorough good soaking once a week will suffice ; attend
to trees against walls or fences, remove superfluous wood,
and nail or tie in that which is to remain ; protect ripening
fruit from birds by netting ; thin peaches, nectarines, and
apricots ; bud fruit trees, and water them freely in dry
weather ; remove suckers and weak wood from gooseberries
and currants ; thin out weak shoots from raspberries, leaving
only those wanted for next year's crop ; attend to the strawberry beds, by preventing the too rapid growth of runners ;
strawberry runners layered last month may now be repotted if well rooted ; break over foreright shoots of pears,
plums, apples, and all spur-trained fruit trees.

Flower Garden.—The flower garden, if well managed,
should now be a blaze of colour ; constant attention must,
however, be paid to rolling, mowing, and staking.   Care
is now necessary in tying up carnations and picotees,
thinning the flower buds, and layering.   When layering, stir
the soil round the plant, and put in a few inches of clean,
well-rotted, sandy turf-loam, in which bend down and hook
the layer, after having slit it upwards from a convenient
joint, about half-way to the one above it.   Let the earth be
formed into a basin around each plant, which will prevent
the water running off, thereby lightening labour, as the
layers may require attention in watering until they are well-
rooted, when they should be taken off and potted.   Mule
pinks and double sweet-williams may also be layered, and
treated in the same way as carnations.   Remove decayed
blooms of roses, or those that are spoiled by continued wet.
Give every attention to staking plants that require it, lest
high winds or heavy rains injure them ; do not trust to one
tie, but make as many as will secure the plant from being
injured, always observing not to bind too tight.   This is
particularly to be attended to in tying dahlias ; for if sufficient room be not left for the swelling of the stem, the
ligature will cut it ; and if, by any chance, the upper ties
give way, the head will snap off.   Most of the hybrid China
roses will now be fit to take buds from.   Select shoots on
which the buds are most plump.   Other kinds of roses may

now also be budded. The plumpness of the eye is the only criterion by which to judge whether the bud is fit to be put in. Examine those previously budded, and slacken the ties. Lift tulips, hyacinths, ranunculuses, and anemones as soon as their foliage has decayed, and store them in a dry, airy place. It is not absolutely necessary that these bulbs should be raised annually, on the contrary, they are sometimes greatly benefited by being left undisturbed for a couple of years. Stake and tie up chrysanthemums, watering freely when necessary, giving liquid manure once a week.

FEBRUARY.

A final sowing of peas should be made in the first week, and may possibly yield a few dishes during the beginning of Winter Cauliflowers and broccoli should be sown about the end of the month for planting out in early Spring. Onions intended to stand over Winter should be sown during this month; if left until next month they are very liable to be thrown out of the ground by the frequent thaws of our variable Winter. A sharp look-out should be kept for slugs and wood-lice, which are becoming a terrible nuisance in some parts of the colony. Trench or dig as either seems expedient, and manure heavily the ground as soon as a crop is off, and let another adapted for Winter and Spring use take its place. Sow as early in the month as possible cabbage seed, to produce plants for putting out in March, August, and September. Sow endive and lettuce thinly where the plants are to stand, and thickly when they are to be transplanted for Winter and Spring use; also radishes and small salading in succession. Plant out cauliflowers and broccoli for Spring use, celery for a full and late crop. Earth up celery, but only when the soil is quite dry; hoe and fork lightly between the lines of all growing crops. Raise and dry early-sown onions as they ripen, also shalots and garlic. Never allow a weed to live, much less to seed in the kitchen garden. Remember the proverb, "One year's seeding makes seven years' weeding."

Vines.—Where the crop has been an early one and the fruit off, all dead leaves should be removed, and the remaining foliage thoroughly syringed. Plenty of air day and night should be the rule, doors and ventilators left open, and occasionally a brisk dash of the syringe given to keep the leaves clean and healthy to the end. If considered desirable, this would be the right time to remove a portion of the surface soil of the border, and replace it with a fresh compost formed of nice fibry loam, with a little bone meal added. In late houses, where the fruit is only showing color, a good soaking of manure water and a light mulch over the surface will tell advantageously. When fully ripe, stop and thin the shoots, and keep the atmosphere rather dry. Remove all young and superfluous growths. Ventilate early in the mornings, and be sure to leave a little air on at night; and in all cases a watch should be kept on the foliage for one of its worst enemies—red spider. Young vines planted this season should be carefully attended to as regards syringing and watering, in order to push on growth and secure an early and thoroughly ripened rod.

Melons.—Stop and arrange the shoots of plants intended for a late crop. Keep the shoots rather thin and clear of secondary growths and tendrils. In the cases of ripening fruit be chary of water, but give air freely, and in order that the fruit may have the full benefit of light and sunshine, elevate it somewhat above the foliage. It is a great mistake to allow melons to get dead ripe before cutting; they will be far better both as regards flavour and keeping if cut the moment the fruit swells and cracks round the connection of fruit and stalk. On the other hand, plants swelling a crop should be liberally watered with manure water.

Flower Garden.—Towards the end of the month numerous kinds of herbaceous plants may be propagated by cuttings. It is much better to do this now than later on, as the cuttings will have a better chance of making the roots which are so necessary to enable them to stand the Winter. The last week of this month—unless the weather be very dry—is the best time for putting in cuttings of evergreen shrubs, such as laurels, sweet bay, escallonias, pittosporum, etc. Cuttings of roses put in towards the end of this month will probably succeed better than at any other time. Seeds of favourite flowers should be carefully gathered as they ripen, and be correctly labelled before putting away. A few small patches of the very hardiest annuals may be sown in the borders; and the utmost attention should be given to keeping down all weeds, so that they may not shed their seeds. Remove suckers from recently-budded and other roses, stake and tie up carefully those whose buds are pushing, lest the latter be destroyed by high winds. Proceed with budding. This is an excellent time to put in cuttings of roses from the wood of the current year, when ripe, with a heel of last year's wood attached. Propagate without delay all sorts of bedding plants, pansies, &c., if not already done. The seed vessels or capsules should be at once picked from rhododendrons ; and, indeed, from all other flowering shrubs. It should be remembered that it is a great waste of power and injury to plants to allow them to ripen seed that is not specially required to save. Pipings of pinks or carnations, and also cuttings and layers now rooted, may be planted out in well-prepared beds, and will require attention as to watering. Finish layering carnations and picotees without delay. Dahlias and other tall-growing plants should be carefully staked. Pot auriculas in compost formed of sandy turf loam and thoroughly decomposed cow-manure, shake out the roots before repotting, place in a close frame, and shade for a few days.

MARCH.

Kitchen Garden.—Sow small quantities of endive and lettuce, and also a little onion seed. The latest crops of celery should now be got in, and those previously planted should be earthed up as soon as they attain a sufficient size. The earthing-up must be carefully performed, when the soil is moderately dry, and may be done two or three times. Cauliflowers and cabbage plants may still be set out for Spring use, and liberally supplied with liquid manure. Prickly spinach for Winter and Spring use should be sown now. It is an excellent vegetable much neglected in the colony. It should be sown in drills in deeply-worked ground, with an abundance of manure, and carefully thinned and kept clear of weeds as it advances in growth. The main crop of onions should now be lifted and spread out thinly on the ground to dry ; if the weather should be damp, it will be advisable to remove them to a gravel path or to some dry place exposed to the sun ; they should be turned over once a-day till they are thoroughly dried, and then stored away in a well-aired loft or storeroom or strung in hanks.   Various kinds of biennial herbs should now be sown.   A final crop of turnips may be tried, the best kind for late work being the Old Snowball.   Remove all decayed leaves, haulms, and the remains of all crops which have been taken up, in order to preserve that neatness which is so desirable in the kitchen garden.   Towards the end of the month prepare the ground where it is intended to plant new fruit trees.   Our reason for recommending the preparation of the ground now is that we are convinced that early planting is very desirable in most of the districts of New Zealand, on account of the extremely changeable nature of the Winter.   Indeed, we are convinced that trees planted in the latter end of April will do better than at any other season.   Raspberries should be pruned as soon as the wood has thoroughly ripened. It is advisable to cut away all except the six strongest canes, and these should be shortened to different lengths according to their strength, and tied together with flax or cord.   Young plantations of strawberries may now be made with every prospect of success. The ground should have been trenched two feet deep and well manured, and should not be dug again, being merely forked over, while the crop remains in the ground, say three years.

Flower   Garden.—This is not a busy time in the flower garden, the principal work being the frequent hoeing of borders, and the gathering of such seeds as are now ripe. A few cuttings of the finer herbaceous plants may be put in now, and most of the deciduous shrubs will be found to strike best if put in at the end of this month.   Cuttings of the various kinds of pelargoniums, verbenas, and all other half hardy plants may be struck now in pots or boxes. Continue to stake and tie up crysanthemums.

APRIL.

Kitchen Garden.—Lettuces may be transplanted into rows in a dry, warm situation where they are to remain during

Winter. It is advisable to plant rather thickly, especially in damp rich soils The remainder of the potato crop should be carefully lifted and stored in a pit or outhouse. Care should be taken not to place them in very large heaps, as they are liable to ferment, and are often very seriously injured thereby. Carrots, beet, and artichokes should be lifted and pitted in dry sand under cover, after removing the tops, but they may be left in the ground for a couple of months longer. Parsnips will be better left in the ground and taken up as required. In digging up the roots of beet, care must be taken not to bruise them, for if this be done they bleed and deteriorate in quality. Broad beans intended for Spring use may be sown now in the sunniest part of the garden. The old stalks of asparagus, &c., may now be removed, and the beds forked and raked, and dressed with a coat of well-rotted manure with a good sprinkle of salt. The last crop of cabbages may now be put out in rows in the usual manner. Celery should be carefully earthed up on fine dry days, so that the soil placed against the stems may be moderately dry. A few seeds of any kind of radish may be sown in the warmest part of the garden. The first sowing of peas should be got in towards the end of the month. The best kinds for sowing now are First Crop and First Crop Blue, from both of which we have had excellent dishes gathered in October ; we must, however, add that we do not advocate sowing out of season, except under exceptional circumstances, as to situation and aspect, we have rarely seen much gained by Autumn sowing. All vacant pieces of ground should be either trenched or deeply dug ; and all decayed leaves, &c., should be buried in digging, which will be found a more profitable and cleaner way of disposing of such rubbish than the old plan of piling it in heaps till the Spring. The ground for young fruit trees having been prepared last month, the planting may now be proceeded with unless the ground be very dry, in which case it will be better to defer it for a week or two ; but if the season is at all favourable, it is decidedly advantageous to plant at once, as the trees will be able to make embryo or young root fibres before the Winter weather comes on, giving them the start of Spring-planted trees. Plantations of small fruits may also be got in now; and cuttings of gooseberries, currants, &c., should be inserted in a sheltered border.

Flower Garden.—In the flower garden department there is much to be done this month. The final clearing and weeding should be given to all the beds and borders; and any dead leaves, rubbish, &c., may be buried. Bulbs intended for Spring bloom should be planted now; and any bulbs at present in the borders may be lifted and divided, or removed to better situations. Herbaceous plants may also be divided and transplanted. All kinds of shrubs and trees may be planted with success after the middle of the month, though in very dry seasons or dry situations it may be better to defer it for a short time. The putting in of cuttings of various kinds of shrubs and such trees as strike freely should be continued during the month, but no more seeds should be sown before Spring.

MAY AND JUNE.

The month of May may be said to close the season in the orchard, the kitchen and the flower ·garden; and all future operations will have in view the necessities ·for the coming year. The successes and failures of the growing months just past will have suggested many alterations which the careful gardener, be he amateur or professional, will not be slow to note and act upon. The usual routine work of pruning, transplanting, manuring, and trenching requisite at this season will claim attention. Continue to clear away the decaying leaves and haulms of rhubarb, seakale, and asparagus, and to treat with a liberal dressing of strong loose manure. Make new plantations of raspberries.

Planting Orchard Trees.—At this season, when planting is being largely carried on, it may be well to warn the inexperienced against the too common practice of planting too thickly. It is an every-day remark that two trees are put in where there is only room for one, yet fresh plantations continually come under notice in which the trees are planted much too thickly. Large, strong-growing kinds of apples and pears should stand at least from twenty-five to thirty feet apart if the soil is strong; for although many planters say they will cut out the supernumerary trees as soon as they encroach on each other, it is very doubtful whether, if they are producing anything like good crops, they are not left long enough to spoil all before any are removed. A good plan in cultivating orchards is to plant the tall standards at the fullest range they are ever likely to occupy, and to fill the intermediate spaces with dwarf spreading bush trees, as orchards thus treated are sooner remunerative than when they are planted with tall growing trees only.

Transplanting and Pruning.—Fruit trees should be attended to as soon as the leaves begin to fall. However carefully young trees may be lifted, some of the roots will be broken, these should be pared clean with a knife. Blighted trees should be carefully dressed with a mixture of soft soap, kerosene, and hot water, applied with a hard brush. Blighted trees should, however, be discarded, and those grafted on blight-proof stocks substituted. Finish pruning gooseberries, currants, and raspberries. In pruning raspberries, cut away the wood which bore this year's fruit, thin out the suckers, leaving five or six of the strongest for fruiting next season, which should be tied together. Black currants will not bear cutting back, they should, however, be freely thinned out when necessary. Clean strawberry beds by cutting away all runners and some of the outside leaves; fork slightly between the rows, removing all weeds; finish off with a dressing of well-rotted manure or short stable litter three to four inches thick.

Tomatoes.—When danger from light frosts is apprehended, the season may be prolonged by protecting the plants, or some of them, by thin canvass or papers Some growers pull up their vines and hang them up in sheds, etc., for the same purpose. Secure the green tomatoes in sufficient quantities for spiced and other pickles, before the frost injures them.

Vines.—In the case of late grapes still hanging, care should be taken to avoid wetting the floor or other exposed surfaces. Keep such houses closed during foggy, muggy weather; but air freely on brisk, dry, bright days, when a little fire heat may, at the same time, be used advantageously. Keep a sharp look-out for the appearance of mouldy or decayed berries, and promptly remove any showing the slightest taint. Vines from which the crop has been removed should be pruned, cleaned, and dressed as soon as the whole of the leaves have fallen off. In the case of vines intended to start only when nature moves them and ripen a crop in ordinary course of the season, the borders may be lightly pointed over with the fork, and then have a good coating of well-rotted farm-yard manure, and over this a coat of stable litter.

Advantage should be taken of fine weather, to form new vine borders or to raise the roots of old vines and replant. In case of the latter, raise the vines carefully, and after draining the border, lay a bottom of concrete or other substance, impervious to the roots, eighteen inches from the surface, and on such a slope as will carry the water from the roots. Where there is no necessity for lifting, vines may be greatly benefited by removing the exhausted surface soil and replacing it with a top-dressing of maiden earth, bone meal, charcoal, and old farm-yard manure.

Outside vine borders should be protected with a good coat of dry leaves, fern, or litter, with a view of conserving earth heat and preventing the border from being saturated. When late grapes, such as Alicante and Lady Downes, have to hang on the rods for some time yet, means should be taken to throw off the wet from the outside border.

Flower Garden.—When the weather is dry and the ground in favourable working condition, proceed vigorously with alterations, but avoid as much as possible any such work in wet, sloppy weather ; and if there be any unevenness or inequalities in the turf, the sod should be lightly skinned, the bare portion made perfectly solid and firm, and the sod relaid and well rolled. Dig and trench all vacant flower beds, leaving them roughly turned up till required for planting. Plant ornamental trees, shrubs, roses, etc., but only in mild open weather—never during frost. Collect fresh composts, and turn and mix old. Take care to have a good supply of all the requisite composts under cover, so that they may be ready for use at all times. Cut out the dead and superfluous wood of rose bushes, leaving, until the first pruning in Spring, the strongest and best of the young wood. Look sharply after rose suckers, remove them at once, and mulch over the roots with rotten manure. If not already done, lose no time in planting hyacinths, bedding tulips, and Spring flowering bulbs of all kinds: also the early flowering varieties of gladioli. In the mixed herbaceous border all old flower stems, withered leaves, in a word — everything unsightly and objectionable should be removed; the surface between the plants lightly dug over, and then, provided the appearance is not an objection, have a sprinkling of mulch or decomposed manure.

Dahlias are destroyed by the first frost. Cut the stalks near the ground and lift the roots, selecting a warm day, doing the work in the morning that the roots may dry all day in the sun. Be sure to securely label the different varieties before putting them away; any place suitable for keeping potatoes will answer.

See about potting the general collection of such bulbs as are required for Winter and Spring flowering, especially hyacinths, which, in common with all plants of a similar nature, evince by their roots beginning to develop that they want to be placed in soil. It frequently happens that the indifferent way in which hyacinths and other bulbs flower is attributed to some deficiency in the strength or maturity of the bulbs, when, in reality, their unsatisfactory blooming is caused by the first efforts of the bulbs to develop roots taking place before they are put into soil, by which neglect the tender fibres are injured. In selecting hyacinths, amateurs should rely upon the good and well proved older varieties: for although they are offered at prices very much below that of the comparatively new and scarce kinds, the difference in price is far from an indication of any superiority in the flower.

The first planting of anemones may be made early in May. Plant in clumps of two or three inches deep; also hyacinths, crocuses, tulips, gladioli, and all other hardy bulbs. Geraniums, if not already attended to, should be lifted and heeled in in boxes or frames, where they may receive the little attention and protection from frost which they will require during the next four months—they must, however, be kept free of withered or mouldy leaves. Rose stocks should now be planted ready for budding or grafting; plant eighteen inches apart, in rows two feet six inches apart. Rose beds should now be dressed with rotten manure, to be forked in in the Spring. Never use a spade, the use of which destroys the surface roots. Fuchsias may remain in the ground where they grew ; a shovelful of ashes or sand thrown over them is all that they will require. Plants treated in this manner make better flowering plants in the following season than those turned out of pots in the Spring.

VEGETABLE GARDEN.

(Arranged Alphabetically for convenience of Reference)

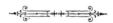

Artichoke (Globe).—The best variety for cultivation is the Globe. Soil—a deep rich loam. Propagation, by seed.—A sixpenny packet sown in a drill two inches deep, thinned out to six inches, and transplanted when strong enough into their permanent position, two feet apart each way ; sow in September. By plants.—Procure suckers from old roots in the Spring, in August or September, select such as are crisp and tender, if tough and stringy they are worthless. Plant in rows four feet apart and three feet in the rows. Plant two or three suckers in each clump, mulch round the roots during Summer, remove all weak suckers about November. The plants will produce a succession of heads from January to the end of March. Winter dressing.—As soons as the stems are cleared of all their heads they should be broken down close to the root. Clear away the old leaves and dress with manure, being careful not to cover the crown. This excellent vegetable, although long in cultivation, is not now nearly so general as it deserves to be.

Artichoke (Jerusalem).—Plant in August or September, in rows three feet apart, and six inches deep, and two feet apart in the rows. They thrive best in a rich pliable loam. An abundance of manure should be dug in in May, in order that it may be well incorporated with the soil at the time of planting. The after culture consists of frequent

hoeings and thinning the stems produced by each set to two
or three at the most.   In May the tubers will be ripe, and
may be dug and pitted as potatoes, or they may be left in
the ground and used as required.   They must not however
remain longer in the soil than the beginning of the following
September.

Asparagus.—Plant in August or the beginning of
September.   The conditions of the successful culture of
asparagus are :—First, deep dry soil, trenched at least two
feet deep incorporating an abundance of manure; second,
leaving off cutting by the middle or end of November ;
third, not cutting down the seed stems till they are quite ripe.
Planting in rows on the flat is now generally adopted instead
of in beds.   Plant in rows at least two feet apart (we would
prefer three feet) and two feet plant from plant, with three-
year-old plants, one or two-year-old plants will answer equally
well, but they will not come into bearing so soon.   The
following is recommended as being the best method of planting :—After the bed has been finally prepared by being
forked over and raked, mark out the rows two feet apart,
placing a stake at each end, stretching a line tightly between,
draw a drill four or six inches deep on each side of the line,
leaving a ridge, over which the plants should be placed,
regulating the long roots evenly on each side and closing in
the earth as the work proceeds, pressing it firmly at the same
time with the back of the rake, or with the foot ; or a deep
trench may be opened and the plants inserted, taking care
to spread out the roots like a fan against the cut, the
crown of the plant being kept two or three inches below
the surface, this latter plan is the most expeditious.   The
young plants should be lifted from the seed rows with
care, injuring the fibrous roots as little as possible.   Beds
formed of three-year-old plants will afford a slight cutting,
the second year after planting ; from the fourth year
out they will be in full bearing, and will last for many
years if properly attended to.   In the matter of not cutting
too closely, be particular to remove all seedling plants
as they appear in Spring, otherwise they will soon spoil the
bed.   Winter dressing.—In May, or as soon as the stalks are
yellow, they may be cut close to the ground and removed,

carefully avoiding the scattering of the seed berries ; if this is neglected trouble will follow in the shape of young plants over-running the bed. Then fork in a good coat of rotten manure, at least three inches thick, and a dressing of common salt, quarter of a pound to every square yard. In August the bed should be forked over carefully, removing all the rough manure. Cutting should not be commenced till the shoots are six inches above ground, and cut them only half-an-inch below the surface. Nearly the whole shoot is then eatable, and the flavour beyond all comparison superior to that which has scarcely seen daylight. A shilling packet of seed will produce plants sufficient for a good bed. Sow in September, in drills one and a half inches deep and one foot apart.

Beans thrive best in strong loamy soil, which should be well manured. A small sowing may be made in May, the main sowing should, however, be deferred till August, making sowings every fortnight or three weeks where a large supply is required till the end of September. Green and White Windsor, Beck's dwarf Green Gem, and the Mammoth Long Pod are well known, and certain croppers, sown in rows two feet six inches apart, in drills four inches deep, and dropped four inches apart in zigzag fashion—° ° °. One pint at each sowing will suffice for a small family. One pint will sow a row seventy feet long.

Beans (French).—There are many varieties, but for general purposes the Caseknife and Scarlet-runner are good croppers. Sow in drills two feet apart, four inches seed from seed, and two inches deep. Stakes will have to be provided for these. Height, from four to six feet. One pint will sow seventy-five feet. For Dwarfs.—Canadian Wonder and Ne Plus Ultra can be recommended as good croppers. Same treatment as given for the runners, except that no stakes will be required. Commence to sow from the middle of October till the end of December. One pint will sow one hundred feet.

Beans (Haricot).—We would recommend this desirable bean to the notice of every one possessed of a garden. They are dwarf growers. Sow in November, and let the crop ripen. They are a delicious and most nutritious vegetable ; the beans are pure white. The simplest mode of cooking is to steep them over night, boil till soft, serve them up with a little butter, salt, and pepper. Half a-pint will fill a large vegetable dish.

Beet.—Of the varieties cultivated for their roots, the Dwarf Red and Dell's Superb are the best. Beet requires a rich, deep, open soil. Manure should never be applied with the crop, but should have been trenched in the previous Autumn. Sow the main crop of Red Beet in September. Sow in drills eighteen inches apart, and thin the young plants to ten inches. The crop will be ripe and may be lifted by the end of May, and stored in sand or earth. In lifting, care must be taken not to break the tap root, otherwise they will bleed, and be much deteriorated in value as a vegetable or salad. They may be left in the ground, if desired, till the end of July. One ounce will sow a row fifty feet long. White Silver Beet is grown for its leaves. It may be sown in February for use during Winter and the following Spring. Sow in drills eighteen inches apart and one inch deep ; thin out the plants to ten or twelve inches ; it must have a deep, rich soil.

Borecole or Kale.—There are many varieties of this useful vegetable, the best being the Dwarf and Tall Curled Kale, only differing in height. Sow in October for planting out in the end of November, for use in Autumn. Sow again about the middle of December, for final planting in February ; and March, for use during Winter and Spring months. Plant in rows two feet apart each way—the last planting may be a little closer.

Broccoli.—There are many varieties, all good in their way, but for general cultivation the following will be found to answer for successional planting :—Commence to sow Veitch's Self-protecting Autumn in October, followed by Snow's Superb White, to be sown at intervals from October till the beginning of December ; followed by Early Penzance, Elleston's Mammoth, and Knight's Protecting. Each variety should be sown separately, and planted in beds three feet wide, for the convenience of weeding. The seed must not be buried more than a quarter of an inch, and the beds must be protected from birds. Quarter of an ounce of any of the cabbage tribe would furnish plants sufficient for any ordinary garden. For small suburban gardens, it may be more convenient to purchase the plants ready for planting out; but care must be taken to deal only with known parties, as the result of the whole year's operations may be frustrated through obtaining plants which have been raised from spurious seeds. October sowings may be planted out in December, and the others in succession, as they become fit, the late crops being put out in February. Any loamy, well-manured soil will suit. Plant in rows two feet six inches apart, and two feet in the rows. The after culture will consist of hoeing between, and drawing the mould up about their stems. Liquid manure may be given with great advantage once a week. It is an excellent plan to cut off the ends of the roots (the tap roots) and dip them in a mud composed of cow manure, earth, and a little soot. These remarks apply equally to all the cabbage tribe. If a dust of superphosphate were added, all the better.

Brussels Sprouts.—This is, perhaps, one of the most delicious of the cabbage tribe, as well as being one of the hardiest, it should find a place in every garden. Scrymger's Giant and Dalkeith are sure croppers. Sow the seed in September and October—same treatment as that recommended for broccoli, except that they may be planted a little closer. Any deep, well-manured soil will answer. Plant out as required. The sprouts are fit for use chiefly in Winter and early Spring.

Cauliflower.—A sowing may be made in March, in a warm, sheltered spot; these will be ready for planting out by the end of August and September. The main crop should not be sown till August or September, to be followed by successional sowings at intervals of four weeks, till November. For Autumn cropping, the Walcheren and Veitch's Autumn Grant; for Spring, Early London, Erfurt, and Mammoth; and for Summer, the Asiatic and Alma will prove good standard varieties. The after culture is the same as that for broccoli.

Cabbage.—Little may be said of this generally-culti-
vated vegetable, except to name a few of the best varieties,
which are Early York, Enfield Market, Large York,
Nonpareil, Sugar Loaf, and Wheeler's Imperial. Make a
sowing in February, and again in March, for planting out in
the early Autumn and Spring. Sow again in August and
September, and plant out as required, following the instructions given for Broccoli. Cabbages are gross feeders, and
therefore require an abundance of rich manure.

Carrots thrive best on deep sandy loam, which must,
however, be rich, having been manured the previous
Autumn. Manure should never be applied with this crop.
Carrots may be sown from August to September. Nantes
Horn and Early Short Horn. Sow thinly, in drills not less
than twelve inches apart, rubbing the seeds between the
hands, with a little sand or dry earth, for the purpose
of breaking the hooked awns—which hold the seeds
together—otherwise they cannot be sown regularly. An
inch of covering will be sufficient, beating the ground
gently with the back of the spade—particularly if the soil is
dry at the time of sowing. The hoe must be kept going
between the rows immediately the crop shows over ground,
for the double purpose of destroying weeds and keeping the
moisture in the ground. When the plants have three or
four leaves they will require thinning to four or six inches
apart. One ounce will sow one hundred feet.

Celery. — Laing's Mammoth Red, Seymour's Giant
White, or Sandringham Dwarf White are all good varieties.
To produce celery of the best quality, the plants must not
be checked in their growth A light, rich, moist soil is
more suitable for celery than heavy retentive soil, however
rich it may be. Although the plants require plenty of
water during the growing season, they are apt to rot in
Winter in cold, heavy soil, if saturated with moisture.
Sowing.—Sow in boxes or pans in August and September.
Plunge in heat if available, if not, in a cold frame, or, failing
this, in a warm corner of the garden ; and again in November for successional planting, covering the seed as lightly as
possible with rich soil. When the young plants have

reached their second or third leaf, they should be transplanted into boxes, or a well-prepared bed, in rows six inches apart each way ; water copiously, shading well till they have recovered themselves. - Care must be taken to keep the roots moist while out of the ground ; shorten a little of the long tap roots before planting. Celery may be grown on the flat. The most general and perhaps the easiest method is in trenches, which should be four feet apart. Throw the soil out on each side to the depth of twelve or eighteen inches, according to the nature of the soil ; dig and fork in four to six inches of the richest manure procurable. As soon as the young plants in the transplanted bed have become robust—which will be in about a month—they may be lifted with a hand fork and planted in the trenches nine inches apart. If the weather should be very dry and hot after planting, the plants ought to be protected in the day from the scorching sun till they start to grow ; water should be given freely after sunset. As the plants advance they will require to be earthed up a little at a time, once a fortnight, taking care not to earth over the centre of the heart. A mere pinch of celery seed will raise hundreds of plants.

Cucumber.—Rollison's Telegraph for the frame, and the long and short prickly varieties for the open ground, have proved themselves to be sure croppers. If it is desired to have early cucumbers, heat must be provided. A hotbed may be formed of stable litter, straw, and leaves ; the mass to be turned two or three times before finally forming the bed, which should be four or five feet high at the back, and three to four feet in the front ; the length and breadth must be determined by the size of the frame at hand. The bed cannot be trodden down too much, the firmer it is made the longer it will retain the heat. The bed should be made a foot wider all round than the frame intended to be placed upon it. Place the frame on the heap, and fill in six inches of soil—a fresh loam, the top spit of a pasture three parts and one part of rich, well-rotted manure, is, perhaps, as fine a soil as can be employed for the cucumber. As soon as the bed has somewhat subsided the seed may be sown, or the plants, which may have been previously raised in pots, may be planted in August or

D

September, watering freely and shading, having due regard
to ventilation every warm day, taking care to close up early
in the afternoon.   As the fruit shows, stop one joint above
it.   For open-ground crops the long and short prickly
cucumbers should be selected.   Any well-sheltered, richly-
manured, fresh soil will answer.   Sow five or six seeds two
inches deep, in clumps five feet apart.   Sow from the
middle of October to the end of November.   Keep a sharp
look out for slugs and birds.   An occasional dust of lime
will secure the plants against slugs.   Birds are not so easily
dealt with.   Excellent crops of cucumbers may be produced
if. planted amongst cabbages and irrigated occasionally.
Beds for cucumbers may be prepared as follows :—Dig a
trench six feet wide and fifteen inches deep, throwing the
soil on both sides in order to raise them.   Fill up to the top with
well decomposed manure, consolidate by tramping, and
cover with four or five inches of the soil taken out of the
trench.   This should be done not later than September, in
order that the bed may have time to settle before the plants
are set out, or the seed sown.   Sowing the seed is preferable
to plants.

Capsicum (Chili and Long Red).—The first of
these is used for pickling when green ; for mixing with other
pickles ; for placing in vinegar, so as to form Chili vinegar ;
and for grinding, when ripe, for pepper.   Unless in warm
situations it does not often ripen sufficiently.   In the North
Island they ripen freely in the open air.   The seed should
be raised in heat, and the plants, when hardened off, may be
planted out in November, selecting warm sunny situations.

Cress.—There are two varieties, plain and curled leaved.
These may be sown in small quantities any time between
August and April, covering with half-an-inch of fine earth.
One ounce will sow twenty feet of a row four inches wide.

Endive.—Used in salads.   The Green Curled is usually
sown for the main crop ; the White Curled is chiefly grown
for Summer and Autumn ; the Broad-leaved, or Batavia, is
preferred for soups and stews.   A light, dry, but rich soil is
most suitable for this crop.   To secure a continuous supply

from April until Spring, sow in drills eighteen inches apart in October, December, and again in February. Thin out the young plants to twelve inches apart when the leaves are six or eight inches long, blanch them by gathering them in the hand and tying them together near the top with matting.

Egg Plant.—This is a decorative plant. Treatment, same as for capsicums.

Garlic.—Autumn is the best season for planting. Plant the offsets or bulbs in rows twelve inches apart and six inches in the row, one inch deep. They will be ready for taking up as soon as the leaves begin to wither, which will be about December or January. Spread out to dry, and tie up in bunches in a cool, dry place.

Shalot.—The directions given for cultivating garlic are entirely applicable to shalots.

Gourd—Pumpkin, Water Melons, or Vegetable Marrow will grow in any rich light soil. Sow in October; plant two or three seeds within a foot of each other in clumps eight feet apart, and thin out to one or two plants. All that is required for the successful culture of these most useful vegetables is that the soil must be as rich as it can be made—the sight of an old hot bed is best. They require no after attention. A sixpenny packet of any of the above will suffice. One good plant of each will suffice for a small garden. Gourds, Pumpkins, and Vegetable Marrows may be used as green vegetables, or allowed to ripen to be stowed away for Winter cooking.

Horse Radish delights in a rich, deep soil. It is propagated either by seeds or by sets, provided by cutting the main root into lengths of two inches. The tops, or crowns of the roots, form the best sets. Each set should have at least two eyes. They may be planted in May or August in trenches eighteen inches or two feet deep, in dry soil. The roots will be ready for use the second year after planting. A few plants will suffice for most gardens.

Leek.—The best varieties for general use are the London Flag and Musselburg. Sow in September for transplanting in December and January. Always lift with ball of earth so as to injure the roots as little as possible. Plant in a shallow trench. The rows should be eighteen inches apart, and the plants twelve inches in the rows—to be earthed up as they grow. The soil cannot be too rich. An abundance of water or liquid manure will very much add to the size, colour, and mildness of this vegetable. One ounce will sow 100 feet.

Lettuce.—All the Year Round, Drumhead, and Neapolitan Cabbage, Wilmot's Giant, and London White Cos, are all excellent varieties. They may be sown in small quantities once a month throughout the season, from August till March or April. Like all other salads, it thrives well in rich, moist soil. Sow in drills fifteen inches apart, and thin out to one foot. Lettuce may be transplanted, choosing showery weather. A quarter of an ounce will sow a fifty-feet row.

Melons.—A very long list of names might be given, but Munroe's Little Heath, Turner's Scarlet Gem, and Gilbert's Green Flesh are good varieties. Melons can not be grown with any certainty out of doors, except in the warmer parts of the North Island. They can, however, be grown with a little heat supplied by a hot-bed (see directions for growing cucumbers in beds). They however differ from cucumbers inasmuch as they require much more sun to bring the fruit to maturity.

Mint—Spear Mint, for soups, salads, and mint sauce. Any soil will suit ; a few plants will suffice. If not looked after it will soon spread beyond its proper bounds. It should be gathered when in flower, dried, and hung up in a dry, cool place for Winter use.

Mustard and Cress may be sown throughout the season, beginning in August, and ending in March. Make small sowings once a fortnight, on rich soil, covering the seed with a quarter of an inch of fine soil. It will not be necessary to sow in drills, as the crop remains so short a time on the ground that weeds have not time to grow. One ounce will sow twenty feet of a row four inches wide.

Onions—White and Brown Spanish, James' Keeping, Zitteau Giant, Giant Rocco, and Silverskin will be found good varieties for general purposes. Sow, for the main crop, in August or September. A sowing may also be made in October, which will answer for salading during the Summer and for small bulbs for pickling. Sow again in January and early in February, for salads in Autumn ; and finally in February to stand the Winter, for Spring and beginning of Summer. Sow in drills, twelve inches apart. As soon as the young plants appear above ground, run the hoe between the drills to kill seedling weeds. If the seed come up thickly and large bulbs are required, thinning will be necessary in about six weeks after sowing, thin out to four inches apart ; if large bulbs are not desired thinning need not be resorted to; in which case the result will be that a sufficient number of large bulbs will be secured, the balance being small will be useful for pickling. When the crop has nearly finished growing, it is a good plan to bend down the stems flat on the ground with the foot. This operation has the effect of causing the bulbs to grow larger, it also prevents any of them from running to seed. As soon as the crop is ripe let it be taken up at once, if left in the ground afterwards they will soon start to grow which completely destroys their keeping qualities. To grow onions successfully the ground must be deeply trenched and well manured. Before sowing the seed, however, the ground should be firmly tramped to a firm surface, and again tramped after sowing the seed. James' Keeping and Brown Spanish onions are the best for storing for Winter purposes.

Silverskin is the proper variety for pickling, they should be sown thickly on rather poor land and should not be thinned. One ounce will sow a row of seventy feet. The Silverskin should be sown thicker.

Onion Potato or Underground.—This plant is not much cultivated in this colony ; it is however worth a place in the garden. It produces a cluster of bulbs or offsets. It is propagated by offsets of the root of moderate size ; plant in September. They should be inserted in drills twelve inches apart each way, not buried entirely, but the top of the offset just level with the surface. As soon as the leaves have attained their full size, and begin to be brown at the top, let the earth be cleared away down to the ring from whence the roots spring, so that a kind of basin is formed round the bulb. They attain their full growth towards the end of January. For immediate use they may be taken up as they ripen, but for keeping, a little before they attain perfect maturity.

Parsnip.—Hollow Crown and Student are the best in cultivation. The soil cannot be too deep and rich for this crop. The manure should be applied the previous Autumn, if manured at the time of sowing the roots will be rusted. Sow in August and September, in drills fifteen inches apart, and half-an-inch deep. When the seedlings are two or three inches high thin to nine inches apart, and keep the hoe constantly going to destroy young weeds. The crop may with advantage be left in the ground till the end of July and taken up as required during the Winter. · One ounce will sow 100 feet.

Parsley.—Sow in September, in drills quarter-of-an-inch deep. As soon as the plants begin to send up flower stems they should be cut close down; and again, in Autumn, if they have become strong and coarse. This will cause them to shoot afresh. One ounce will sow a row of 100 feet.

Pea.—For first sowing, William the First (three feet), Kinner Gem (two feet and a half), McLean's Little Gem (eighteen inches), Multum in Parvo; late and medium, Yorkshire Hero (two feet and a half), Veitch's Perfection (three feet), Epicurean (three feet), are all good croppers. Sow from August to middle of December. Peas thrive best in light loamy soil. Commence sowing in August and continue throughout September and until December once every three weeks. A pint at a sowing will suffice for a moderate-sized family. Sow the dwarf varieties in drills two feet six inches apart and two inches deep; the tall-growing kinds will require three or four feet. If the seed is good they may be dropped two in an inch for dwarfs; tall-growing kinds may be dropped one inch apart. When the plants are two or three inches high the rows should be hoed between, and the earth drawn up to each side of them. Sticking is not required until the plants show their tendrils. As these successional crops ripen they should be immediately cleared away, the ground dug over and planted with cabbage, broccoli, cauliflowers, or Brussels sprouts. One pint of dwarf peas will sow a drill sixty feet long, and eighty feet of tall varieties.

Potato.—The varieties are too numerous to be named The following will, however, be found good early ripening sorts and keep well :—Walnut-leaved, Royal Ash-leaved, Snowflakes, Early Lapstone Kidneys. A dry, pliable, fresh, and moderately rich soil is the best for every variety of potato. In warm well-sheltered situations a first planting may be made in July, and again in August, and up to November for late crops. It is a good plan to plant when sufficient ground is dug for receiving a row, in rows two feet apart and twelve inches set from set. Plant six inches deep. For very early planting use whole potatoes, weighing from two to three ounces. If sets are used, let each one have not less than two eyes. Hoe as soon as the plants are well over ground, and earth up. This is more particularly necessary for early crops, to save them from cold cutting winds and late frosts. As the early-planted crops are removed from the soil, the ground should be freshly dug and sown with peas, turnips, or planted with cabbages, cauliflowers, or French beans, as required. One peck of potatoes will plant 100 feet, cut into sets with two eyes in each set.

Radish.—Long Scarlet, Short Top White, Red Turnip, and French Breakfast, are the best for general cropping. For Autumn and Winter varieties, White and Black Spanish. These latter varieties are not grown nearly so often as they deserve to be. Radishes may be sown from July to March, at intervals of three weeks. Quarter-of-an-ounce at a time will suffice. The ground should be rich and thoroughly well pulverised; manure should not be applied at the time of sowing. Cover the seed a quarter-of-an-inch, and protect from birds. These seeds may be sown broadcast, as they occupy the ground only for a short period. During dry weather water should be liberally supplied in the evenings. This applies to all kinds of saladings. Four or five ounces of superphosphate of lime or guano to the gallon of water will have a magical effect. One ounce will sow twenty feet.

Rhubarb. — Wyatt's Victoria, Royal Albert, and Mitchell's Early Albert are good early and late varieties. Rhubarb thrives best on deep, strong, moist soil, heavily manured. It may be planted in June, July, or August. Plant in rows four feet apart and two feet in the rows. Seed may be sown in September, in drills three feet apart, and half-an-inch deep, the plants to remain where raised.

Thin out as they make their appearance the following Spring to the required distances.   Rhubarb may be forced by driving stakes into the ground, say three or four feet round each plant, inclining together at the top ; surround these with stable litter, leaving the top open.   Chimney pots, cement casks, or boxes with the bottoms knocked out, will also answer for forcing purposes.   Rhubarb may be forced without either pots or frames, by merely covering the plants six or eight inches deep with light litter, care being taken that the plants are not injured.   Flower stems should be broken down as they appear.   Continue pulling the leaves for use as required till November, after which they should not be touched.'   The more they are stripped after this date, the less productive they will be next year.   In Autumn, remove the decayed leaves and cover up with light, rich manure.

Propagation by Division.—When rhubarb is propagated by division of the root, care must be taken to retain a bud on the crown of each piece, together with a small portion of the root itself, with, if possible, some fibres attached to it.   Rhubarb is benefited by being taken up when old, and the large stools cut in pieces, with a bud on each, and these planted where they are intended to remain, at the same distance as indicated above. In dry weather a good soaking of water or liquid manure will, be of great service.   Four ounces of superphosphate to three gallons of water is a good dressing, equally suitable for all kinds of vegetables.

Sea-Kale delights in deep, rich soil.   It may be raised from seed sown in September ; in drills three feet apart, and finally thinning the plants to two feet apart in the rows. Liquid manure applied once a week to the growing plants, will improve its growth very much.   The better plan is to purchase one-year-old plants, and plant them three in a clump, three feet clump from clump, and eighteen inches plant from plant ; or they may be planted in rows singly, similar to rhubarb.   Those who have but few plants, and have not a convenience for either forwarding by the use of pots or fermenting materials, may produce excellently blanched Sea-Kale in the Spring months by covering the crowns with light friable earth, fine cinder ashes, old tan, or leaf-mould, to a depth of about a foot. As soon as the flower stems begin to appear, all covering should· be removed and the plants allowed to grow, removing all blooming shoots as they appear. Sea-Kale may also be forced by taking up a supply of old roots and stowing them thickly in the corner of any outhouse or stable, and filling in with light soil and litter, and watered occasionally. In this way several excellent cuttings may be obtained in the early Spring. Let the roots be stowed as described any time from May till July.

Spinach. — The Round-Leaved (or Summer) and Prickly-Seeded (or Winter) are the best varieties. Spinach prefers a light, friable loam, enriched with well-decomposed manure. Make a first sowing of the Round-Leaved in August or September, to be continued every three weeks until the end of October. Sow in drills eighteen inches apart, covering the seed half-an-inch. Sow the Prickly or Winter Spinach in February. The outer leaves only should be gathered at a time, the centre being left uninjured to produce successional crops. This direction applies chiefly to the Winter standing crops , those of the Summer may be cut off close to the roots. Successional sowings will only be necessary where large supplies are required. One ounce will sow sixty feet.

Spinach, New Zealand.—This plant is sometimes used as a substitute for Summer spinach—it is not, however, recommended. The seed may be sown in September or October, in drills three feet apart, in rich soil, and thin out to two feet apart. A dozen or twenty plants will afford an abundant daily supply for a considerable period. It will be ready for use in five or six weeks after sowing.

Sage thrives in any light, friable soil. It is propagated by cuttings of the preceding or same year's growth ; if of last year's growth, plant in October ; but, if of the latter, not until December. The most robust shoots should be chosen, and cut six inches in length ; all but the top leaves being removed. Plant in rows six inches apart, four inches deep, in a border facing south, chosing showery weather.

Thyme. — Broad-leaved Green, Narrow-leaved Green, and Lemon-scented. Thyme thrives best on rather poor soil. Propagate by taking up an old plant and divide into as many rooted portions as possible ; plant out in August or September. Although thyme is a perennial, yet after three years it becomes stunted and unproductive, and consequently requires to be raised periodically from seed.

Turnip. — Early Snowball, Early Whitestone, and Golden Ball are all good varieties. A first sowing may be made in September, to be followed by another in October, and again in January and February. Turnips thrive best in a light, rich loam. Sow thinly, in drills twelve inches apart. Thin the plants to nine inches when they have four or five leaves. A sowing may be made broadcast in March, these may not bulb but will make excellent Spring greens when they begin to run to seed in August. They are particularly wholesome at this season of the year. One ounce will sow 150 feet.

Tomatoes thrive best in a rich, light soil. They are particularly susceptible to frost, and should not be planted out till the end of October, safer still in the middle of November, when all danger of Spring frosts has passed. Sow the seeds in pots or boxes in a greenhouse or frame, in September, and as soon as the young plants are tall enough to handle they should be transplanted into three or four-inch pots, and watered well and shaded. They will soon strike, and should then have plenty of sun and air till the time appointed for planting out. This may seem a troublesome plan, but it will repay the trouble where only a few plants are required. They may also be taken from the seed box and planted out where they are to grow. Tomatoes cannot have too much sun, in fact they will not ripen properly lacking heat. Plant in rows four feet apart, the drills running north and south, so that both sides of the drills will have the full sun all day long. Train to a trellis three feet high, or stake in the same manner as peas. As the plants branch out, let the side shoots be thinned out and shortened back to the blossom bunches. After the fruit has been well formed, the superabundant leaves may also be thinned out, exposing the fruit as much as possible to the sun. If any quantity of small green fruit is required for pickling, they should be pulled when no larger than marbles. These form a most excellent pickle. Green tomatoes may also be preserved as chutnee.

THE ORCHARD AND THE
FRUIT GARDEN.

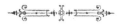

IN selecting a piece of land for a garden or orchard, there are two extremes which should at all times be avoided. The one is when the soil and subsoil are too retentive of moisture ; the other, when the soil is so sandy and poor, that the roots become exposed to sudden droughts. In the former case the trees become choked with lichens, and the points of the branches die prematurely, and the fruit is starved and stunted. If possible, select land intended for fruit trees free from either of the above extremes. A deep, rich, sandy loam is the most suitable. If of sufficient depth let the land be trenched two or three feet deep, as directed for the vegetable garden. Should that method be considered too expensive, a deep ploughing followed by a subsoil plough in the same furrow will answer admirably.

The Planting Season for all kinds of fruit trees commences in April, or as soon as the leaves begin to fall, provided the soil is in a mellow state. In the case of cold

retentive soils—which, however, should be avoided unless
they can be thoroughly drained—the business had better
stand over till Spring; but the ground may be rough trenched
and left exposed to the Winter frosts and rain, and be much
improved for planting purposes ; and then planting may be
continued up to the end of August or first week in September, after which the work should cease.   Nothing can be
more injurious, either to the present or future success of
the trees, than to bury the roots away from the influence of
heat and air ; so long as the roots are sufficiently covered,
so as not to be exposed to the direct influence of the air,
they have all that is necessary for their prosperity.   There
are, however, some essential points to be kept in view in
forming an orchard, which, if not attended to, must lead to
failure.   The soil should be deep and dry ; the situation
should be well sheltered, if not naturally, artificial shelter
must be provided.

Shelter Belts.—Where space is plentiful and land
cheap, a belt of trees may be planted, extending round the
orchard, or at least round those portions exposed to the
strong prevailing winds.   Cupressus Macrocarpa may be
planted on the outer edge, to act as nurses, to be cut out
when the deciduous trees have grown sufficiently.   The
inner rows to consist of ash, oak, elms, and poplars.   The belt
should not be less than one and a half chains wide ; the trees
to be planted in alternate rows ·.·.·.   A row of walnuts may
be planted next the orchard, fifty feet apart. These in themselves will form good shelter, and will yield abundant crops
after a few years.   The inner row of shelter trees should
be at least one hundred feet from the fruit trees. Deciduous
trees are recommended for shelter belts for orchards, for
the reason that while evergreen trees answer admirably in
Summer, they shelter the fruit trees too much from the blasts
of Winter, thereby offering a safe refuge for blights of all
kinds.

Number of Varieties to Plant.—The majority of
fruit-growers cultivate too many kinds of apples.   Ascertain,
if possible, what kinds have been proved by experience best
adapted to soils similar to your own, and then confine yourself to a few of the best varieties.

The Selection of Fruit Trees is a matter of the utmost importance. It is well to remember that a good tree occupies no more room than an indifferent one. Never plant a poor specimen or an inferior variety : such trees are dear at any price. · The best safeguard is either to grow them yourself, or to deal only with a nurseryman who has gained for himself a good repute for clean stocks, well-formed trees, and true to name. Far better pay twenty-five per cent more to such a man, than buy at a much cheaper rate where the same care has not been taken in working up the stock for sale. A few really good varieties will be found more profitable than a large number of mixed kinds. It must, however, be observed that in a country with such a range of climate as New Zealand, it is impossible to give a single list of apples which will be found suitable for all districts. All that can be done is to recommend a really good selection of dessert, cooking, and keeping apples. Should any of them prove failures, let them be cut back and grafted with a variety which has proved itself suitable to the district. This is a better method than. rooting up the tree and planting another ; for the reason that a couple of years at least will be gained by adopting this plan. The following list, with accompanying remarks, have been supplied by Mr. Adams, of Greendale, Canterbury, who has for some years past been testing the qualities of over four hundred varieties of apples in his orchard. He says : The following dozen have proved the most profitable, taking all things into account. They ripen in the order given.

1. Irish Peach—A regular bearer, and free from American blight.

2. Gravenstein—A fine habit of growth, comparatively free from blight.

3. Benoni—Of good habit ; apt to overbear ; the fruit must be thinned or it will be small.

4. Cellini—A handsome fruit, and good cropper.

5. Nelson Codlin—Always fruits well ; fruit smooth and fair.

6. Prince Bismarck—A most profitable apple ; not much attacked by scale.

7. Wagener—An American apple of finest quality; an enormous bearer; not much subject to American blight; adapted for small gardens as it makes but little wood.

8. Scarlet Nonpareil—First-class dessert.

9. Wooling Favourite: a variety of Beauty of Kent— one of the most beautiful as well as profitable of apples; not easily shaken from the trees.

10. Rome Beauty—An American apple; a grand cropper, and good keeper; with exceedingly showy fruit.

11. Morgan's Seedling—A good bearer; very suitable for small gardens.

12. Boston Russet—A heavy cropper.

Dessert Apples.—The same authority has selected the following twelve varieties as of first quality all the year round :—Early Joe, Kerry Pippin, Mother, Ribston Pippin, Cox's Orange, Melon, American Golden Russet, Wagener, Marston's Red Winter, Romanite, Scarlet Nonpareil, Russet Nonpareil, Newton Pippin, and London Pippin.

Keeping Apples.—The following have been selected — Stone Pippin, Stephenson's Winter, Newtown Pippin, Winter Strawberry Pippin, Winter Greening, Rushock Pearmain, Kentucky Readstreak, Chronicle, Allen's Everlasting, Beefing, Cullasage, and Winter Peach. This last variety will keep good for twelve months.

The largest apples are Mobb's Royal, Gloria Mundi, Twenty Ounce, Warner's King, Emperor Alexander, Peasgood's Nonsuch, Lady Hennicker, Lord Nelson, Beauty of Kent, Carter's Blue, Waltham Abbey Seedling, and Yellow Bellefleur, all of which are splendid exhibition apples, and in sheltered places most of them will be found profitable. Adam's Birthday, a fine dessert apple; Baron Ward, a long keeper; Norfolk Bearer, almost blight proof; Cornish Aromatic, a very showy apple; Rawles Janet, and Shockly, two popular American apples, are remarkable for holding their fruit through the strongest winds.

Planting.—Choose well-formed, young trees, two or three years old; insist on having them on blight proof stocks, which means that the roots should be free from blight (such as the Northern Spy), that blight proof scions should be grafted on the blight proof roots, and that ultimately the varieties of apples required should be grafted on these stocks. With such precautions, properly carried out, the trees will be free from American blight (or woolly aphis). Trees are frequently sold purporting to be so worked, which are really only worked above the ground, and which is no advantage at all. Strong and vigorous growing apples should be worked on Northern Spy stocks ; the small and weakly growing varieties, on the Majetin. Young trees should be lifted carefully, and, before planting, cut off every root that grows downward—the surface roots are the most valuable—take off all bruised or ragged ends with a sharp knife. Mark off your land for planting, placing a peg in the ground where each tree is to stand, in alternate rows ∵ ∴ ∵ , twenty feet tree from tree, and twenty-five feet row from row. Some orchardists advocate planting much closer and thinning out afterwards. The former plan is the better for permanent orchards. Make holes, not more than nine inches deep, and larger than required to admit the roots, place the tree in the centre, carefully spreading out the roots all round, then cover up with fine mould, treading gently but firmly with the foot. The stem must stand a little higher out of the ground than required, to allow for settling down. The surface should just cover the collar and no more. If the orchard is in an exposed situation, the trees will require staking as directed for transplanted trees. The soil must be dry at the time of planting: this is essential to success. If the trees have been well-formed from the nursery, they will require very little pruning for some years, beyond Summer stopping or pruning, which is the best treatment of all (see Summer stopping). During the early years of their growth, the trees should be encouraged to assume a bowl-shaped appearance, which can easily be done if they have been attended to from the first. The ground should be kept free from weeds or grass for at least six or eight feet each side of the tree. The intervening space may in the meantime be cropped with roots , do not plant small fruits such as currants, gooseberries, or raspberries, which would prevent the free use of the drill grubber during the Summer months. Never use a spade within six feet of the stems. Use a flat-tined fork, which will not injure the surface roots, which are the most valuable and most essential to the production of the best fruit.

Pruning may be classed under three heads, viz :—
Rest or Winter pruning, Summer pruning, and root pruning.
A very great diversity of opinion exists on the subject of
pruning apple trees'; while some advocate a vigorous use
of the knife, others condemn the practice.   Our own
opinion is that the knife should be sparingly used on
young standard trees : which must, however, be worked
into symmetrical form, and this should be done in the
nursery ; when this has been properly attended to, the
only after pruning necessary will be to keep the centre of
the tree as open as possible, and to remove all branches
which have a tendency to grow out of their place.   This
may be achieved by the simple but much neglected system
known as Summer pruning or stopping.   If this is attended
to, there will be little necessity for the knife.

Large orchard trees, when in their prime, require very
little pruning ; once in three years may then suffice to
regulate them.   Their pruning will simply consist of a
slight thinning out of exhausted or cross boughs, which,·
situated in the interior of the tree, cannot bring fruit to
perfection, and, in bearing, rob the superior parts of the
tree.   When, however, the trees become somewhat aged,
they require more attention ; for when it is found that they
cannot bring all the fruit which may "set" to perfection,
it becomes necessary to sacrifice some portion, in order to
throw strength into the remainder.   As long as the tree
continues to bear at all, the best fruit will ever be at the
extremities of the boughs ; nature, therefore, must be
followed, or rather in this case anticipated.   Once in a
couple of years the trees should be gone over, and much
of the interior wood cut away.   The wearing-out wood
may readily be distinguished by its stunted character, and
frequently by its dead parts, which may be taken as an
indication of the breaking up of the constitution of the tree.
There is no occasion to prune the extreme points ; the
removal of the larger decaying branches will suffice.   It
often happens, nevertheless, that a good deal of young
annual spray grows out of the old branches ; such, occasionally, should be thinned away, or it will decoy the sap
from the more important portions of the trees.   Winter
pruning may be performed any time between May and
the middle of August.

Root Pruning.—A writer in *The Garden* gives the following practical instructions as to how this operation should be performed :— " A tree from ten to fifteen years old should have a trench cut half way round it at a distance of five or six feet from the bole. The trench must be deep enough to enable the operator to cut through all the roots ; then take a fork and work well under the ball of earth, cutting off all roots that have struck deep into the ground. For the soil that has been thrown out, some from another part of the garden should be substituted ; the new soil will be better for the tree than the old exhausted material. In applying the new soil endeavour to get the roots nearer the surface than they were before. The object in doing half the roots only is to prevent the tree from receiving too great a shock to the system. During the following season new fibres will be formed where the roots were cut, and the other half of the tree can be done the following season. When the work is done in this way there is no danger of the tree being blown over, nor will the crop of fruit be lost the first year after the pruning.

Transplanting may with advantage be resorted to under totally different circumstances. When young trees exhibit a tendency to make too much wood and not many fruit spurs ; or in the case of trees which have got their roots into a cold ungenial sub-soil, and whose timber assumes a weakly appearance, being cankered or decayed at the points. By transplanting a too vigorous tree it will be thrown into bearing, and by lifting the unhealthy tree and planting it on the surface, health and vigour will be restored. In either case, care must be taken to lift the tree carefully, injuring as few of the fibrous roots as possible. The strong roots which have been broken off must be pared with a clean cut. In proportion as the roots have been destroyed while lifting, a corresponding quantity of the branches must be removed. When planting, spread the roots out carefully, and fill in with fine, dry mould, pressing the soil round the stem gently but firmly with the foot ; then drive a stout pointed stake firmly into the ground, a few inches from the stem ; to this fasten the tree with some soft material such as soft rope or native flax. Some gardeners prefer three stakes driven in at equal distances

E

from the stem (say two feet), fastening a piece of sacking loosely round the stem to prevent the band from chafing, passing a soft rope round this band, and tying to each stake in the following manner, the centre dot representing the stem of the tree. We have seen young trees almost barren rendered abundantly fruitful the following season after having been shifted. Transplanting may be done any time from May till August. A barrow load or two of manure or litter spread round each shifted tree will preserve the fibrous roots from being injured by drought or hot winds ; in dry weather a few buckets of water occasionally administered will be of benefit to the tree. This will only be necessary in protracted droughts.

Apples and Pears treated as Espaliers.—This mode of growing fruit trees requires constant attention and skill, it is therefore not suitable for amateur gardeners. A trellis four to five feet high, formed of battens, wire, or iron rods will answer, placed along the side walks three or four feet from the edging To these the trees are trained as on a wall, with this difference, that instead of being nailed, the branches are usually tied ; the fastenings should be soft hemp cords or strips of bass or native flax. In selecting trees for espaliers it will be well to select those which have been worked upon *quince* or some other slow-growing stocks. Summer pruning and stopping is indispensable to successful fruit growing under these conditions.

The Pear.—This delicious fruit does not receive the attention it deserves in our gardens : the reason probably is that it is rather longer in bearing than the apple. With judicious treatment this may in a great measure be obviated. Any good, dry soil will do for pears. By careful selection the ripening period may be extended over several months. The first point to consider is the stock upon which the pear should be grafted. Considerable diversity of opinion exists on this head, some recommending the quince, others again condemning it, and preferring the pear stock. Our opinion is that they are both good when the soil is suitable. The pear stock produces a stronger growing tree and more enduring than the quince ; but it is longer in coming into bearing. Rampant growing varieties should therefore be grafted on quince stocks, and the shy growers on the pear stock. Where the situation is naturally damp, and the soil rich in character, the quince will thrive ; but where it is very dry and sandy, it will make little progress, and the fruit will be small and gritty. Common observation will, however, easily enable any one to determine whether the soil is suitable for the one stock or the other.

The mode of training is another subject deserving attention. If the espalier system is preferred, it must be remembered that it involves a considerable outlay in the first place if a permanent railing of iron is erected, and if wooden stakes are employed, then these are constantly giving way, and fresh ones are required ; endless expense is consequently incurred. Dwarf standards, if properly managed, will obviate the use of these expensive props. If the ground is properly drained—an essential point as regards the flavour of the fruit as well as the productiveness of the trees—they may be planted ten or fifteen feet apart. Should they grow too vigorously—which is often the case with pears grafted on their own stocks—this may be counteracted by simply sticking a few strong stakes into the ground, to which the branches should be tied, drawing them gently towards the earth till the bark begins to creak. This system checks the flow of sap, and causes the formation of fruit buds. If this treatment has not the desired effect, then judicious root pruning or transplanting must be resorted to. The most important point in the management of pear trees hinges on the Summer pruning. Many imagine that when the trees are planted there is nothing more to be done, except picking the fruit. This notion has converted some little gardens into little forests. During the Summer let the superfluous shoots be stopped back to within three inches of the old bearing wood—broken off rather than cut. This will cause flower buds to be formed at the base of the shoots so treated. The projecting part can be removed in Autumn or Winter, close to the fruit buds. By following this mode of treatment the trees will be kept within a limited space and their productiveness secured. The following varieties will be found suitable for general purposes :—Williams' Boncretian and

Jargonelle, Marie Louise, Easter Beurre, Napoleon, Beurre-bosc, Beurre d'Amaulis, Winter Nelis, Autumn Bergamot, Pitmaston Duchess, Louis' Bonne of Jersey, Beurre Clairgeau, Beurre Baehlieu, Vicar of Winkfield.

Almonds.—Any light rich soil will suit almonds. The same mode of treatment as that indicated for plums will suit for almonds. The Soft shell is the most generally useful.

The Apricot.—This delicious fruit does not bear freely in all localities, it requires plenty of shelter and a deep moist soil, so long as stagnant water does not lie about the roots. It bears freely when treated as a wall tree—at least in the South Island. It however grows to a large size, and bears well as a standard in many. localities. As a standard it requires very little pruning, simply cutting out superfluous or exhausted wood. Apricots, treated as wall trees, like plums, are prone to produce coarse shoots ; these should be pinched in during the Summer, if not done at that period they must be cut away during May, June or July. The apricot, when in proper condition, produces, perhaps, more natural spurs than most of our fruit trees ; and although some kinds will blossom and bear on the young wood, yet on the true spurs we must mainly rely, for blossoms from the young shoots most generally develop imperfectly. The pruner, therefore, must, with some precision, cut away cleanly all immature-looking sprigs which may tend to shade the blossom-bud and produce too much spray in the succeeding Summer. The following varieties can be recommended:— Moorpark, Kaisha and Royal.

The Cherry will thrive in any deep sandy loam. They are propagated by budding or grafting on wild cherry stocks, after the same manner as pears and apples. Cherries require very little pruning. No shortening back is necessary. Pruning resolves itself into thinning away cross shoots, and those interior branches which become crowded. Plant out in May, June or August. The following varieties may be relied on :—May Duke, Amberheart, Blackeagle, Blackheart, Bigarreau, and the Morrello for preserving.

Blackberries.—Great improvements have been made of late years in this useful fruit. They will grow in any soil, but they prefer a moist, shady situation. They may be planted against any back fence or outhouse. The Lawton may be grown in rows like the raspberry, and pruned in the same manner. The Italian is a late variety, ripening towards the Autumn; the fruit is not quite so large as the Lawton, but the flavour is much finer: it is not however so profuse a cropper.

The Currant.—The red and white will thrive in any light, rich soil, and may be produced from seed, but the more general mode of propagation is by cuttings. Select strong shoots of last season's growth, from six to twelve inches long, cutting off a few inches of the top, then remove all the eyes except three or four at the top, plant in rows one foot apart each way, this may be done at the same time as pruning. The young plants will be ready for planting out the second year. On the first formation of the head much of the future symmetry of the bush depends. The heart of the bush must be kept well opened by pinching out or rubbing off all the young shoots which have a tendency to grow inwards. The leaders, that is the main branches, must have each season's growth cut back at least one-half its length, the object being to encourage side spurs, which should be cut back to within half-an-inch of the base. These are the spurs which bear the fruit. A well-formed tree should have ten or a dozen main stems. Suckers must be removed as soon as they appear above ground. Another system of training currant and gooseberry bushes is by tying the main stems down to a hoop which has been fastened to stakes stuck in the ground; the hoop (wood or iron) being fastened with copper wire. The centre of the bush is kept clear of all spray or superfluous wood, the spurs or side branches which grow from the main stems are pinched back in Summer, or cut back to within a couple of eyes in Winter. This system of training entails some extra trouble without, in our opinion, producing commensurate results. The best varieties are the Red and White Dutch. There are several new varieties possessing great excellence.

Black Currant.—This currant delights in a rich, moist soil, and will thrive in shady situations. Differing from the white and red from the fact that very little pruning is required, this operation being simply confined to thinning out superfluous shoots and cutting out the old exhausted branches. When the bushes begin to grow too large and inclined to straggle, the best plan will be to take out each alternate bush and plant a young one, rooting out the others as soon as the young stock begins to bear. The principal crop of fruit is borne on the annual shoots rather than on the spurs; means must therefore be taken to excite and sustain a regular sprinkling of such wood all over the tree, and in this case there is not the same necessity for keeping the middle of the bush open as in the red and white currant and gooseberry. Black Naples and Lee's Prolific are good varieties.

The Fig.—Propagated by seeds, layers and cuttings, by suckers, and by grafting. Almost any moderately-rich soil, provided it is not too dry, will answer for fig trees. Figs cannot be successfully grown against walls or fences unless attention is paid to disbudding. In vigorous health they always produce a host of superfluous suckers from the roots. On examining the character of the wood as it springs forth, two or three distinct kinds of wood may be clearly traced. One will be found of an over-luxuriant character, long in the joints, and thick or succulent in substance; a second kind will be found almost as weakly as straws, lanky and spongy; and a third kind will be found robust, but short-jointed and compact. The last is the kind of wood to reserve for bearing. *Stopping.*—Fig trees which bear an abundance of short-jointed wood will require attention in the way of stopping—but they are the exception. It is therefore well to stop all those of a doubtful character at the end of February or early in March, merely pinching off or squeezing flat the terminal growing point. This will induce the fruit for the ensuing year to commence forming, so as to receive a decisive character. A too-early stopping with some figs would cause them to develop the fruit for the ensuing year too early, when they would be likely to perish, should the following Winter prove a severe one. Figs may, however, be successfully grown in this climate as standards, with little attention, save an occasional thinning of superfluous shoots.

Plant in rows fifteen feet apart and twelve feet tree from tree. The North Island is generally better suited for the fig as a standard tree than Canterbury or Otago. The best varieties are Black Bourjassotte, Brown Turkey and varieties, Brunswick, and Castle Kennedy.

The Gooseberry may be propagated as directed for the currant. Plant in rows six feet apart and four feet in the rows. Pruning may commence as soon as the leaves begin to fall, and on till July—leave only such branches in the tree as contain good firm buds. The shoots which are left should be well ripened. Having selected such well-ripened wood to be left on the tree, all spindly and weak shoots should be removed. The wood to be removed should not be cut off close to the main branches, but sufficient should be left on to form "spurs," say three-quarters of an inch long. All coarse thick shoots should be cut clean away to the stem. Suckers must also be removed. To sum the matter up concisely, pruning a gooseberry bush properly consists in cutting away, as directed, at least two-thirds of the annual shoots, and leaving the remainder shortened to two-thirds of their length, and all pointing away from the centre of the tree, which should be open like a shallow basin. The hoop system, as described in the culture of currants, answers admirably for gooseberries. A top-dressing of manure in the Autumn will ensure a good crop the following season, unless the soil is naturally rich, in which case the manure had better be dispensed with. Gooseberries will not thrive in soils with a cold subsoil. The following will be found useful varieties—Early Sulphur (yellow), Golden Purse, Ironmonger (red), Lancashire Hero, Warrington, and Champagne (red and yellow.)

Medlars are grown from seeds, which should be sown as soon as the fruit is ripe. They take two years to come up. These merely require thinning out occasionally to prevent the centres of the trees from becoming too dense, thereby excluding the necessary sun and air. Varieties—Dutch and Nottingham Medlar. As soon as the trees begin to fruit, the ground surrounding them should be sown with grass, as the fruit should be allowed to fall and remain on the grass for a week or so till quite soft, or they may be gathered and stored in a dark and airy place on shelves.

Mulberries.—Young trees must be prevented from becoming too crowded with wood. There are several varieties. The black mulberry (*Morus nigra*) produces the best fruit. Every garden should have a tree or two ; they are a delicious fruit, requiring little or no attention. The varieties of the white mulberry *(Morus alba)* are the most useful for producing leaves for feeding silk-worms.

Nuts.—The best varieties are the Red and the White Filberts. Almost any light loamy soil will answer. Dig or trench the ground deeply. The main thing in the majority of soils is to guard against over-luxuriance. This has the tendency of producing only male flowers. *Planting.*—When planted in rows they should be set not nearer than ten or twelve feet apart. If after a few years the bushes grow too gross, root-pruning may be resorted to, and a corresponding thinning out of rampant shoots or branches. The nut produces both male and female blossoms on the same bush. The male blossoms may easily be known by their gay dangling appearance, and by the yellow dust they shed on being handled—this dust is the fertilizing pollen. The female blossoms, on the contrary, are so obscure that they have to be sought for. When in full blossom they are of a lively pink colour, and appear like little brushes at the tips of the side shoots produced by mature wood. The cultivation of nuts is by no means difficult ; indeed they are more likely to be injured by over-cultivation than otherwise. They should, in all cases, be trained to a single stem ; for the production of suckers (shoots from the roots). or rather, the permitting them to remain is most injurious to their future success. Suckers will spring up, but they must be removed every year. The only pruning necessary will be an occasional thinning of the inner branches, that light and air can circulate freely through those that are left. Nuts are propagated by seeds, layers, and suckers.

The Peach.—A few years ago this delicious fruit was as easy and as certain of culture as the apple. Planted as standards they required little attention, save an occasional tying-up or supporting of the over-laden fruit-bearing branches. Almost in every garden in the colony, North and South, luxuriant trees were to be found. Within the last few years, however, things have changed, and now a really healthy peach tree is rarely to be met with. Premature decay seems to have attacked old and young trees alike : so much so that many orchards which were once noted for the quantity and quality of their peaches have almost died out. Unfortunately no specific has as yet been discovered for the prevention of this blight. Exhaustion of the soil is not the cause ; for we have seen trees planted in virgin soil and in the course of two or three years they have shared the same fate as those of longer growth. Vigorous cutting back and top-dressing with half-inch bones and with lime has been suggested; while some experienced gardeners think that a total change of stocks for grafting upon would have a beneficial effect. Almond stones have been imported with this view. Professor Kirk, in his report on fruit blights and deseases of fruit trees in New Zealand, recommends the use of the mussel plum stock. He thinks that its adoption would once more allow of the profitable cultivation of the peach. *Planting.*—Peaches are very impatient of wet ; they require a light rich loam. Plant almost on the surface, as directed for apples, and stake if necessary. Pruning has not been practised much in the past, but as the trees are now more difficult of growth it may be better to pay a little attention to it in the future. The principal points to observe will be to thin out or remove superfluous shoots, in order to ensure sufficient light and a due circulation of air to the remainder.

The Nectarine.—This fruit requires exactly the same treatment as that recommended for the peach. It is, however, more susceptable to injury from exposure to hot parching winds.

Select List of Peaches and Nectarines.— *Peaches :* American Pound, Early Beatrice, Lady Palmerston, Late Admiral, Noblesse, Red Magdalene, Tunmer's Surprise, and Royal George. *Nectarines :* Red Roman, Stanwick, and Oldenburg.

The Plum.—A good sound loam is the soil best suited for plums. Plant in rows fifteen feet apart each way. They require little pruning as standards, except thinning out to give light and air, and to throw additional vigour to the bearing branches. Some varieties of the plum : such, for instance, as the Washington and Magnum Bonum, &c., if planted in a liberal soil, produce excessive growths of rampant wood, which is very detrimental to the well-being of the tree, and should not be allowed to grow.   They should be removed during the growing season ; if not done then they must be .cut clean out in Winter.   The gross shoots having been cut clean away, and the remainder thinned duly out, little remains to be done with old or bearing trees, unless they are producing too much gross wood, when they should be root-pruned as directed for apples and pears.   List of 12 select plums given in their order of ripening :—Early Mirabelli, middle of January ; Early Rivers, last of January ; Early Orleans, beginning of February ; Brahy's Greengage and Belle de Louvain, middle of February ; Jefferson and Pond's Seedling, end of February ; Late Black Orleans, Damson, and Coe's Golden Drop, early in March ; Reine Claude Bavy, middle of March ; Coe's Late Red, 'April.

Quince.—Every garden should have at least one or two quince trees.   Grown as standards, they require a loamy soil. They occupy but little space, and require no pruning except an occasional thinning of the over-crowded inner branches.

The Raspberry succeeds in any rich garden soil that is not too stiff, but prefers one that is very rich and rather moist.   It grows exceedingly well in sandy, alluvial ground, also in peat and soils that are mixed with peat ; but those that are heavy and compact, becoming hard in dry weather, do not suit it.   In all cases abundance of decomposed manure should be applied when the ground is trenched before planting, and afterwards every Autumn as a top dressing, to be forked in in the following Spring.   The ground should be trenched at least two feet deep, and if to the depth of three feet so much the better.   Raspberries are culti-vated by suckers or by seeds, the usual mode being by suckers.   Select young canes, with plenty of fibrous roots. Plant three in each clump, six inches apart, in rows four feet apart, and three feet clump from clump.   Another plan which commends itself for its neatness is to plant single canes, two feet apart in rows, along a trellis composed of three wires ; the canes to be tied to the wire.   Before or after the young canes are planted they should be cut back to half their length.

Pruning—It is good practice to go over the plantation in December and thin out the young suckers or rods of the current year's growth, leaving five or six of the strongest to each stool—this will save much work in the Winter pruning, and will materially improve the quality of the fruit. Should this thinning be omitted, as is usually the case in colonial gardens, all the weak shoots must be cut away as soon as the leaves begin to fall, and four or five of the strongest left, which must be shortened one third of their length, leaving the canes from four to five feet long, according to growth. The wood which has borne fruit this year must also be cut away. Tie the canes in bunches of four or five. Plantations may be made any time from May till August If properly attended to in the matter of thinning, pruning, and manuring, a plantation will last for ten or a dozen years. The following are good varieties :—Red and Yellow Antwerp, Kentish Fill-basket, and Carter's Prolific.

Strawberries.—No plant makes a more profitable return for good treatment and cultivation than the strawberry, although they will grow and fruit in almost any soil and situation, as is evidenced by the unfavourable places one occasionally meets them in, and the conditions under which they exist. To do them really well they require a good, deep loam, resting on a clayey subsoil, as the roots delight in a cool, moist bottom ; and when this can be secured for them, no amount of sunshine will harm them, but, on the contrary, they will be all the better for the exposure, especially as regards the quality and flavour of the fruit. When huddled together, with a mass of foliage overlapping, or grown under the shade of fruit bushes or trees, as is frequently the case, they never attain that degree of perfection they do on a nice, sunny border, or in an open situation in the vegetable quarters of the kitchen garden. Shade is fatal to flavour and the other good qualities for which the strawberries are prized ; for without moderate sunlight the crude juices are not converted into saccharine matter, without which they are little better than so much pulp and water, insipid and flavourless. To grow strawberries to the greatest perfection the beds should be renewed every three or four years, at most. For forming new beds, runners should be taken off the old plants in December, or early in January, and planted in nursery beds in a shady situation, until they form strong, well-rooted plants ; this should be in March or April. They should then be carefully lifted with a trowel (taking care to saturate the bed with water the previous evening), and planted in their permanent quarters. This is a far better system than trusting to runners rooting in the rows. Before planting, the trenched ground should be tramped as firm as possible, otherwise the young plants will run too much to leaf. This is an important point in successful strawberry culture, and should not be neglected. Plant in rows two feet apart, and eighteen inches plant from plant in the rows, press the soil firmly round each plant, and give a good soaking of water, which must be continued a couple of times a week in the event of continued dry weather. A plantation made in this way will bear a moderate crop the following season.

The plants must be cleared of all runners as they appear. This will concentrate the energies of the plant in developing strong, fruity crowns for the following season. Another system in strawberry culture is to allow the runners to grow, but to prevent them from rooting, by simply passing a dutch hoe along the rows under the runners, and lifting them up. Unless constant attention be paid to cutting the runners, two or three will grow for every one which has been cut, and the energies of the plant will be more heavily taxed. It is a common practice in the Old Country to spread clean drawn straw along the rows of strawberries, under the leaves, just before fruiting commences. Grass mowings from the lawn would answer equally well. This serves the double purpose of keeping the fruit perfectly clean and of keeping the soil shaded from the sun. Strawberries are very impatient of drought and will not produce freely without plenty of moisture, especially when the fruit is forming—afterwards much moisture is detrimental to the flavour of the fruit. Watering in this country is not often necessary ; but, when required, it should consist of a thorough soaking or irrigation if possible. In May, the beds should be cleared of all stray runners and withered leaves ; but on no account should green leaves be removed, as their function is to mature the crowns for next year's crop.

The spade should never be used among strawberries, as the roots lie close to the surface, and, if destroyed, the healthy vigour of the plant will be impaired. A light forking is all that is necessary, top dressing with decomposed manure.

The following are good varieties :—Black Prince (early), Keen's Seedling, La Marguerite, Rifleman, Sir Joseph Paxton, Trollope's Victoria.

The Vine can be successfully grown in any light porous soil. The most suitable, however, being a calcareous loam on a dry subsoil. Whatever be the character of the surface soil, the substratum (or subsoil) must be free from stagnant water. Unless these conditions are observed it will be useless to try to grow vines successfully. If the ground is naturally deep and dry very little will be required beyond deep trenching and the application of well-rotted manure. One of the most important improvers or correctors of soil is lime- rubbish. A great deal of trouble is sometimes gone to in preparing vine borders, such as excavating the soil for three feet deep, paving the bottom of the trench with lime rubbish, old bones, and fresh soil. We do not consider this necessary, provided the soil is naturally good, when the treatment above referred to will suffice. The requisite nourishment can be supplied by liberal top-dressing each season, which should be applied in May or June. One of the main features in vine culture should be to encourage a vigorous surface root action. This can only be done by a generous treatment of the surface soil of the border. Writing on this subject Mr. Thomson (an authority on vine culture) says :—

The fact that the roots of vines require to be as carefully cultivated as their stems is in numerous instances not systematically recognised nor acted upon. What is considered an orthodox border is made, and young vines planted, and while every necessary detail connected with the welfare of the stems is attended to with care, that upon which success mainly depends—namely, the culture of their roots—is not attended to with the regularity and care that is necessary to keep them where they ought to be—near the surface of the border.

The first step in leading the roots in their downward course is in mixing into the border a quantity of ordinary manure from the farm or stables. Naturally, the roots have the instinct, if the term may be applied, of going where they get most to feed upon ; and planted in a border thus enriched, with the surface of it left uncovered, the roots go down in search of the more moist and consequently more available elements of nutrition at a distance from the exposed, drier surface. If at first no such manure is mixed in the soil, but instead of it bones and other appropriate manures, and immediately the vines are planted the farm-yard manure be placed on the surface as a mulching, and it be kept moist all through the season of the growth of the vines, the moisture and elements of nutrition in the surface dressing will attract the roots. It is not necessary nor desirable —should the first Summer be dry and hot—that more water should be applied than will keep the surface of the border moist by artificial waterings. The bottom will take care of itself, and if the upper portion is thus kept moist the roots will keep to it as sure as water runs downhill.

Every third year, some time late in Autumn or in Winter, when the vines are at rest, the mulching should be removed, and also the surface soil till the roots are reached, and immediately over them should be laid three or four inches of fresh loam and horse droppings in the proportion of four parts of the former to one part of the latter, and also a few barrowfuls of old mortar or charcoal rather finely pounded, then over the whole throw as much rough stable litter as will keep the frost out. After the vines have begun growing in Spring remove the dry litter ; then, or some time before there is any chance of drought affecting the surface of the border, carefully lay on three or four inches of good farm-yard manure, and keep it moist. This process, if attended to, will keep the roots at the surface in the greatest health and activity. This is termed " root cultivation ; " and if neglected the roots go down in search of moisture and nourishment, because they cannot get such at the surface, and the fruit is not so fine.

As we are addressing ourselves to amateurs it may be necessary to explain the technical terms in common use amongst practical men, the principal ones have the merit of being peculiarly expressive.

Disbudding signifies the removal of every opening bud, at the period of leafing, which is not needed for the present year's crop, or for filling up some space on the wall or trellis which would otherwise remain bare.

Thinning out.—This process consists of going over the vines again about the period they commence blossoming, and then making a final selection of the shoots to be allowed to remain. This is an operation too often neglected, and ends in the vine speedily becoming a confused mass of shoots.

Stopping.—This is pinching off the ends of those shoots which are to remain, and is generally performed at one joint beyond the one bearing the bunch. The best time for stopping will be about a week or so after the young bunch is well developed. At this early stage, the house should be kept moist by constantly wetting the floors and walls. It should be borne in mind that leaf should not be permitted to overlap leaf, and, above all, that no growing spray, whether lateral or terminal, should be allowed to shade the principal leaves. As the berries advance in size, thinning will be necessary : of course, where vines are grown on a large scale out of doors, for wine purposes, thinning will be out of the question, but against fences and in houses thinning must be attended to if fine, large, well-ripened berries are to be obtained.

Thinning.—When the grapes are well set the bunches should be looked over and thinned, removing one-third of the young berries, reserving always the most promising ones. The quantity of bunches to be left on each vine must depend upon its size and age. The bunches should be handled as little as possible. Immediately after thinning the bunches the vine should have a good syringing (it must, however, here be stated that many experienced vine growers object to the use of the syringe, asserting that it should never be used after the vines have burst into leaf). Where artificial heat is used, it should now be increased to 80° during the day, and from 65° to 70° at night. This will be in September.

Pruning.—There are commonly three distinct methods of pruning practised—First, spur-pruning ; second, long-rod pruning ; third, ordinary pruning. Pruning should commence as soon as the leaves are all off, on no account deferred till Spring on account of the rapid rising of the

sap, when the loss of sap would be great, thereby impart-
ing the vigor of the plant, by what is called bleeding.
Pruning on the spur system consists in carying up one
leading shoot to the back of the house, establishing thereon
what are termed spurs, at regular distances. About one
to every foot is sufficient. These spurs are first developed as side-shoots, and in order to insure their full development, they are produced during about three seasons. A
good cane nearly the length of the roof, and about three-
quarters of an inch diameter, may be pruned to one-third
the rafter length the first year, another third the second
year, and the remainder the third year. By this plan sup-
posing a rafter 15 feet long, there will be about five large
bunches the first year, ten the second, and fifteen or more
the third year; and this will be found to tax the powers of the
vine rather severely. By this mode every side shoot will be
strongly developed, and consequently a selection may be made.
The subsequent pruning simply consists in cutting each of
these back annually to what has been termed the "spawn
eye" that is to say, the last eye at the base of the young
side-shoot, although some leave another eye.

Ordinary pruning is such as is commonly practised on
outdoor vines trained against a house or fence, where the
leading shoots are carried almost at random, and at first
chiefly with a view to get the house or fence covered. Here
the pruner selects according to the character of the wood,
little heeding its situation, reserving the short-jointed and
strong, and cutting away the weak. The shoots reserved are
shortened back with reference to the space they have to occupy,
say from three to six or eight eyes, as the case may be.

In all pruning it is an axiom to cut an inch or so above
the eye or bud.

The following varieties are the best for the following
purposes :—*For Early Grapes*—Black Hamburg, Black
Fontignan, Madresfield Court (also black) ; (white) Royal
Muscadine, Buckland's Sweetwater, Foster's White Seedling.
Middle Season Grapes (Black).—Black Hamburg, Madres-
field Court. (White).—Buckland's Sweetwater, Muscat of
Alexandria. *Late Grapes.*—(Black) Black Alicante, Lady
Downes, Gros Guillaume. (White).—Muscat of Alexandria,
Golden Queen, Calabrian Raisin. The Black Hamburg and
Muscat of Alexandria are the two best for general culture.

Propagation.—Vines may be propagated either from seed, eyes, cuttings, or by grafting. Propagation by seed is resorted to for the purpose of producing new varieties. The seed should be sown in August in heat, and transplanted into four-inch pots, increasing the size as required. The great element of vine-culture is to secure a continuous vigorous growth. Propagation by eyes is accomplished in the following manner :—Shoots for eyes must be obtained from well-ripened wood, selecting short-jointed lateral shoots, which will be taken when the vines are pruned in May or June. They should be labelled and heeled in soil till required in Spring. The eyes are prepared for planting by cutting them out, inserting the knife half-an-inch above the bud and cutting them out the same distance below ; or by simply cutting the shoot across, an inch above and as much below the eye. The young roots will proceed from the wood *below* the eye. These are planted round the sides of a five-inch pot, three or four in each pot. Or the eyes may be inserted in a piece of turf about six inches square, having a hole scooped out large enough to contain the eye, along with a little mould. The vines are set close together on a bench in a warm vinery, and kept moist. This is a favourite plan with many vine growers in England. Vines grow freely from cuttings, which should be selected at pruning time, choosing only well-ripened and short-jointed wood. The cuttings may be planted in pots, boxes, or out-of-doors. Each cutting should have two eyes over ground and one or two under the surface.

Planting.—The following method is considered a suitable one for most cases, presuming that the border has been prepared as directed. The vines should be planted three feet apart, allowing one rod to each vine. Plants one year old should be used, and the canes should be cut down to within two or three feet : this length of cane will be required to reach the bottom wire to which the cane is tied after it is planted. Care must be taken in planting not to bury the cane. The roots should be evenly spread on the border prepared for them, and covered with four or six inches of soil. Before planting, the canes will have to be pushed through the hole in the wall and tied to the wire inside. Vines thrive best when planted outside the house. The

F

best time for planting will be from the beginning of August up to the first week in September, according to locality. The plants must be watered if the soil and weather be dry at the time of planting. When the planting has been completed the border should be covered with ten or twelve inches of litter. Vines grown under glass, without artificial heat, take about eight months to ripen their fruit.. As the warm weather advances air must be given freely, and a moist atmosphere must be maintained by syringing and watering the floors. It is a good plan to give a little night ventilation during the months of October and November.

Rules as to Temperature.—During the nights, beginning with a newly-started vinery, no harm will result if the temperature fall to 35° every night till the buds break; such a low temperature is preferable to a high one by means of hot-water pipes or flues. After the bud breaks, and from that period onward till the branches come into flower, a night temperature of from 45° to 50° will be sufficient in cold weather. During the flowering period the minimum should be 50° at sunrise, and after flowering and onward till the grapes are ripe, it may range at from 60° to 70° (by fire heat, if necessary), according to the weather.

Day Temperature.—From the time the vinery is started till the buds break much should be made of the sunlight, aided by fire heat. The heat should be got up early in the day: on dull days the maximum should be 60°, and on sunny days 70° to 75°. After the buds have broken, and from then till the vines come into flower, the maximum by sun should be 80°, and in dull weather from ·65° to 70°, according to the temperature out-of-doors. When the berries are all set, it should be raised to 85° or 90° on fine and 75° on cold and dull days, and a lower temperature should not be given till the fruit is ripe. Space will not permit in this treatise of going more fully into the culture and management of the vine, which would require a volume of itself. We can, however, with confidence recommend to our readers a little work on the " Grape Vine : its Propagation and Culture," by John Simpson, from which we have obtained some of the above information.

The insects and diseases injurious to the vine are the vine-louse (Phylloxera vastatrix, which pest has not yet made its appearance in New Zealand); mealy bug, red spider and thrip; mildew shanking, rust, warty leaves, and scorching of the berries. For the prevention of which, see chapter on "Injurious Insects," &c., &c.

Walnut.—There are several varieties of this favourite nut. They require a deep loamy and fertile soil. They are propagated by seeds, grafting and budding; by seed is however the most general method. Select the finest and best nuts; when thoroughly ripe bury in sand till Spring. Sow in rows two feet apart, covering the nuts with two inches of soil. The young trees should be transplanted every second year till permanently planted out. Plant seventy feet apart, in an open, airy situation. The only pruning they require is to remove straggly branches, so as to preserve the symetry of the tree. Walnuts will commence to bear in this colony when six or seven years old, increasing with age. Few fruit trees will be found more profitable than the walnut. As yet they seem to have resisted the attacks of parasites. The only drawback we are aware of to the successful culture of the walnut are the late frosts which occasionally destroy the chances of a crop for the season. This refers more particularly to the South Island. By planting the late varieties this may to some extent be avoided. For pickling, the fruit should be pulled while it can be easily pierced by a needle. Walnut orchards have been known to yield £150 per acre for little more than thirty trees.

GRAFTING, IN-ARCHING AND BUDDING.

(See Plate No. 1, with references attached.)

Grafting is one of the most simple and yet most important operations in the orchard, as by its means a worthless tree may be converted into a valuable one. The operation should be performed in Spring (September and October), when the sap begins to circulate freely. The art of grafting is of very ancient origin: it may be described as the application of a portion of the shoot or root of one tree or plant to the stem, shoot, branch, or root of another, so that the two shall coalesce (or join) and form but one plant. The

shoot which is to form the summit of the new individual is
called the Scion ; the stem to which it is affixed is called the
Stock ; and the operation, when effected, the Graft As the
graft is merely an extension of the parent plant from which
the scion came, and not, properly speaking, a new individual;
so it is found to be the best method of propagating approved
varieties of fruit-trees without any danger of altering the
quality of the fruit. Scions for grafting should be selected
in July or August, and heeled in in a shady place till required.
In selecting these make choice only of those varieties which
have been proved by experience to be well adapted to the
locality. There are many varieties both of apples and pears
which do admirably in one locality but are comparatively
worthless in others. (Where there has been no previous
planting of course this precaution cannot be adopted.) The
principal points to attend to in the process of grafting are,
first—whatever be the plan—to use sharp knives, make the
joints fit close, tie them firmly, but not too tight ; let the
barks of the scion and stock always be close on one side,
whatever be the state of the other, for on that depends
everything ; cover the graft, when tied, with proper grafting
clay, which will keep the air from the join until it is united.
This grafting clay is made adhesive by mixing, according
to its stiffness, with a quantity of new cow manure, beating
them together ; for if it were not tempered with the cow
manure it would bake hard on the trees, and crack, and
fall off in the dry weather. Some use grafting wax, formed
of resin and beeswax, in equal parts, and tempered with
tallow, a small portion of which will reduce it so as to be
laid on while warm with a brush, and cool sufficiently to coat
over the join properly, as a body to resist the wet and the
air. But upon the whole the clay is preferable, as it retains
moisture. One particular point should always be attended
to in grafting The stock should, at its highest point, have
a bud, because nothing is more common than stocks dying
down to the first joint, so that a graft would, in such case,
be lost ; because if the stock died back to the first eye, and
the graft were above it, however well it may be done, it must
fail ; whereas the eye or joint being at the very top of the
stock secures it. The different methods of grafting are
known as whip grafting, cleft grafting, saddle grafting, crown
grafting, and shoulder grafting.

Whip Grafting, also called tongue grafting, is the most generally used when the stock and scion are about equal size. The head of the stock is pruned off at the desired height, and then a slip of bark and wood removed at the upper portion of the stock with a very clean cut, to fit exactly with a corresponding cut, which must be made in the scion. A very small amount of wood must be cut away, and the surface made quite smooth; care must be taken that no dirt be put upon the cuts in this, and indeed, in all the other modes. The scion must now be prepared; this should have, at least, three or four buds. A sloping cut must now be made in the scion; this cut must correspond with that in the stock. The two are then fitted together, care being taken that the divided bark of the scion is exactly adapted to the divided bark of the stock; for unless the bark of one side of the scion, at least, meets exactly with the bark of the stock failure is sure to be the result. On this hinges the success or otherwise of the operation. When the scion and stock differ in point of size, of course only one side can touch. These remarks apply equally to all kinds of grafting. The two are then bound firmly, but not too tightly, together with matting; flax will answer. The bandage is carefully covered with well-tempered clay, or grafting wax (which may be had from any seedsman), in order to exclude air from the wound; and the operation is finally left to nature, with the precaution, that any buds from the stock below the scion are removed as soon as they begin to sprout. In about six weeks or two months the young scion will have made growth, the union is then effected, and the ligature, as well as the clay or wax, may be removed; care being still taken that the scion is not blown off the stock by high winds. To obviate this danger the grafts are sometimes staked on removal of the ligature.

Saddle Grafting is practised only where the stock is of moderate dimensions. The stock is cut into a bridge-like form, and the scion slit up the middle, so adapted that it shall be seated across or ride upon the former; but as in whip grafting the bark must at least on one side be neatly fitted to the bark on the other. This mode of grafting is particularly adapted to the propagation of rhododendrons.

Crown Grafting is practised on old trees, either for their total renewal, or upon large amputated branches, to renew by degrees. The scions are simply placed between the bark and the wood.

Side Grafting is, in general, performed on a stock, the head of which is not cut off, or on a branch without its being shortened. The great utility of this mode is the facility it offers of supplying branches to parts of trees where they may have become too thin, or making a branch in case of accidents. It is well adapted for espaliers, where a branch is sometimes wanted to fill a vacancy on the wall or trellis, and for the insertion of new kinds of fruits on established trees, in order to increase the collection. It is also usefully employed upon wall or espalier trees that have become naked of fruit buds near the centre, while they may have abundance towards the extremities. This kind of grafting is, however, not much resorted to.

Grafting Clay—How to Make It.—Take some strong and adhesive loam, approaching to a clayey character, and beat and knead it until it is of the consistency of soft-soap. Take also some horse droppings and rub them through a riddle of half-inch mesh, or wanting a riddle beat with a spade until thoroughly divided. Get some cow manure, the fresher the better, and mix about equal parts of the three, kneading and mixing them until perfectly and uniformly incorporated with each other. It is a good plan to have a vessel with a little finely-sifted ashes by the side of the grafter, and after the clay is closed round the scion the hands should be dipped in the ashes; this enables the person who applies the clay to close the whole with a perfect finish. It must be so closed that no air can possibly enter; and it is well to go over the whole of the grafts in three or four days afterwards, when, if the claying of any is cracked, it may be closed finally. Grafting wax is now much used instead of the above.

Budding.—While grafting must be performed in the Spring, budding should not be commenced till Midsummer when the leaves have fully matured, and the buds in the axles of the leaves are plump and ripe. While grafting is practised in the Spring, by the union of one piece of wood upon another, budding is the insertion of a bud of the current season into the bark of a tree which is intended to be budded. Budding is more suitable for most of the stone fruits, such as peaches, nectarines, and apricots, than grafting. The time when budding is most successfully performed is when the young shoots, from which the buds are intended to be taken, have all but perfected their growth, and which will generally be from the beginning to the end of February, and when the buds on the lower part have become firm and set. With a sharp knife cut out a bud from the shoot, having about half-an-inch of bark both above and below it: this is called a shield (and is the most general method adopted). Then dextrously pick out the piece of wood which is found in the shield, leaving nothing but the bark and the axis of the bud. Should the axis of the bud be removed in the act of taking out the wood, the bud will be valueless and another should be taken. (If there is a deep hollow behind the eye when the bit of wood has been removed, then the axis has been destroyed. Some gardeners say, how-ever, that it is not necessary to remove this bit of waste wood.) In removing this bit of wood care must be taken to draw it upwards, if drawn downwards the axis of the bud will probably be destroyed. The bud is now ready for insertion. Having fixed upon the spot where the bud is to be inserted in the stock or tree, make a transverse cut and a perpen-dicular one up to it. Cut as deep as the wood ; these two cuts will make a figure like the letter T. Then with the bone end of your budding-knife raise the bark on each side of the perpendicular cut, and slip in the shield ; then make a clean cut across the top of the shield where it joins the upper edge of the bark of the stalk, the two barks thus united will allow the descending sap to flow into the shield. The shield or bud must not be allowed to get dry before in-serting it into its berth. Bind round with a piece of soft matting. In the course of three weeks they should be seen to, when, if much swollen the matting should be unbound, and again tied a little more loosely for a month longer, and afterwards entirely removed. Insert the bud if possible on the shady side of the stem. Buds usually remain dormant till the following Spring ; at this period the stock should be cut three or four inches above the bud ; and the shoot, as it grows, should be slightly tied to the portion of the stock left on above the bud, in order to prevent its being injured by high winds. The second year this portion of the stock may be cut off close to the bud.

In-arching.—This is, perhaps, the most ancient of all methods of grafting—indeed, it is supposed that the Ancients first learned the art from observing a case of natural grafting. In-arching consists of bringing the branch of one tree or shrub in contact with another ; both branches should be as nearly as possible the same size. A slice is cut off both branches, as nearly as possible the same size and shape, so that the bark of both scion and stock may exactly meet, they are then bound with matting. In-arching should be performed in Spring. As soon as the union takes place, which will be in three or four months, the shoot may be separated from the mother plant. In-arching used to be practised in the propagation of rhododendrons and other hard-wooded plants. These plants are now, however, more frequently propagated by grafting.

FLOWER GARDEN

 LORD BACON said that a garden affords the " purest of human enjoyments." Great men of every age have found their chief recreation in their gardens. Indeed, it may be said that the love of flowers is inherent in human nature. Wherever civilization has obtained a footing, the love for flowers has developed itself. Many of our most beautiful flowering plants are the result of scientific culture ; while others, equally beautiful are, as we find them in nature, incapable of further improvement. Verbenas, dahlias, geraniums, and a host of others, belong to the first class of plants. Heaths, and a numerous list of bulbs, including the magnificent Lilium Auratum (Japanese Lily), belong to the latter. The most successful growers of all kinds of plants, are those who know most of the natural habits of the plants they cultivate. Gardening in New Zealand is a comparatively easy matter when compared with the same operations in Britain, owing to the general mildness of our climate. Any tolerably good soil will grow flowers, provided always that it is well sheltered.

Soils—Their Selection for Garden Purposes.—If in the cultivation of plants one thing is more necessary than another to be attended to, that thing is the proper prepara-

tion of soils and composts; for, however great the care
bestowed upon the potting and watering of a plant may be,
if the soil is unsuitable, or not in a proper condition to
supply the requirements of the plant, every other care is
thrown away; but if the soil is suitable it is surprising
with what tenacity a plant will cling to existence, under
very unfavourable circumstances. Every person who has
paid any attention to the management of plants knows
that in the open garden as well as in pots the sweeter
the soil is—that is, the more it has been exposed to
the ameliorating influence of atmospheric changes—the
more suitable it becomes for all horticultural purposes. Even
maiden soil, fresh from an old pasture, is materially improved by exposure to atmospheric changes for a few
months; while in the case of soil from a wet locality, it
should never, under any circumstances, be used in the cultivation of choice plants untill it has been exposed to the
varied changes of the Winter; and if afterwards it can have
a few months' exposure through the Summer, it will be much
improved thereby. This improvement arises principally
from the expulsion of deleterious matters, the decomposition of vegetable substances, and the thorough disintegration
of the mass of soil. The surface sods pared from old pasture
land, if loosely stacked in some out-of-the-way place for
twelve months, will become a valuable compost for potting
plants. Such a pile should be found in every well ordered
garden.

Hedge Plants.—The following is a list of shrubs suitable for this purpose :—Cupressus macrocarpa and Law-
soniana, Arbor vitæ, Holly, English Beech, Pittosporum, (or
Matopo), African Box Thorn, Laurel (common), Osage
orange, Evergreen Privet, New Zealand Broadleaf, Berberis
Darwinii, Retinospora pleumosa, &c. The common English
Laurel is our favourite for general purposes. These should
all be planted at such distances from the plants they are
intended to shelter so as not to injure them by the encroach-
ment of their roots. *In forming a flower garden* for the
first time, the ground should be trenched—(as directed for
vegetables). Where the space is limited, we prefer beds and
gravel walks neatly lined with box, or some other plant.
Tiles and bricks can also be used with advantage. Grass

edgings are troublesome to keep neat, and should therefore
be avoided. The pattern of the garden must depend upon
the shape and size of the ground. Where the ground is not
so limited it may be laid down to grass and may have beds
cut in it ; but grass requires incessant care to keep it nice—
if neglected, it soon becomes unsightly. Dandelion, cape
weed, and other abominations soon take possession, when
the desired effect will be completely frustrated. Then comes
the grub to complete the ruin. We shall have more to say
of this pest under the heading of " Lawns "

Shrubs suitable for Small Gardens.—A common
mistake frequently made by amateur gardeners in laying out
their plots of land, is the planting of trees and shrubs which
are quite unsuited for the purpose intended, viz., ornament-
ing the beds and borders. It is no uncommon thing to see
Cupressus macrocarpa, Pinus insignis, and Wellingtonias
planted in gardens containing only a few square perches.
This is an obvious mistake, as they soon outgrow everything
else and have to be cut down ; whereas, if a little judge-
ment were exercised when first planting, the collection would
consist of a few dwarf-growing shrubs. These would remain
for years " a thing of beauty," especially if occasionally transplanted. The following can be recommended for small
gardens :— Retinospora obtusa aurea, plumosa, aurea,
argentea, filifera, and ericoides. These are all Japanese
plants and are dwarf, compact growers. Berberis Darwinii
and Japonica, Daphne indica and rubra, Deutzias, Kalmias,
Azaleas, Rhododendrons, Ribes aureum and sanguineum.
Numbers of others might be mentioned, including many
beautiful native shrubs, such as the Veronicas, &c., &c.
Collections of which can be seen at the public garden'
Christchurch, and elsewhere.

Laying down a Lawn.—When it is desired to form
a lawn, the ground should be trenched as directed for the
vegetable garden—any time during the Autumn. If the
plot can be prepared in March a season may be gained by
sowing the grass seed during that month ; the surface must
be thoroughly pulverised and trodden down firmly. The
following is a good mixture, if procurable :—Crested dog-
tail, 2lbs.; Festuca tenuifolia, 4lbs.: Festuca duriuscula, 2lbs.;

Lolium tenuifolia perenne, 20lbs.; 2lbs. White clover; 8lbs. Trifolium minor; Poa nemoralis and sempervirens, 4lbs. of each. This mixture will suffice for half an acre, and will form a very good lawn, and if kept cut close answers most soils. Special mixtures for laying down lawns may also be had from any seedsman. Some of our native poas and other grasses would answer admirably for lawn purposes. If the ground is of a retentive nature, sowing the seeds should be deferred till August. Commence to cut as soon as the machine will act. Some prefer the scythe for the first time of cutting. Roll previous to mowing; this will save the knives of the mower. Cut at least once a fortnight during the growing season.

The Grub.—Every one who has had anything to do with grass lawns is familiar with this pest. The pest, when in the beetle state, may be heard and seen in the warm Summer evenings humming in myriads over the grass preparatory to laying the seeds of future destruction. The best preventive we know of, is the constant use of a heavy roller, and an occasional flooding of water when possible. The rolling should be the most frequent in the evenings, when the beetles first make their appearance. In the Autumn well-rotted manure or crushed bones should be applied if the soil is not naturally rich; if manure be objected to as unsightly, bone meal, soot, and salt may be substituted, and rolled in during moist weather 7lbs. bones, 7lbs. soot, and 1lb. of common salt will suffice for every square perch (or 5½ yards square), or 2lbs. of superphosphate to the same area will be found beneficial, if applied in August.

Plants and Grasses which resist the Grub.— Yarrow (Achillea Millefolium). The grub will not touch this plant; it also resists drought in a remarkable degree. Its fine dark-green foliage, close set to the ground, suggests it as a plant which would prove admirably adapted for lawn purposes. It is however not well suited for tennis lawns, the foliage being too soft and easily bruised. Poa pratensis resists the grub better than any grass we know of, but it gets hard and matty, and is therefore not so desirable. White Dutch clover, in moist deep soils, if well attended to, forms a handsome green sward. It is also unsuited for tennis lawns.

Annuals.—If properly grown and attended to will well repay the trouble bestowed upon them. If allowed to grow in masses, unthinned and uncared for, they soon become untidy and unsightly. On the other hand, if they are sown at proper times, and thinned out as they grow, they will make robust flowering plants ; and the flowering season may be prolonged by cutting off the seed-vessels as soon as they appear. Such annuals as Godetia Lady Albemarle, Lupins, Phlox Drummondii, &c., may be kept blooming for a couple of months longer than if allowed to ripen their seeds. Mignonette may be kept flowering nearly all the year round by adopting this treatment.

Sowing.—Hardy annuals may be sown any time from the middle of August to the end of September, to be followed by tenderer kinds, which may be sown up to the end of November. A little rich compost, finely pulverised, should be prepared for covering the seeds with a small rake ; draw a portion of soil from the places where you intend to sow. Make as many of the hollows as you have varieties of annuals to sow ; if the weather is dry at the time, give a good soaking of water a few hours before sowing. Large seeds, such as Sweet peas, Lupins, Convolvulus major, &c., should be placed at the back of the border amongst the shrubs and herbaceous plants. Sow thinly, cover with a little fine soil, and press firmly with the back of the spade, rake or trowel. The quantity of covering must, in all cases, be regulated by the size of the seed. Portulaca, for instance, does not require any covering ; a gentle beating with the back of the spade will be sufficient. The following is a list of a few of the many annuals which can be recommended for general purposes:—Bartonia aurea, yellow, one foot high ; Tagetes signata pumila, bright orange, nine inches ; Clarkia integripetala, rose-coloured flowers ; Dianthus of varieties, one foot ; Larkspurs, in varieties, two feet ; Linum grandiflorum rubrum, scarlet, one foot ; Marigold orange, African striped unique, and dwarf yellow or pigmy, one foot ; Nemophila insignis, blue, maculata, spotted, six inches ; Portulaca mixed ; these showy annuals (Portulaca), thrive best in light sandy soil ; scatter the seed thinly, and beat gently with the back of the spade. No other covering is necessary. This lovely little annual will reproduce itself each year where the soil is warm and

dry ; it delights to grow on gravel walks amongst the stones.
Zinnia elegans, one foot ; Asters, double-quilled German, and
double ,globe German, ten-week stock, one foot ; Phlox
Drummondii, of sorts, nine inches ; Lobelia pumila , mag-
nifica, Compacta, and Crystal Palace, blue ; Mignonette,
hybrid, spiral, and giant pyramid ; Godetia, Lady Albemarle,
Princess of Wales and Dutchess of Albany, all good, one
foot ; Sunflower, double and single, four to six feet ;
Nasturtium, King of Tom Thumbs, six inches ; Perilla
Nankinensis, foliage deep bronze, one foot.   Abronia,
umbellata, Acroclinum (mixed), Amaranthus tricolor,
Anagallis grandiflora (mixed), Canna, dark leaved (mixed),
Celosia cristata, Clianthus Dampieri, Clintonia pulchella,
Datura Wrightii Helichrysum, double (mixed), Leptosiphon
carmineus, Linaria reticulata aurea, Matthiola bicornis
(night scented stock), Martynia fragrans, Papaver umbrosum,
vermilion with shining black spots on each petal, Rhodanthe
maculata, Saponaria Calabrica, Schizanthus (fine mixed),
Tropæolum Canariensie, and Lobbianum.   Should the
ground be dry at the time of sowing, it will be well to give
a good soaking of water a few hours before sowing.   Cover
lightly with fine soil ; the depth of covering must be regulated by the size of the seed ; the smaller the seed the less
covering will be required.   If watering should be necessary
give a good soaking always after sunset.   Occasional surface-
sprinkling does more harm than good.   These remarks
apply to all plants.   Packages of choice annuals ready made
up may be had from any seedsman.

`   **Biennials** are those plants which, being sown in one
year, flower and die in the next.   The best time for sowing
will be in October, in moderately rich soil.   Sow thinly, and
transplant into their positions; for blooming in the beds or
borders, when the plants are sufficiently strong, which should
be in January or February.   A better plan, although
entailing a little more trouble, is to transplant the young
plants, as soon as they can be handled with ease, into a prepared bed, in rows six inches each way ; here they will become nice bushy plants, and may be planted out as required
to take the place of annuals—any time up to the middle of
March—or they may remain in the nursery-bed till the
following August or September.   Where only a few plants

are required it will be better to procure them from some florist. The following is a list of hardy Biennials—Canterbury Bells, two and a half feet high ; Foxgloves, three to four feet, suitable for shady places ; Sweet Rocket, one foot ; Sweet William, one foot ; Wallflowers, two feet ; purple and scarlet Brompton Stocks ; the Scarlet Brompton and Queen Stocks, and the intermediate resemble the habit of the Brompton. Double Stocks may be perpetuated by making cuttings of well-ripened shoots which sometimes appear after they have flowered. Treat the cuttings as directed for geraniums, &c.

Perennials (or Herbaceous Plants).—Perennials are sown in one year and flower in the next ; but although they die down in Winter, the roots remain alive and the plants spring up every year. This section of plant life embraces by far the largest number of plants cultivated in our gardens. They may be propagated either by seeds, cuttings, or by division of the roots. The seed may be sown any time from 1st October till the end of November, and transplanted, when fit, as directed for biennials.

Propagation.—Such plants as the Phloxes, Penstemons, Campanulas, Delphiniums, &c., may be propagated in December by cuttings, if desired, planted in a cool, shady border ; or they may be lifted either after they have done blooming, and the leaves have withered, or early in Spring, and divided into as many plants as the tuft will permit of, taking care to have a good bundle of fibrous roots to each piece. Pæonies, Salvias, Dielytra spectabilis, and a host of other plants may be increased in this manner. Where perennials are extensively used for border decoration, they should be planted with a view to furnishing flowers the whole of the season. This may be done in the following manner : put in one that flowers in Spring, then one that flowers in Autumn, then one that flowers in Summer, then an Autumn one, next one of the Spring flowering, and then one of Summer flowering. Mix the colours in the same manner. By this means the general effect will be good, and no part of the border will be at any time without bloom. The following are a few of the most suitable (in addition to those already mentioned) for general cultivation.

Tritoma Uvaria and varieties (commonly called Red-hot Poker plant) from three to four feet·high, bright orange red, propagated by suckers, or division ; Ageratum Imperial dwarf blue, and Mexicana, one foot ; Amaranthus melan-cholicus ruber, a fine foliaged plant with blood-red leaves, one foot ; Calceolarias, golden yellow, one foot ; Del-phiniums, of varieties, two feet ; Fuchsias, of varieties ; Gazania splendens, deep orange, a fine plant for planting in lines for effect, four inches ; Mimulus, of varieties, thrives best near water, or in moist soils ; Pyrethrum, golden and hybrid double, good for effect, six inches , Verbenas, of varieties ; Viola cornuta, flowers mauve ; Lutea, yellow, golden gem, and true blue, all admirably adapted for beds, patches, or lines, four inches ; Petunias, of sorts ; Geraniums, golden tricolour, Zonale and plain-leaved; Pansies, of sorts ; Campanula pyramidalis, the finest of all the bell-flowers, easily cultivated either from seeds, cuttings, or by offsets, three feet ; Chrysanthemums, Pompone, and large flowering, two to three feet ; Pœonias (including Tree Pœonies) all gorgeous flowers and free bloomers, of various colours, two feet ; Salvia fulgens, bright scarlet, patens deep blue, and alba white, height two to three feet ; Lobelia cardinalis and fulgens, deep scarlet, one foot.

Spring Blooming Perennials.—Double yellow, white, crimson, and lilac primulas, three inches ; Polyanthus primroses, of sorts ; Iberis sempervirens (Evergreen Candy-tuft) nine inches ; White Hepatica ; alba and cærulea, white and blue, three inches , Helleborus niger (Christmas Rose), one foot, pink ; Gentiana acaulis (Dwarf Gentian), four inches, deep blue ; Dodecatheon giganteum (Giant American Cowslip); Anemone Appenina (Mountain Anemone), six inches, blue ; Alyssum saxatile (Rock Madwort), six inches, yellow ; Lily of. the Valley ; Phlox verna ; Saxifraga oppositefolia (opposite leaved Saxifrage), three inches, purple. These charming Spring flowers, although common in England, are comparatively rare, as yet, in New Zealand, excepting the double primulas, which are now plentiful. Fancy primulas are to be had from several of the nurserymen who make specialities of these things.

HARDY BULBS FOR SPRING & SUMMER BLOOMING.

Procure some well known bulb grower's descriptive catalogue and make your selection therefrom.

It will be impossible with our limited space to do more than name a few of each of the best of the numerous plants in this section   Hyacinths rank first amongst hardy Spring. bulbs—flowering from September till the end of October. Hyacinths delight in sandy loam, deeply trenched; if manure is used it must be thoroughly rotted and well buried in the soil.   Old cow manure, or decayed vegetable mould is best.   The bulbs may be left in the soil from year to year ; but they will degenerate sooner than if taken up. . As soon as all the leaves have withered away the bulbs will then be ripe ; lift and put into brown paper bags, label and put away in a dry, cool place till the time for planting comes round again.   It is unnecessary to give a list as new varieties are being brought out every season.   They can, however, be purchased at from 4s. per dozen upwards.   Plant four inches deep.

The Narcissus Tribes are now very numerous, and form a most attractive feature in the flower garden from early Spring to Summer.   The Polyanthus, Narcissus, Poeticus florepleno, and their numerous varieties, are all adapted for planting in rows, patches, or beds.   These, with such small bulbs as Crocuses, Snowdrops, and Jonquils, intended for planting in patches amongst shrubs, or the mixed flower borders, should have the places where they are to be grown enriched with well-rotted manure some time before planting.   Mice sometimes make great havoc amongst the Crocuses.   A little finely cut gorse spread over where they are planted will protect the roots.   The following. bulbous plants are also admirably adapted for planting in beds or patches ; plant from three to four inches deep :—

Anemones, single and double, may be had in flower for months by planting at different seasons.   Plant in May and again in August and September.   Plant three inches deep.

G.

Early Tulips.—The varieties of these are endless, beginning with the single and double Van Thol, which begin to flower in September and continue in succession till the end of November. The double yellows are remarkably showy, as are also the parrot tulips. Tulips are very effective when planted in masses or in beds, having regard to height and colour. Any tolerably good garden soil will answer for tulips, so long as it is not too heavy in texture ; they must not be treated with fresh manure. The soil must, however, be in good heart from previous manuring. Plant five or six inches apart, and three inches deep. Plant in May. A few may be planted in pots at the same time (three or four in a pot) for early flowering in the greenhouse.

Scillas are lovely little bulbs, Scilla Siberica and præcox are the earliest bloomers. Scilla bifolia, Peruviana and alba are also good.

Dog's Tooth Violets are more conspicuous for the beauty of their foliage than that of their flowers. Plant in Autumn.

Colchicums (Autumn flowering).—The following are good varieties, the pencilled white single, and a double variety. Plant in Autumn.

Amaryllis, of varieties, are gorgeous plants, principally with brilliant crimson flowers ; flower stalks one foot high ; thriving well out of doors in good soil. The bulbs may be left in the ground.

Valloto purpurea, a lovely bulbous plant.

Ixias and Sparaxis may be planted in Autumn or Spring. They are now to be had in great variety. Muscaria botryoides (grape hyacinth) and its varieties are pretty plants with white and blue flowers. Plant in Autumn and Spring.

Iris.—There are several beautiful bulbous varieties of Iris, which are worthy of a prominent place in the flower border.

Crocuses.—These well-known and beautiful Spring bulbs should be planted in May, in patches. There is a great variety of colours ; but few, if any, excel the common yellow for out-door blooming. The bulbs should be lifted as soon as the foliage has died away after flowering. As soon as quite dry, put them in paper bags named, and stow away in a cool, dry place, or they may be allowed to remain in the ground from year to year.

Snowdrops (single and double).—These charming little gems may be planted in May, and remain in the ground where planted.

Cyclamens.—These lovely plants are more suitable for pot culture, although they can be grown successfully out of doors.

Anemone Nemorosa (Wood anemone).—Single and double. Although rare in the Colony they should be procured. They raise their welcome flowerets early in Spring, and continue to bloom for a month or more. As their name indicates, they thrive best in a shaded situation.

Lilies. — These glorious flowers are best adapted for planting among shrubs or at the back of borders, or in the middle of large beds, the most of them being tall-growing. All the varieties of this family revel in deep, rich, moist soil, which must, however, have plenty of drainage. Trench two feet deep, and incorporate with soil plenty of well-rotted manure mixed with peat mould if procurable. Lilium giganteum is a noble plant for effect where it can have plenty of space and shelter. It grows eight or ten feet high, flowers white marked with crimson. Lilum auratum and its varieties also flourish in the open garden if sheltered from high winds, perfuming the atmosphere for several yards in circumference : height from three to four feet. The following are also worthy of prominent positions,—as, indeed, are all the lilies—and should be found in every garden where the soil is suitable :—Lilium japonicum, height two to three feet, flowers large trumpet-shaped, colour white ; Lilium eximium, height two feet, flowers trumpet-shaped and pure white ; Lilium candidum (called the Christmas lily), height three to five feet, flowers pure white ; Lilium lancifolium album, height three feet, flowers white. There are several varieties of this charming lily marked with red and spotted with rose and other colours. Lilium excelsum, height four to five feet, flowers deep buff ; Lilium Humbolti, height four to five feet, flowers rich golden yellow spotted with crimson, Lilium chalcedonicum; height three to four feet, flowers brilliant scarlet; Lilium superbum, height four to six feet, flowers orange beautifully spotted with black; Lilium tigrinum, height three feet, flowers reddish orange spotted with black; the flore pleno (double tiger lily) is also a beautiful variety; Lilium Thunbergianum, and its varieties, are all good, height from one foot to eighteen inches, colours from pale yellow to rich orange-red and spotted with black; Lilium umbellatum, and varieties, are all good, height two to three feet, varying in colour from deep orange to orange crimson, more or less spotted with black. When lilies have finished blooming, and the stalks have withered, they should be removed, if necessary, and a stake placed in the ground to mark where the bulbs are. Lilies should not be lifted oftener than once in two or three years, when it is necessary to reduce the size of the plant. When they have to be lifted they should be planted with as little delay as possible. Bulbs composed of fleshy scales soon perish if left long out of the soil.

The Guernsey Lily is a beautiful Autumn flowering plant; the varieties are scarlet, pink, purple, and red. Plant in a mixture of peat, sand and good garden soil. Plant in September or October. The bulbs must not be kept long out of the ground.

Belladonna Lilies also flower in Autumn, and should be treated in the same manner as the last mentioned.

Tigridia Pavonia, and the new varieties are gorgeous bloomers, and will thrive in any good garden soil. No garden should be without them.

Lily of the Valley.—This charming Spring flower is so well known that it requires no description. It delights in a moist, shady situation, where it will get either the morning or evening sun.

The Tuberoses.—The double-flowered American, and Italian are deliciously fragrant plants. The bulbs should be planted in August.

Schizostylis Coccinea.—Autumn Ixia; scarlet. Plant in May or August.

Fritillarias.—(Crown Imperials), are useful for contrast; they are not showy, and therefore they are not favourites. Plant in Autumn or early Spring.

Violets.—To grow these universal favourites to the best advantage they should be taken up at least every second year, after they have finished blooming, any time in October, March or April. Break each tuft into separate plants, and plant either in beds or as edgings. Procure young plants from the sides of the old tufts, if possible. Violets delight in a rich sandy loam. The following are all good kinds :—*Single.*— Lee's Victoria Regina, Czar, purple and white. *Double.*— Maria Louise, Neapolitan, and Belle-de Chatney, Compt-de-Zabna, pure, double white, and very large.

Hardy Climbing Plants for covering verandahs, fences, arbours, or outhouses—Virginian Creeper, Clematis Jackmani, Miss Bateman, and Sieboldi are good varieties. The Native Clematis is also a desirable plant. Honeysuckle, Flexuosa, and Sempervirens, and the Japanese Honeysuckle (Lonicera aurea reticulata), are all good. Passiflora Cœrulea, Solanum Jasminifolium, Bignonias with either red, crimson, yellow, blue or purple flowers. Roses of sorts, Double-flowered Bramble, Banksian Rose, Cobaes scandens, purple flowers; Lophospermum scandens, rose-coloured flowers; Maurandia Barclayana, blue and white flowers; Tropaeolum Lobbianum, crimson; Triomphe de Grand, scarlet; Canariensie, bright yellow. The following plants may also be used as climbers, although not climbers by nature :— Cratægus Pyracantha, with clusters of bright red berries during Autumn; Cotoneaster microphylla, with bright red berries, admirably adapted for covering rocks or low walls; Pyrus Japonica, scarlet crimson flowers early in Spring. These plants may be propagated by layers, cuttings or seed.

Primroses. — Double yellow, white, crimson and purple. These charming Spring plants are easy of culture, they revel in moderately rich moist soil, with plenty of sun. They commence to bloom in August, and continue on till the end of October. They may be taken up, divided, and replanted in March or April.

The Polyanthus Primroses.—These are charming Winter flowers, particularly in places where there is little or no glass.   If such plants as are showing bloom are taken up towards the end of April out of the borders and potted they will soon make a very pretty display by being simply protected, either in a frame, cold house, or in the window of the dwelling-house, giving them all the air and light possible. Under this treatment they will present a delightful realization of the coming Spring during the following two months, and they will require very little care.

FLORISTS' FLOWERS.

FLORIST FLOWERS are distinguished from others of the same kind by approaching a standard of perfection by which such plants are judged in relation to the form of their flowers, colour, markings, and regularity of the petals, &c. Only such plants as produce flowers in accordance with the hard and fast rules laid down are considered worthy of the Florist's care and attention. The following is a list of plants cultivated under this heading, treated of in alphabetical order :—

Anemone.—*Properties of a Double Anemone.*—The blossom should be from two and a-half to three inches in diameter, consisting of an outside row of stout, large, well-rounded petals, called the guard-leaves. These should spread out horizontally to the edges, which latter should turn upwards slightly, so as to present a saucer-like appearance. Within these guard-leaves, and at a little distance from the edges, there should be such a number of long, small petals, longest at the bottom, and gradually shortening to the centre, as to form a half ball. Self-coloured flowers should have the colour clear, bright, and distinct, whether it be blue, crimson or scarlet. If variegated, that is, the interior and exterior petals striped, the colours should be very distinct, for even cloudiness, or irregular broken stripes, are objectionable. The stem should be elastic, yet stout enough to bear the flower erect, and should be, at least, from eight to nine inches high.

Soil and Situation.—The Anemone requires a pure loamy soil, well mixed with sand. Choose a situation that is open, but sheltered from violent winds, or strong twisting currents of air. Mix the soil with sand if it require it, and dig in a thin covering of thoroughly decomposed hotbed manure or cow manure; the latter is to be preferred. No manure must be among the top stratum of soil, because it causes the peculiar disease called *mould* to attack the bulbs that come in contact with it.

Planting.—The best season is from about the middle of April to the end of May; the bulbs then form roots before severe frosts set in. Some, however, prefer planting in August, especially if the Autumn be wet. Choose a time when the soil is moderately dry, and the day fine. Draw drills across the bed two inches deep and five or six inches apart, and plant the tubers five inches apart in the rows. For choice varieties, a thin layer of sand scattered under and around each tuber will be useful. As soon as the bed is planted, cover the tubers with sandy loam. Take care that the tubers are placed the right side up, by observing the side that has the old small fibres on it, that side being placed next to the bottom of the drill. When all are planted and covered up the right depth (two inches) then level the surface with a garden rake.

After-Management.—Should the weather prove dry in Spring give a thorough watering now and then. The bloom will be greatly prolonged if an awning of canvas be stretched over the bed, upon a frame of hoops, to shelter the flowers from the sun, from high winds, and heavy splashing rains; but measures of this kind are rarely resorted to in this country, it would, however, repay the trouble to do so All weeds must be pulled up as they appear, and a deligent watch kept for slugs.

Taking up and Storing the Roots.—Very little trouble need be taken with the common single varieties, especially if they have been planted in clumps. But the fine double varieties should be taken up annually. As the foliage decays the real roots will decay also ; the tubers will then gradually mature, when they should be placed in paper bags, labelled and put away in a dry, cool place till required for planting.

Propagation : by Seed.—For double flowers save seed only from semi-double blooms with well-formed flowers, and bright, distinct colours. As the seed ripens at different times, and is downy, it is in danger of being blown away with the wind ; therefore it must be carefully gathered daily as soon as it is ripe. Spread the seed on a sheet of paper, lay it in a window facing the morning sun for a few days until it is perfectly dry ; then put it in a bag, and keep it dry till the sowing season.

The common single Anemone seed may be sown immediately it is ripe, in a prepared bed in the garden ; but seed saved carefully, as described above, is deserving of a little more trouble. Pans, pots, or boxes well drained may be used, filled to within an inch of the surface with rich compost, having a large proportion of sharp sand ; water a few hours previous to sowing. Let this be done in August. Prepare the seed for sowing by rubbing it between the hands for a considerable time amongst some dry earth. This should be done until the seeds are divested of their downy covering, and separated from each other. Then sow the seeds evenly and cover with some light sifted earth, using only sufficient to cover the seed. The boxes and pans may be covered with sheets of glass, and placed in a cold frame or greenhouse. The surface should never be allowed to become quite dry. Give air on all fine days ; as soon as the young plants have made two or three leaves, they may be exposed fully to the light and sun. Keep them duly supplied with water until the leaves decay ; then sift two inches of the surface through a very fine sieve, and carefully pick out all the young tubers. Plant them in the following August in the open bed, and treat them afterwards exactly like old tubers until they flower, which will be in the second year.

Dividing the Roots.—Anemones are easily increased by breaking off one or more of the little knobs of the full-grown tubers. These may be planted and managed exactly like the old-established roots.

Antirrhinum (Snapdragon).—*The characteristics of a perfect Antirrhinum :—*

1. The plant should be dwarf, the flowers abundant; the mouth wide, and the more the inner surface turns up to hide the tube the better. 2. The tube should be clear and pure if white, and if any other colour it should be bright; and the mouth and all the inner surface, should be of a different colour and texture, and form a contrast with the tube. 3. The petal should lap over at the indentations, so as not to show them; the texture of the tube should be like wax or enamel; the inside surface, which laps over, should be velvety. 4. When the flower is striped or spotted, the marking should be well-defined in all its variations; the colour should be dense, whatever that colour may be. 5. The flowers should form spikes of six or seven blooms, close, but not in each other's way; and the footstalks should be strong and elastic, to keep them from hanging down close to the stem, which they will do if the footstalks are weak.

Propagation : by Seed.—The Antirrhinum may be sown in the open border of the garden. Procure a few of the best sorts in cultivation, grow them one year, and save seeds from them, keeping the seed of each variety to itself.

The time for sowing is about the second week in October. Sown in March they will flower the following season When the seedlings have attained an inch or two in height, they may be planted out, and they will thrive in any good garden soil.

Propagation : by Cuttings is the easiest method; they grow freely if placed in a shaded border either in Spring or in Autumn This is the best method for perpetuating really good kinds.

If it is desired to have a long season of bloom, cut down the first flowering spikes before the seed is formed, then fresh flower-spikes will push forth from the base of each plant, and there will be a succession of bloom.

The finest flowers will always be produced on young plants; therefore, whoever wishes to excel in blooms should renew his bed and plants annually.

Auricula.—Terms used in describing an Auricula.—
Thrum, the stamens shown beyond the throat. *Pin-eyed*,
the pistil showing beyond the throat. *Paste*, white circle
next to the tube in the florist's flower. *Ground colour*, circle
next to the paste, being the distinctive colour of the variety.
Edge, outer circle or border. *Pip* is a single flower. *Truss*,
a number of flowers on a common flower-stalk : it is desirable
there should not be less than seven pips on each flower-stalk.

Characteristics of a good Flower.—The pip should consist of four circles, formed at equal distances round a given
point. The first, the *tube*, round, of a yellow colour, the
thrum rising a little above the eye, or paste. The *paste*,
pure white, dense, and round. The *ground colour* should be
dense and distinct, perfectly circular, next the paste, slightly
feathered towards the edge. The *edge* should be distinct in
colour, whole and circular, instead of starry in outline. The
whole *pip* should be round, flat, and smooth at the edges.
All the pips in a *truss* should show boldly, without overlapping. The *stem* should be strong, and the foliage healthy.

Propagation · by Suckers.—These are generally removed
at potting time, because the plants are thus dressed at once.
Those rooted should be placed in small pots in proportion
to their size, or two or three in a pot. Those not rooted
should be placed two or three inches apart round the sides
of a pot, in rich, sandy soil, and kept under a handlight in
a shady place till they are rooted, when, according to their
strength, they may be potted separately in small pots, or, as
will generally be preferable, kept in store pots all the Winter,
and shifted early in Spring. Except for show purposes,
Auriculas may be grown out-of-doors in the same manner as
Primulas.

By Seed.—Cut off the seed-vessels as they become brown,
and place them in a dry sunny place on a sheet of paper
until they open. When this takes place, the seeds may be
sown at once on rich light soil, under a handlight, or better
still, in a box that may be protected, and easily moved
under cover in Winter. It is, however, better practice to
sow in August or September, as in that case the plants attain
a good size before the first Winter. The seed, in either case,
should not be covered more than the eight of an inch. As
soon as the seedlings can be easily handled, they should be

pricked out into a bed, about five inches apart, supplied with a frame, so as to be wintered there, and many will show bloom the following year, when the good ones may be potted and placed with the florists' flowers, and the others transferred to the border.

Soil.—Take one part of dry, well-rotted old cow manure, free from worms, add to this two parts of well rotted grass sods, with a little sharp sand. If cow manure is not procurable manure from an old hot-bed will answer, but it must be at least two years old. Blend well together, and pass through a ¼ inch mesh riddle. The compost will then be ready for use.

Time and Method of Potting.—The best time for re-potting will be soon after the blooming season has passed. This will probably be towards the end of January. If potted much earlier there is a danger of the flower-stems showing early in Winter before they are required, if much later, the roots will not have occupied the main soil suffi-ciently before Winter. In turning the plants out of the pots after blooming, shake out all the old earth, shorten back the longest roots and thin out the weakest ones ; place a few crocks in the bottom of the pot with an inch of rough soil or bits of broken sods over them. Place some compost in the pot, hold the plant in it with the left hand, regulate the roots all over the space nicely, and shake the soil among them, settling it by striking the pot on the bench, and then firm the soil a little with the fingers, and especially near the collar or stem of the plant. Place the pots on a raised platform, on rough coal ashes, beneath the lights of the frame, which should be set with a south-west aspect, water with a fine rose, and keep them rather close, and shaded from the mid-day sun for a fortnight or three weeks.

Summer Treatment.—As soon as fresh growth is pro-ceeding the shading may be dispensed with. More air may be given at first, and then the sashes may be taken off completely ; the frame being elevated on bricks, that the air may have free access all round the pots. Let waterings be duly given, the surface soil frequently stirred, decayed leaves removed, and slugs and worms hunted out. If the position

is at all exposed to the mid-day or afternoon sun, shading
will be required in the hottest hours. Mild, warm rains
will be beneficial, but heavy rains must be guarded against,
either by canvas or glass.

Winter Treatment.—From the first to the middle of
April is a good time for removing the plants to their Winter
quarters. This may be a cold frame ; the pots should stand
on rough coal ashes. The frame should face north. Plenty
of air must be admitted on all fine days. No rain should
fall on the plants in Winter, and, if they become dry, the
foliage should not be wetted, as, if long wet, mildew is
likely to seize them. Nothing in the shape of a yellow leaf
should be twice seen. The pots should stand within six
inches of the glass. The general stock of auriculas may be
successfully wintered in the open if provided with shelter
from excessive wet and wind.

Spring Treatment.—In August, during a fine day, pick
up the surface soil, throw off as much as you can without
injuring the roots, and refill with rather rich, dry compost of
equal parts of old, decayed manure, sweet loam, and sharp
sand, using it in a dry state and pressing it firmly against
the collar. Take this opportunity to add or replace fresh
ashes, and thoroughly to clean and whitewash the frame
inside with fresh lime. A watering will, before long, be
wanted. When water is given after the end of August, it
should be carefully applied to the soil, without touching the
leaves, or the heart of the plant. As the flowering period
approaches, remove the plants individually to a south aspect
in a frame, and give air and shelter according to the weather.
A little manure water once a week during October and
November will be of great advantage in giving size to the
flower and strength to the stem. This treatment refers only
to those plants which are grown for show purposes.

Calceolaria, or Lady Slipper.—Calceolarias are

divided into two classes herbaceous and shrubby ; the former
are only suitable for pot culture, the latter for open borders
and flower beds.

Characteristics of a good Flower.—If the flowers are
equally good, the more shrubby the plants are the better, as
the foliage makes a fine background for the flowers. The

larger the flower the better it will be, provided it is circular
in outline, without crumples or seratures, and convex or
globular in shape instead of flat; the mouth of the purse
cannot be too small; the colour should be bright, if a self
(all one colour); and if spotted, or blotched, the ground
colour should be clear and distinct, and the spots, &c., well
marked, not running or fouling into each other, or feathering into the ground colour.

Propagation by Seed.—Time of Sowing.—If sown in
January and February, large flowering plants may be had in
November following. They grow very fast at the end of
Autumn, and after the turn of the day in Spring. The
second and third week in February may be considered a
good time for sowing. Take an earthen seed pan (or pot),
half fill it with drainage covered with rough soil, fill up to
within half an inch of the top with finely sifted compost as
recommended for auriculas, press firmly with a slate or bit
of board to make the surface perfectly level, then water
with a fine rose till the earth is thoroughly soaked, allow
them to drain for a day, then sow the seed on the surface,
a pinch of seed will suffice for an ordinary seed pan, cover
slightly with sand, then place a sheet of glass over the pan
and put it in a cool place. When the young plants are
fairly up, edge up the square of glass over the pot or pan,
first at night, and then during the day. When a little larger,
move the square of glass altogether. By this time the tiny
plants will have a few leaves, though it would be difficult, as
yet, to handle them singly. To prevent them damping at
the surface, lift little patches of several plants together, and
prick out these patches an inch or so apart, in pots or in
shallow pans. In two or three weeks it will be necessary to
prick out the plants in the little patches separately, leaving
about one inch or so between each two. As the Autumn
advances, the strongest, to bloom in October or November,
may have each a four-inch pot, and be shifted to a larger
one before the end of April; but the chief supply may be
pricked out into shallow pans a couple of inches apart, or
four may be placed round the side of a five-inch pot.
Moisture, if not stagnant, will do little injury to them in
Winter. They may be grown with the protection of a cold
frame in Winter, paying great attention to air, and just secur-

ing them from frost. They will do well in a temperature ranging from 35° to 45°, with air and moisture in proportion. They will grow rapidly, even in Winter, at 45° to 55°, standing on ashes to keep them free from worms, and having plenty of air. Whenever the pots are full of roots the plants will be inclined to throw up their flower-stems, and therefore they must be potted on, to prevent the roots matting, when large specimens are required. Seedlings will bloom well in six-inch pots, plants sown in February would fill that size, and bloom in November. To bloom in December and January, they must be shifted at the end of October and the end of November. Seeds sown in September, or October, will produce plants to bloom in Autumn; they should be kept under glass at first, but after December will do best in a shady place out of doors.

Cuttings.—The best time for making cuttings from old plants will be as soon as the young shoots can be had after flowering, though cuttings will root at any time. They also strike freely in the Spring with a mild bottom heat. Those truly herbaceous may likewise be divided. The pots should be prepared as for seeds, only having very sandy soil, or half an inch of sand on the surface. A south border, under hand-lights, is the best place for cuttings in Summer and Autumn; they should have no heat then. They will strike very fast in mild bottom heat in Spring. Shrubby varieties, for flower-beds, strike well in a shady place, with or without glass, during the month of March. They will strike in a quarter of the time, in Spring, in a mild heat.

Soil.—Rich light, sandy loam grows them to perfection. Four parts of sweet, fibry loam, one of sand, and one of flaky, dry cow manure, or thoroughly decomposed leaf mould, will grow them admirably. Calceolarias are very impatient of drought.

General Treatment.—From the time the seedlings are up, or the cuttings inserted, they should never be allowed to get quite dry. If well drained, and in open material, there is less danger from damp than dryness. In all shiftings see that the ball is wet before giving it another pot, and use the soil in a condition neither hot nor dry. In Winter they should be as near the glass as possible. In frosty weather, when much artificial heat is used, the plants should stand on a moist bottom, and frequent gentle syringing over the foliage in sunny days will help them to a moist atmosphere. The moisture should be in proportion to the artificial heat. In pits or frames where, little or no artificial heat is given, the plants will be moist enough; and if young plants, and well-drained, and not in too large pots, they will seldom suffer from damp. Small sticks, as inconspicuous as possible, should be used for supporting the bloom. When in bloom they will be the better of a little shade. When saving seed is an object, the plants should have a drier atmosphere. When done flowering, those intended for propagating from should be placed on the south side of a fence, and the old flowers, &c., removed. When handlights are not to be had, many of the semi-herbaceous kinds will root freely if a very little sandy soil is heaped up to the base of the young shoots. Every one of these would make a better plant next year, wintered in a four-inch pot, than if you took the greatest pains with a plant in a twelve-inch or sixteen-inch pot.

Calceolarias are subject to the attacks of green fly. When they make their appearance, let the house be well fumigated with tobacco or tobacco paper, syringing the plants next morning with clean water. The fumigation should be done in the evening when the foliage is dry. The smoke should never be so dense as to prevent seeing from one end of the house to the other. Much harm is frequently done to plants by giving too much smoke.

How to Fumigate.—See Useful Hints.

Carnation and Picotee.—The Carnation has the marks on its petals from the centre to the edge, and through the edge in flakes, or stripes of colour.

The Picotee has its coloured marks only on the outer edge of its petals.

Properties of a Show Carnation. — Carnations are divided into five classes, namely :—1. Scarlet Bizarres. 2. Pink or Crimson Bizarres. 3. Scarlet Flakes. 4. Rose Flakes. 5. Purple Flakes.

Bizarre is a French word, meaning odd or irregular ; the flowers in these classes have three colours, which are irregularly placed on each petal. Scarlet Bizarres have that colour predominating over the purple or crimson, but the Pink or Crimson Bizarres have more of these colours than the scarlet. Scarlet Flakes are simple white grounds, with distinct stripes or ribbons of scarlet. Rose and Purple Flakes have these two colours upon a white ground. The properties in other respects are—

1. The flower should be not less than two and a-half inches across. 2. The guard or lower petals not less than six in number, must be broad, thick, and smooth on the outside, free from notch or serrature on the edge, and lapping over each other sufficiently to form a circular rose-like flower; the more perfectly round the outline the better. 3. Each layer of petals should be smaller than the layer immediately under it; there should not be less than five or six layers of petals laid regularly, and the flower should so rise in the centre as to form half a ball. 4. The petals should be stiff, free from notches, and slightly cupped. 5. The ground should be pure white, without specks of colour. 6. The stripes of colour should be clear and distinct, not running into one another, nor confused, but dense, smooth at the edges of the stripes, and well defined. 7. The colours must be bright and clear, whatever they may be; if there be two colours, the darker one cannot be too dark, or form too strong a contrast with the lighter. With scarlet the perfection would be black; with pink there cannot be too deep a crimson; with lilac, or light purple, the second colour cannot be too dark a purple. 8. If the colours run into the white and tinge it, or the white is not pure, the fault is very great, and pouncy spots or specks are highly objectionable. 9. The pod of the bloom should be long and large, to enable the flower to bloom without bursting it.

Properties of a good Picotee.—Picotees are divided into seven classes. 1. Red, heavy-edged. 2. Red, light-edged. 3. Rose, heavy-edged. 4. Rose, light-edged. 5. Purple, heavy-edged. 6. Purple, light-edged. 7. Yellow grounds, without any distinction as to the breadth of the edge colour.

The characteristics of good *form* are the same as for the Carnation, but with regard to *colour*—1. It should be clear, distinct, confined exclusively to the edge of the petals, of equal breadth and uniform colour on each, and not running

H

down (called sometimes *feathering* or *barring*), neither should the white ground run through the coloured border to the edge of any one of the petals.   2. The ground must be pure white, without the slightest spot.

Disqualification of a Carnation or Picotee.—1. If there be any petal dead or mutilated.   2. If there be any one petal in which there is no colour.   3. If there be any one petal in which there is no white.   4. If a pod be split down to the sub-calyx.   5. If a guard petal be badly split.   6. Notched edges are glaring faults, for which no excellence in other respects compensates.

Soil.—Fresh loam is absolutely necessary, procured from an old pasture if possible.   Add to this about one-fourth of two-year-old well decomposed cow manure, and the same quantity of leaf mould.   A small quantity of finely sifted old lime rubbish will be found useful to mix with it.   Wireworms are very destructive to all of the Carnation tribe ; a good look out should be kept for them when planting the beds.

Thinning the Buds.—Select three or four of the most promising on each stem, and strip off the remainder.   This rule applies only to such as are intended for exhibiting as cut blooms.

Propagation : by Seed.—A perfectly double flower cannot produce seed ; to do so the flower must be only partially double, and the seed-pods will be shorter, and the seeds fewer in such flowers than in single flowers.   Save seed from flowers as double as possible ; gather it as soon as it is ripe, and keep it dry and cool through the Winter.   Sow in boxes in September, placed under glass or on a warm border.   In November, or as soon as the young plants are sufficiently large to handle, transplant them on a bed enriched with leaf mould, or very decayed hotbed manure.   Plant them nine inches apart, and let them remain in that bed through the succeeding Summer and Winter.   They will all flower the season following.   Mark such as are good, name them, and layer them in the way to be described presently.   Afterwards treat them exactly like your old varieties.

By Layers.—A layer is a branch or shoot brought down to the ground, and when rooted, separated from its parent. The materials wanted for layering are a sharp small knife, a quantity of hooked pegs (strong hairpins will answer), and some finely-sifted soil. When the shoots round each plant have made five or six joints, choose a dull cloudy day on which to perform the work Commence by trimming off the lower leaves of each shoot all round the plant. When this is done, steady the shoot with the left hand, then pass a sharp knife through the second or third joint from the base, cutting upwards and half-way through. Then pass a hooked peg, or stout hairpin, over the layer (where cut) and press it firmly into the soil, taking care not to separate the layer from the parent plant. Do the next in the same manner, and so on till every shoot is layered ; then cover them all with the sifted mould about three-quarters of an inch deep, and that plant is completed. Then give a slight watering, and the layers want no further care till they are rooted, which will be in about a month or six weeks, when they may be removed and planted out where required.

By Pipings.—Carnations and Picotees may be propagated by this mode. It is, however, not so safe as layering, but where there are more shoots than can be layered, and it is desirable to propagate largely, the superfluous shoots may be piped. Cut off the lower part of the shoot up to the third joint, trim off the lowest pair of leaves, and pass the knife just through the joint. Plant in sandy loam in a shaded situation. The young plants will be fit for planting out in the following Spring.

Chrysanthemum.—The characteristics of a show Chrysanthemum are as follows :—1. The plant should be dwarf, shrubby, well covered with green foliage to the bottom of the stems ; the leaves broad and bright ; the flowers well displayed, abundant and well supported by the stems, which should be supported by stakes painted green. If the stems are more than eighteen inches high they are gawky, and show too much green in comparison with the bloom. 2. The flower should be round, double, high in the crown, perfect in the centre, without disc or confusion, and of the form of the segment of a ball. 3. The petals should be thick, smooth, broad, circular at the ends, and the point where they meet hardly perceptible. They must not show their undersides by quilling, and should be of such

firm texture as to retain themselves well in their places.   4.
The flowers to be large in proportion to the foliage, but the
size only to be considered when plants are in all other
respects equal.   5. The colour, if a self, is superior in proportion to its purity and brightness ; if the colours are more
than one they should be well defined and distinct.   The
worst of all colours are those which are mixed or clouded
together ; and we are inclined to place more than usual
emphasis upon colour in the case of the Chrysanthemum,
because many flowers now admitted even into exhibition
stands are odious in this respect.   We have given no rules
for judging either *the quilled* or *the tasselled* varieties, because
these should never be admitted to be shown, except in a
separate class, as " Fancy Chrysanthemums."

Soil.—Chrysanthemums thrive best in good fresh loamy
soil two parts, and one of well decomposed manure.   When
grown in pots they must be kept liberally supplied with
water and weak liquid manure once a week while growing
vigorously.   Water must not, however, be allowed to
stagnate about the roots.   Watering overhead in the evening
will be beneficial.   In potting care must be taken that there
is proper drainage.   The pots should be plunged half their
depth in coal ashes, or even earth.   This will keep the
plants steady and the roots cool.   The best position to
arrange them in is a single row in a sheltered position but
not shaded, with a foot of space between the pots.

Propagation : by Cuttings.—The best are made of the
young tops an inch long ; and the best time is in August or
September.   They may be managed in two ways—either
put them singly into two-inch pots, or place a number round
the inside of a five-inch pot.   Use sandy loam to strike
them in ; they may also be struck in beds in the open
ground.   Place them in a frame and shade them from the
sun for a few days.   They will quickly root, and should then
be potted off, and replaced in the frame, if in five-inch pots ;
but if singly in small pots they may be placed out of doors
as soon as they are rooted, and repotted when the pots are
filled with roots.

Chrysanthemum blooms may be grown to a great size by
planting in rich soil, and thinning out all the branches but
one or two well-selected stems, and removing all side shoots

as they appear ; the blossoms must also be removed with the exception of one or two on each stem. Liberal supplies of weak liquid manure must be given while the plants are blooming ; with this treatment blooms may be produced as large as good-sized roses. This treatment is only desirable when blooms are required for exhibition. The following are a few of the best large and small flowering Chrysanthemums :— Aurea multiflora, bright yellow ; Beverly, large, ivory white; Empress of India, white ; Globe, white ; Gloria Mundi, brilliant golden yellow ; Golden Beverly, canary colour ; Hereward, purple ; Lady Harding, deep rosy lilac. Small flowered or Pompones—Amphilla, bright red ; Bou le Rose, orange ; Golden Aurora, yellow ; Mrs Talfour, white.

Chrysanthemums out of doors. — The treatment just described is that suitable for growing plants for exhibition or for greenhouse decorative purposes. The out-door treatment is of the simplest character, consisting of dividing the plants every second year, keeping the ground enriched by well decomposed manure, an abundant supply of water ; thinning out the superfluous branches, and staking as required.

Cineraria.—In cultivating the Cineraria there are three principal points to be aimed at. First, never allow the slightest frost to touch them ; but avoid the opposite extreme, for they should be kept as cool as they can be conveniently without the temperature falling to 32°. The green fly is particularly addicted to cinerarias, and must be kept under if fine plants are to be grown.

Characteristics of a Show Cineraria.—1. The petals should be thick, broad, blunt, and smooth at the ends, closely set, and form a circle without much indentation. 2. The centre or disc should rise boldly, and almost equal to half-globularly, above the petals, and be not much more than one-fifth the diameter of the whole flower. In other words, the coloured circle formed by the petals should be about twice as wide all round as the disc measures across. 3. The colour of the petals should be brilliant, whether shaded or self; or if it be a white it should be very pure. That of the disc should harmonise with that of the petals. 4. The trusses of flowers should be large, close, and even on the surface—the individual flowers standing together, with their edges touching each other, however numerous they may be.   5. The stems should be strong, and not longer than the width across the foliage.   In other words, from the upper surface of the truss of flower to the leaves where the stem starts from should not be a greater distance than from one side of the foliage to the other.   6. The leaves should be broad and healthy.   No worse symptoms of bad cultivation can be apparent than the leaves being stunted, discoloured, and showing other symptoms of having suffered from green fly or drought.

Propagation : by Offsets.—When a Cineraria has done blooming, remove it from the greenhouse, cut down the old flower stems, excepting such as it is intended to save seed from, and place the pots out-of-doors upon a bed of coal ashes in an open situation.   Give water moderately in dry weather, and as soon as the offsets appear, and have attained a leaf or two, take them off with a sharp knife, with the roots uninjured ; plant them in small pots, and place them in a cold frame, shading them from the light for a fortnight, and from bright sunshine for another week.   They will then be well rooted, and will require a pot a size larger.   This mode of propagation is seldom resorted to except where it is desired to perpetuate exceptionally good varieties.

By Seed.—Sow the seed as soon as it is ripe in shallow, wide pots, in light, fine soil, and slightly covered.   As soon as the seedlings have formed two or three leaves, prick them out into the same kind of pots in a somewhat richer soil.   They may remain in these pots till they have made some more leaves and fresh roots, then pot them off singly into small pots, shading for a few days.   Afterwards, and at the proper time, repot them in the same manner as the offsets.

Soil —The offsets and seedlings having attained the proper size for potting into larger pots, prepare the following compost :—Turfy loam, two parts ; fibrous peat, one part ; decayed leaves two years old, one part ; very rotten cow manure, half a part ; and a small addition of sharp sand.   Prepare, also, a sufficient quantity of broken potsherds of two sizes, one as large as walnuts, and the other about the size of peas.   Have also a sufficient number of either new or clean-washed pots, two sizes larger than the plants are in.

Winter Culture.—By the time the plants, whether offsets or seedlings, are ready for repotting out of their first-sized pots, cold nights will have begun to occur, which brings the time of culture under this head. Bring the plants on to the potting bench ; prepare a pot by placing a large piece of potsherd over the hole at the bottom of the pot, then a layer of the larger size, and a second layer of the smaller size ; place a thin layer of the rougher parts of the compost upon them and as much soil as will keep the plant just level with the rim of the pot ; set the plant in the pot, and fill round it with the compost, pressing it gently down. Be careful not to break the leaves, as they are very brittle and tender. When the pot is quite full, give it a gentle knock upon the bench, to finally settle the soil. When all are finished, give a gentle watering, and place them in a cold frame ; shade them if they flag·from the sun, and water when necessary. They will soon require another shift. To know when they require it, turn a plant carefully out of its pot, and if the roots have reached the sides of the pot, and through the drainage, repot again immediately ; for, if the roots once become closely matted, the plants will be, crippled in their growth. The grand object is to keep them growing freely till they make large, broad-leaved plants, in eight-inch pots, before they begin to show their flower-stems. Keep them in the cold frame or pit through the Winter ; only take care to cover them up securely every night. On all fine days give abundance of air ; pick off all decaying leaves should they appear, and only water when absolutely necessary. They grow and keep healthy much better in such a situation than in a greenhouse.

Summer Culture.—As soon as the warm mild days of Spring arrive, give the plants their last shift, and, if desirable, remove them into the greenhouse at once, placing them as near the glass as possible. The flower stems will now be advancing rapidly. Cinerarias are very subject to green fly before they flower. The safest preventive is a daily syringing with soft water. If this is not effectual the plants must be fumigated with tobacco in the evening, and when the foliage of the plant is dry, syringe the plants well next morning.

Dahlia.—*Characteristics of a Show Flower.*—1 *Form*—
Viewed in front the flower should be a perfect circle ; the
petals broad at the ends, smooth at the edges, thick and
stiff in substance, perfectly free from indenture or point,
and should cup a little, but not enough to show the under
surface.   They should be in regular rows, each row forming
a perfect circle, without any vacancy between them ; and all
in the circle should be the same size, uniformly opened to the
same shape, and not rubbed nor crumpled.   2. Looked at
sideways, the flower should form two-thirds of a ball.   The
rows of petals should rise one above another in rows: every
petal should cover the join of the two petals under it, which
the florists call imbricating ; by this means the circular
appearance is perfected throughout.   3. The *centre* should
be perfect ; the unbloomed petals lying with their points
towards the centre should form a button, and should be
the *highest* part of the flower, completing the ball.   4. The
flower should be very double.   The rows of petals lying
one above another should cover one another very nearly ;
not more should be seen in depth than half the breadth ;
the more they are covered, so as to leave them distinct, the
better in that respect ; the petals, therefore, though cupped,
must be shallow.   5. *Size.*—The size of the flower when
well-grown should be not less than four inches in diameter.
6. *Colour.*—The colour should be dense, whatever it may
be—not as if it were a white dipped in colour, but as if the
whole flower were coloured throughout.   Whether tipped or
edged, it must be free from splashes or blotches, or indefi-
nite marks of any kind ; and new flowers, unless they beat
all old ones of the same colour, or are of a novel colour themselves, with a majority of the points of excellence, should
be rejected.

Defects.—If the petals show the under side too much,
even when looked at sideways—if they do not cover each
other well—if the centre is composed of petals pointing
upwards, or if those which are round the centre are confused—if the petals are too narrow, or exhibit too much of
their length—or if they show any of the green scale at the
bottom of the petals—if *the eye* is sunk—if the shoulder is
too high, the face flat, or the sides too upright—if the petals
show an indenture as if heart-shaped—if the petals are too

large and coarse, or are flimsy, or do not hold their form—in any or all these cases the flowers are objectionable ; and if there be one or two of these faults conspicuous, the flower is second or third rate.

Propagation : by Cuttings.—Cuttings may be made as soon as the young shoots are long enough to be taken off. The young shoots that spring from the tubers make the best cuttings, and are the most sure to grow ; but the young tops taken off at a joint will strike root and form small tubers even so late as February, and often are more sure to grow in the Spring following, if kept in small pots, than roots that have been planted out late. If the shoots on the old tubers are numerous, or there appear many buds ready to start, the shoots that have grown three inches long may be slipped off with the finger close to the tuber ; but if the shoots are few, or only one, they must be cut off so as to leave two buds at the base of the shoot to grow again. The cuttings, or slips, must be put in pots filled with light earth, with a layer of pure sharp sand on the surface, and placed in a gentle hotbed. If the pot of cuttings can be plunged in coal ashes or other material, the cuttings will strike the sooner ; water very moderately and carefully, and shade from bright sun. They will strike root in a fortnight or three weeks, and should be immediately potted in three-and-a-half-inch pots, and kept close for a few days, till they make a few more roots. They may then be placed in a cold frame, shaded from the sun. Pot them again into four-and-a-half-inch pots before the roots become matted, and then begin to give air daily, and keep them well watered. This system is not recommended except for the propagation of rare and choice varieties.

By Division.—The roots may be divided from the crown downwards, taking care to have a bud or two to each division or tuber. Pot them, if too early to plant out, or plant the divisions out at once in their places, but not earlier than the end of October. In dry situations dahlias may be left out all the Winter ; but they degenerate much sooner than if lifted and separated each season.

By Seed.—Save the seed from such double flowers as are partially fertile, having bright, distinct colours and good form. Gather as soon as ripe, and hang the pods up in a dry place. When the scales of the pod turn brown, separate the seeds, dry them in the sun in the morning only, and when dry store them in a dry room. Sow them in September in shallow pans, and transplant the seedlings singly into small pots or into a seed bed as soon as the frosts are passed, plant them out a foot apart every way, and allow them to flower. All badly shaped or dull-coloured flowers throw away , there is no hope of their improving by culture. Such as have good-formed petals and bright colours, though not perfectly double, may be kept another year for further trial.

Soil.—The Dahlia requires a rich, deep, friable soil ; and, as the branches are heavy and brittle, a sheltered, but not shaded situation should be chosen. The ground should be trenched, if it will allow it, eighteen inches or two feet deep, and a good coating of well-decomposed manure spread on the surface after the trenching is completed, and immediately dug in one spit deep.

Summer Culture.—Prepare the plants for planting out by constant and full exposure when the weather is mild The season for planting is as soon as there is no fear of any more frost. Five feet apart every way for the dwarf-growing kinds, and six feet for the tall ones, will not be too much. It is a good method to have the places for each marked out by driving in the stakes in the exact places first, and then there is no danger of the stakes injuring the roots. As late frosts frequently occur, especially in the South Island, it is safer to cover the plants at night with clean empty garden-pots, of a sufficient size to cover them without touching the leaves, until all fear of frost has subsided. When the plants have obtained a considerable growth, cover the surface round each plant with some half-rotten, littery stable manure ; this will preserve them from drought, and afford nutriment when the plants are watered.

Tying.—As soon as the plants are high enough they should be tied to the stakes with some rather broad shreds of soft bass matting ; and the tied shoots must also be secured by longer pieces of matting, to prevent the winds and heavy rains from breaking them off.

Winter Treatment.—As soon as the Autumn frosts have destroyed the tops of the plants, cut down the stems, and take up the roots immediately. If the roots come clean out of the ground, they will only require gently drying, and may be stored at once in some dry place where they will be safe from frost.

Pompone or Dwarf Growing Dahlias require the same treatment as ordinary dahlias. They should be grown in all gardens where there is a good herbaceous border or shrubbery border.

Single Dahlias.—Few plants are more effective for shrubbery or herbaceous borders than the above. Their bright and many coloured blooms render them most effective as decorative plants; but like the double dahlias they are more suited for large than small cottage gardens. They may be left in the ground from year to year, covering them with a shovelful of ashes or a little litter. They are, however, improved by being lifted every second year and divided.

Fuchsia.—*Characteristics of a Show Fuchsia.*—Commencing with the tube a first-rate Fuchsia should be well-proportioned, neither too thick, nor too long; one inch and a-half is a fair length, but if it is stout in proportion two inches might be allowed; the sepals or flower cups should stand at equal distances, and should be broad at the base, gradually tapering to the end; they should be refixed a little above the horizontal line, but not turned up so high as nearly to meet the tube; the corolla should be large and well rounded at the end, so that when the flower is turned up it may have the appearance of a little cup; the stamens and anthers at the top of them should project well out of the corolla; and the filament bearing the stigma must project considerably beyond the anthers, the stigma itself should be larger than the anthers, and should be of a clear white, so as to contrast well with the purple or crimson corolla. The colours should be clear and bright; the tube would be improved if of a waxy appearance, bright, and shining. If white, that white should be pure, not a pinkish white, but clear as the driven snow. The corolla should be of a clear colour, untinged by any other. The flower-stalk should be long enough to allow each flower to be seen distinctly from amongst the leaves. The habit should be rather dwarf than tall, and the plants should produce bloom when a foot high.

Soil.—Mellow, strong, yellow loam, one-half; well-decom-dosed hotbed manure, one-quarter; and one-year-old decayed tree leaves, one quarter; with a little sand all thoroughly mixed will form a suitable compost.

Propagation: by Seed.—The seed should be carefully gathered when ripe. As the seeds are developed in a pulp, it is necessary, in order to preserve them, to cleanse them effectually. This is done by washing; bruise the berries with the hand, and mix them with water; as soon as the pulp is all washed off, pass the liquor through a hair sieve fine enough to catch the seed, wash it repeatedly till it is quite clean (a fine gauze bag will answer the purpose equally well), then dry it gradually, put it up in brown paper, and keep it in a dry place till Spring. Sow early in September in a mixture of light sandy loam and peat, cover slightly, and place the pots in a gentle hotbed if available. When the seedlings are half-an-inch high transplant them in rows across pots five inches wide—these will hold about twenty or thirty plants each—and then replace them in a hotbed, cold frame, or greenhouse. In these pots they may remain for a month or six weeks, and then they will require potting off singly into three-inch pots. Place them for a few days in a cold frame, and keep pretty close and shaded till fresh roots are formed, and they are then able to bear the full light and a moderate admission of air. Give plenty of the latter as they acquire strength, and when the pots are full of roots give another shift into four-inch pots, and let them remain in these last till they flower. Many of them will flower the first year, and then is the time to make a selection. The selected ones should be repotted, and grown on to the end of the season to prove them. Cuttings of the best may be taken off and propagated, and the whole kept in the coolest part of the greenhouse or cold frame during the Winter.

By Cuttings.—There are two seasons when cuttings may be made with advantage—early in Spring and in Autumn. In September, when the old plants will be sending out young shoots, these should be slipped off as soon as they have formed two or three leaves—remember the cuttings can hardly be too short—insert one each in a thumb pot filled with fine compost, largely comprised of sharp sand; place under glass, water and shade for a week. They will strike in about three weeks, and should be shifted into larger pots as they grow. These plants if attended to will form fine flowering plants for Autumn and early Winter blooming. Cuttings may again be made in February or beginning of March and treated as above. These will make fine young blooming plants in the early Spring and Summer, but to effect this they must be kept growing throughout the Winter. This can only be effected where heat is regularly supplied. Fuchsias require plenty of water .and shade during the following season. Some of the finest flowering plants we have seen were flowered under calico.

Summer Culture.—The plants struck in the Autumn make the finest specimens for Midsummer blooming. When the young plants have filled their pots with roots, shift them immediately into five-inch pots, in a compost of light loam and leaf mould, in equal parts, adding a due portion of sand to keep it open ; this will be rich enough for the first two shifts. Let them stand pretty close to the glass to cause a stout growth. Now is the time to determine upon the form the plants are to take when fully grown.

Pyramidal Form.—To furnish side-shoots nip off the tops when the plants are six inches high. Side-shoots will then be produced, and these should be tied out horizontally. The uppermost shoot should be tied upright, to be stopped again when eight or nine inches have been added to its stature. By the time this has taken place a fresh shift will be necessary. The diameter of the pot at this shifting should be seven inches. This shift should take place about the beginning of October. Replace them in the house or cold frame again as near the glass as their shoots will allow. Give them every attention to cause strong quick development by watering freely at the roots, by syringing them overhead in the evening, especially in sunny weather, and shutting up early in the afternoon, at the time the syringing is done. This will create a moist stimulating atmosphere, and the plants will grow fast and produce broad healthy foliage. Stop them again, and tie the side shoots out in such a way as will furnish every side of the plant with horizontal branches equally distributed. If the house is a lean-to it will be necessary to turn the plant round every three or four days to cause every side to be well proportioned and equally furnished. As soon as the plants commence to blow they will require an abundance of light and shade as before directed.

Winter Treatment.—As soon as the bloom is over, set the young plants out-of-doors in some open place in the garden. When the frost begins to appear take the plants under cover, either under the stage of the greenhouse or in a back shed, where the severe frost cannot reach them. Here they may remain without water till the potting time comes round again.

Fuchsias will flower admirably in the open borders, commencing to bloom about Midsummer, until cut down by the frost; spread some ashes over the roots until Spring when they will start with renewed vigour. .

Hyacinth.—*Characteristics of a Show Hyacinth—Size and Form of Spike.*—To be a fine specimen the spike ought to be at least six inches long, and two inches in diameter at the lower and broadest part, tapering gradually up to a single pip. But form or proportion is the greatest merit; and the handsomest proportions for the spikes are for its length to be twice the diameter of its lowest part, and for the whole spike to form a cone.

Size and Form of Pips.—The outline of each, looking at it in front, should be circular; and looking at it in profile, it should be semi-circular. In other words, each pip should be half a globe. To effect this the petals (if the flower is single) require to be strongly bent back, or reflexed, so as to throw forward the centre. In double flowers it is not needed for the outer petals to be much bent back, as the semi-globular form in them is partly attained by the inner petals being imbricated, or lapped over each other in tiers, like the tiles on a roof. The lower pips should be large— an inch and a quarter in diameter is a superior size; and the pips of each circle should gradually diminish in diameter as they approach nearer to the summit. The petals should be thick, glossy surfaced, as if made of wax and rounded at the end. Sharp-pointed petals always injure the outline of the form of the spike.

The footstalk, or stem, of the spike should be straight, stout, and of a height sufficient to raise the lowest part of the spike just above the points of the leaves. The footstalk of each pip should be gradually shorter as it approaches nearer the top; and each should spring from the stem at an angle just a little less than a right angle, so as to aid the pips in adapting themselves to a conical form, and yet to keep their broad faces, or discs, full before the eye.

Colour.—What we say on this point is applicable to competing flowers of every species, for in all it should be esteemed as entirely subordinate to form and size. The reason for this is sound; for form and size, if no accident interferes, are superior just in proportion to the skilfulness of the cultivator. Colour, therefore, should have no further weight than to turn the scale in favour of the best coloured, provided that two specimens are equal in form and size. In the case of selfs—that is, flowers of one colour—the most uniform and brightest are best; but in flowers of more than one tint the colouring is best where the colours are distinct, and not clouded into one another.

Fragrance.—When flowers, such as the Hyacinth is, are of a kind yielding a perfume, if the rivals are equal in other qualities, we should award the prize to the most fragrant. It is even a criterion of good cultivation

In Glasses.—The glasses ought to be at least nine inches long, with a cup at the top to contain the bulb. The bulbs should be put into the glasses at two or three times, commencing in May, if a lenthened season of bloom is desired; the glasses should be filled with soft clean water, just up to the neck, but not actually to touch the bulb. A few bits of charcoal in the water will be an improvement. Place the glasses in a dark, cold room for a fortnight, to cause roots to be formed previously to the bloom-buds appearing. Examine them occasionally, and remove gently any scales that may be decayed, but be very careful not to injure the young roots. Should the water become foul, let it be changed, keeping each glass filled up to within a quarter of an inch of the bulbs, but do not let it actually touch them. When the buds and leaves have made a little growth they should be brought into the full light of the window, but even then, if possible, avoid a window facing the mid-day sun, or one in a room where there is a fire. These precautions produce a gradual growth, and, consequently, a much stronger foliage and finer bloom.

When the roots have nearly reached the bottom of each glass there will be seen, at the extremity of each, a pellicle or covering of mucous matter. This soon stops up the mouths of the roots by which the food of the plant is conveyed to the leaves. To prevent this the roots should be drawn carefully out of the glasses, and a wide vessel should be placed handy filled with clean water. In this immerse the roots of the bulb, and draw the mass carefully through the hand, pressing them gently. Do this two or three times until the roots appear quite clean and perfectly white. Whilst one person is doing this, let another be washing out the glass, and wiping it quite clean and dry. Then gradually work the clean-washed roots into the glass before putting in any water. To get them in when numerous it will be found necessary to twist them round and round till they reach their old quarters, and the bulb rests upon the neck of the glass. Then fill the glass with clean water, and replace it in the window. It will generally be found that one washing will be sufficient. After this no more care will be necessary, excepting occasionally changing the water. Bulbs bloomed in glasses are afterwards only fit for the border. As soon as the bloom is over, the bulbs should be taken out of the glasses, preserving all the roots. Plant them in a border in the garden, and give a good watering. Here the bulbs will gradually ripen and the leaves will turn yellow and decay. Then take them up, and keep them dry and cool until April or May, they may then be planted in the borders in the flower garden.

Culture in Pots.—Soil.—This should be rich and not over light, such as sound loam of rather a strong texture, mixed with about one-fourth of horse-droppings. Well-rotted cow manure will be a good substitute for the horse manure, provided the compost has a liberal addition of sharp sand added to it.

Size of Pots.—The kind denominated "hyacinth pots," which are at least one-third deeper than the ordinary ones, are the best for these bulbs. Three, or even five, bulbs might be planted in pots large enough to contain them, with good effect, where they are to bloom in a greenhouse.

Potting.—Whatever kind of pots are used they must be well drained. Then upon the drainage place a thin covering of very rotten sods broken into pieces. This has been used with great success in a green state. Then put a layer of the compost and press it down very firmly, only take care that it is in a proper state, neither too wet nor too dry. Keep adding more soil, and pressing it down till the pots are full enough to receive the bulbs. When the bulb is placed in the pot upon this firm bed of soil, the top should be about a quarter of an inch below the level of the pot rim; then fill in more soil around it, pressing it also firm, and close to the bulb. If this is not properly done, when the roots begin to push they will lift the bulb out of its place, and these roots will be liable to be broken. The season for potting is the last week in March, or the first week in April, for early blooms; but bulbs may be potted to the end of June.

A bed, four feet wide, in an open place in the garden, will be suitable to plunge the pots in. If the situation is dry the soil may be excavated about four inches deep, and a layer of coal ashes spread over the bottom to keep worms out of the pots. Place the pots containing the bulbs on the bed, and cover them over with spent tanners' bark or coal ashes about two inches above the pots. Here they may remain till they are required, either for forcing into flower or till the Spring.

To have them in flower in Midwinter they should be placed in heat about the middle of April, so that the forcing may be gradual. If forced too quickly the flower-stems will be weak, and the colours anything but bright; whereas, if they are brought on gradually the flower-stems will be strong, the flowers large, and the colour better. Some sorts of Hyacinths are better adapted than others for either growing in glasses or forcing in pots. For growing in pots to flower late in the Spring, almost any variety will answer.

When the bloom is in perfection the pots should be taken into a cool greenhouse or window, and plenty of air given. They will last much longer in bloom than if kept in

I

heat.   After the blooming is over the pots may be placed behind a wall and duly watered to perfect the bulbs.   They will not answer again for forcing, but may be planted in the borders the April and May following

Culture in Beds.—Soil.—To grow Hyacinths well in beds the soil should be rich, light, deep, and dry.   Manure must not be applied at the time of planting, but should be well incorporated with the soil in the previous Autumn.

Planting.—The best time is in April or May, although, if the weather is mild, they may be planted as late as the middle of June.   The soil should be moderately dry, and, therefore, it is better to wait a week or two should the season for planting be wet.   To prevent treading upon the bed lay upon it a narrow piece of board long enough to reach across it.   Plant them with a dibber thick enough to make a hole as wide as the largest Hyacinth is in diameter, and the end that is thrust into the ground should be cut across, and a mark made just as far from the bottom as the bulbs should be covered with soil ; the proper depth is three inches from the top of the bulb.   Each Hyacinth should have at least five inches square of surface to grow in, but six inches would not be too much space for the leaves to expand, especially if the same bulbs are to be planted again the following season.   If the colours are to be mixed, place the bulbs so that the colours will succeed each other in rotation, as, for instance—1, red ; 2, blue ; 3, white ; 4, yellow ; then 5 red, and so on, till the bed is full ; or, if there are several beds, and it is desirable to keep the colours separate, so that one bed shall be red, another blue, another white, and another yellow, then plant accordingly.   Cover the bulbs carefully three inches deep, then rake the bed lightly.

Shelter.—The blooming season may be prolonged for a considerable time by covering the beds with hoops and scrim.   This may appear troublesome, but the trouble will be more than repaid by the prolonged period of blooming.

Water.—During dry parching winds, which sometimes occur in October, a slight sprinkling over the beds will be acceptable to the rising buds.   This sprinkling may be continued with advantage till the blooms begin to expand.   As soon as the leaves turn yellow, the bulbs should be taken up and laid upon a mat to dry. When the leaves are all quite decayed remove them carefully, without bruising the bulbs, and then put them away in a dry cool room till the planting season comes round again.

Pansy.—There are three classes—1. Selfs, all of one colour. 2. Having yellow, orange, sulphur, or straw-coloured ground, with margins of maroon, crimson, chocolate, bronze, puce, and their intermediate tints. 3. Having a white ground with margins of purple, blue, mulberry, and their intermediate tints.

Characteristics of a Show Pansy.—Many have written upon the characteristics which belong to it when really a superior flower, and their opinions are combined in the following :—1. Each bloom should be nearly perfectly circular, flat, and very smooth at the edge ; every notch or unevenness being a blemish. 2. The petals should be thick, and of a rich velvety texture. 3. Whatever may be the colours, the principal, or ground colour of the three lower petals should be alike ; whether it be white, yellow, straw colour, plain, fringed, or blotched, there should not in these three petals be a shade difference in the principal colour ; and the white, yellow or straw-colour should be pure. 4. Whatever may be the character of the marks or darker pencillings on the ground colour, they should be bright, dense, distinct, and retain their character, without running or flushing, that is, mixing with the ground colour. 5. The two upper petals should be perfectly uniform, whether dark or light, or fringed or blotched. The two petals immediately under them should be alike ; and the lower petal, as before observed, must have the same ground colour and character as the two above it ; and the pencilling or marking of the eye in the three lower petals must not break through to the edges. 6. If flowers are equal in other respects, the larger, if not the coarser, is the better ; but no flower should be shown that is under one inch and a-half across. 7. Ragged or notched edges, crumpled petals, indentures on the petal, indistinct markings or pencillings, and flushed or run colours, are great blemishes ; but if a bloom has one ground colour

to the lower petal and another colour to the side ones, or if
it has two shades of ground colour at all, it is not a show
flower. The yellow within the eye is not considered ground
colour.

Cultivation in Beds.—A suitable *situation* is the chief
point in its cultivation ; this should be one sheltered from
all cutting winds, as these often kill the plants by twisting
them about. The situation should be open to the free
circulation of the air, and exposed to the influence of the
morning sun, but protected from the mid-day sun ; cool and
moist but thoroughly drained: for although the Pansy requires
considerable moisture during the blooming season, and
through the Summer months, yet it is very impatient of
superabundant moisture.

The Soil should be rich and tolerably light. Decayed
cucumber-bed manure is better than any other manure, and
the soil which suits best is a light hazel loam, thoroughly
mixed with a good portion of decayed turf from pasture land,
by frequently stirring and digging ; and to three barrow-
loads of this soil add one of the cucumber-bed manure two
years old. Manure water, particularly guano water, applied
during the blooming season, is very beneficial.

The Plants.—Those who intend to grow the Pansy for
Spring blooming should select young plants well established
from cuttings made the previous Autumn, and for Autumn
blooming select plants struck early in the Spring ; and after
these have produced their bloom save them for store plants
to produce cuttings, always having a constant succession of
young plants for the purpose of blooming.

The Propagation of the Pansy is very easy ; indeed they
are the most easily grown of all florists' flowers, provided the
conditions regarding shading and moisture are properly
attended to. The young side shoots are to be most preferred
for cuttings, as the old hollow stems seldom strike freely,
and do not grow so strong. For Spring blooming take off a
quantity of these side shoots in February or the beginning
of March, and for Autumn blooming in October and
November. Plant in compost mixed with a good quantity of
sharp sand, taking care to keep them moderately moist, and
shading them from the sun. Pansies are prone to damp
off without any apparent reason.

Propagation: by Seed.—Seeds may be saved from the best blooms and sown in pans as soon as ripe or in August; place a sheet of glass over the pan. As soon as the plants are sufficiently large to handle they should be planted in a finely-prepared bed. Plant six inches apart; they may remain in this bed till they bloom; select the best and discard the rest. Unless the seed is very choice indeed, we need not expect many choice flowers from a moderately sized packet of seed.

Pelargonium.—*Propagation : by Seed.*—When the seed is ripe gather it carefully and divest it of its featherlike appendages, wrap it up in paper and keep it in a dry cool room till Spring. Sow it early in September, in pots or pans well drained, in a light rich compost, press the seed down gently, and cover it about a quarter of an inch deep. If the seed is good it will quickly germinate, and should then be placed near to the glass. Water very moderately, or the plants will be apt to damp off. As soon as the seedlings have made their second leaf, pot them off singly into two-inch pots, in a compost of loam and well-rotted leaf mould in equal parts, with a liberal addition of sharp sand. Replace them on the shelf, and shade for a time from the hot sunshine. The seedlings will soon fill these small pots with roots. They must then be repotted into pots a size larger, and may afterwards be treated in the same way as those which have been propagated by cuttings. Keep them close to the glass, and give abundance of air on all favourable occasions. As soon as the weather will permit place them out-of-doors upon a bed of ashes of sufficient thickness to prevent worms from entering the pots. The situation should be an open one, to ripen the wood and induce a stocky or bushy habit, so as to insure their flowering the following season. The size of pots to flower them in need not be more than four inches and a-half. When there is a fear of Autumnal frosts, remove them into the greenhouse and place them on a shelf at such a distance from the glass as will serve to keep them dwarf and bushy. There is no need to top them in the manner recommended hereafter for plants raised from cuttings, the object being not to make fine specimens, but to get them to flower as quickly as possible the Spring following. This brings us to consider what are the *characteristics of a first-rate Pelargonium.*

Form is the first ; the flowers should be nearly flat, neither too much cupped nor in the least reflexed. Each petal should be nearly equal in size, rounded at the end, and quite smooth at the edges. The whole flower should be as near a perfect circle as possible. It should be of such a *substance* as to keep its form when expanded. If thin and flabby it will turn backwards and forwards as it advances in size, and the general effect will be marred. The *size* of each bloom should be at least one inch and a-half in diameter. The *colours* should be clear, distinct, and bright ; the edging of the upper petals should also be uniform ; the dark blotch should never run into the edging. The *habit* should be rather dwarf than otherwise, and it should flower freely ; the *truss* should stand well up above the foliage, and the number of blooms forming the truss should never be less than five ; each flower-stem should be long enough to bear the flower as high as to form an even truss.

By Cuttings.—Cuttings may be put in and struck from September to February ; the general time, however, is when the plants have done flowering, and require cutting down to make bushy plants for the next season. This generally happens from the end of December to the beginning of February. The best place to strike the cuttings is in a well constructed propagating house ; but they may be very successfully propagated in a frame set upon a thick coat of coal ashes to keep out the worms. Upon this coat place another of dry sawdust to plunge the cutting pots in. This dry sawdust will serve to absorb the moisture from the earth in the pots and the necessary waterings. The best soil is pure loam mixed with sharp sand. The pots must be well drained ; fill them to the top with the prepared loam. It should not be pressed down too hard, but made firm enough to hold the cuttings fast. Use it in a state neither wet nor dry. The side shoots which have not flowered and are not more than two inches long, make the best cuttings. These should be cut off close to the stem. If taken off with a sharp knife they will not require to be cut again at the bottom, unless the cutting is too long ; then they should have a clean horizontal cut just under a joint, to make the cutting the right length. Cut off the bottom leaves close to the stem, leaving only two of the uppermost. Place the cuttings in a shady place to dry up the wound ; this will take an hour on a dry day. Then put them in the prepared pots, round the edge, inclining the leaves inwards, so that they may not touch the leaves of those in the contiguous pots in the frames or in the propagating house. When a pot is filled give it a gentle watering, and set it on one side to dry up the moisture on the leaves and surface of the soil ; then plunge the cuttings in the frame, and shade them from the sun, or even from the light for a day or two. A little air may also be given every day by tilting up the lights behind, if in a frame. When the cuttings commence to grow they should be potted off into pots two inches in diameter. A small addition of well-decomposed leaf mould may be mixed amongst the loam with advantage. When potted off give another gentle watering, and replace them in a frame or propagating house until fresh roots are formed : renew the shading, but disuse it as soon as it is safe to do so, and then give plenty of air to prevent them from being drawn up and spindly. To cause them to be bushy plants, nip off the top bud ; the lower side-buds will then break, and the shoots from them must be again stopped as soon as they have made three leaves. The plants will then be ready to receive a second potting, and should be removed into the open air. The above directions, as far as the cuttings are concerned, relate only to the *show* varieties, as they are called ; but *fancy* varieties are more difficult to increase by cuttings. Insert the cuttings of these in shallow pans, one inch and a-half deep, with a hole in the centre, in the usual loam and sand, placing them on a shelf in the propagating house, or in the frame, close to the glass, upon inverted pots. The after treatment is the same as that recommended for pelargoniums.

House.—Pelargoniums require a house to themselves. The span-roof form is the best, because the plants in such a house grow on all sides alike. The sides should be of glass, the side windows should move up and down to allow a large circulation of air, and the top lights should also be movable to let out the heated air. The plants should be placed upon stages near to the glass. These stages ought to be broad enough to allow large specimens to stand clear of each other upon them.

The heat wanted is just enough to keep out the frost, and the best mode of obtaining that heat is by hot water circulating through cast-iron pipes. They should be placed near, but not close, to the walls, and about a foot from the floor. A couple of kerosene lamps suspended from the roof will keep out a considerable amount of frost.

Compost.—Procure from an old pasture where the grass is fine as much turf three or four inches thick as will serve to pot the collection for one year; have it chopped up into small pieces and lay it up in a heap. The grassy surface and green roots will soon begin to ferment; let it be turned over every three months in the year, when it will be fit for use. Unless it is very heavy, or of a close texture, it will not require any addition. The grand object is to have a soil just rich enough to grow a plant to a certain size, without too much luxuriance of growth, but still of such a stimulating power as to enable a plant to grow three feet high, and as much through, and to produce so many flowers as to completely cover a plant. If, however, the soil should be so poor as to need a supply of manure, then use well-rotted hot-bed manure a year old, and mix the necessary quantity, one-fourth in most cases being amply sufficient.

Winter Management.—Strict attention to giving air on all favourable occasions; keeping the house as dry as possible; giving a due supply of water, but no more; pulling off every decaying leaf, and keeping the surface of the soil frequently stirred, are the main points to be attended to during Winter. A good look-out should be kept for green fly, which must be destroyed by syringing or by fumigation. The temperature of the greenhouse during Winter should never exceed 50°, nor fall lower than 40°. If kept too warm the plants will draw up weak and spindly; if too cold, the leaves will turn yellow, or spot, or damp off.

Training.—During Spring attention must be given to tying out the plants. Use but few sticks, and those keep out of sight as much as possible. A good plan is to tie round each pot a piece of strong bass mat, or wire, and when the shoots are long, to bring them down with short pieces of bass tied to the piece which goes round each pot. This does away with the sticks in a great measure, gives a direction to the branches, and opens out the centre.

Summer.—The plants will now require shading to prolong the season of bloom, too much air cannot be given. A much larger amount of water is now required ; it will frequently be necessary twice a day. If a can or two of water is thrown upon the floor occasionally during hot sunshine, it creates a moist and cooler atmosphere. Smoke frequently with tobacco to destroy the green fly. As the plants go out of bloom cut them down, and set them out-of-doors to be repotted, as directed for Autumn treatment.

Pelargoniums may be grown out of doors in beds and borders. Plant out in November.

Petunia.—*Characteristics of a Show Petunia.*—1. *Form.*—The flower should be round, without notches on the edge, and it should be rather inclined to cup, that is, the outer edges should not bend back. 2. *Substance.*—The petals should be stout, and able to keep the form nearly as long as the colour lasts perfect. 3. *Colour.*—When a self, it should be clear without fading at the edges ; when striped, each stripe should be well defined, and each colour distinct. 4. *Size.*—Each flower should be at least one and a-half to two inches across ; if large they are liable to bend back. 5. *Habit.*—The plant should be rather dwarf, and produce flowers abundantly ; the foliage should be rather small, in order that every flower may be seen distinctly.

Propagation: by Cuttings.—Petunias are easily propagated by cuttings from August to April. The best cuttings are the young tops of rather weakly-growing plants. In Spring the cuttings require a gentle hot-bed ; but in Summer and Autumn they strike root readily enough in a cold pit or frame or shady border. The cutting pots should be drained in the usual way ; then place a layer of rich, light, very sandy compost nearly up to the rim of the pot ; and lastly, fill up the pot with fine sharp sand ; then give a gentle watering to make it firm. For the cuttings, choose young weak shoots, and cut them off close to a joint, dress off the lower leaves so as to allow about an inch to be planted in the sand, and not more than three or four leaves at the top. Plant them with a short stick, pressing the sand closely to each. The pot may be filled with cuttings in rows across it, or, if space is plentiful, place them out round the edge. Observe that the holes made by the planting stick are filled up with dry sand ; it runs more readily into the holes than moist sand would do ; then give a gentle watering again, which firmly fastens the sand round each cutting ; leave them on the bench for an hour to dry off the surface moisture.   After that, place them, if in Spring, in a gentle hot-bed, or, if in Summer or Autumn, in a pit or frame ; shade from bright sunshine, and water when the surface becomes quite dry. Mind the watering-pot, and do not use it too freely upon Petunia cuttings until they are fairly rooted and show evident signs of having made roots and growth.   Then give plenty of air, and expose them fully.   The Spring and Summer cuttings should be potted off immediately when rooted ; but those struck late in the year may remain in the cutting pots through the Winter.   When they are potted, whatever may be the period, they should be placed in a frame or pit where they can be shaded and kept close for a few days until fresh roots are produced ; let them then be gradually inured to bear the full light and air.

By Seed.—The seed should be gathered as soon as it is ripe, carefully cleaned from the seed vessels, and kept dry and cool through the Winter   Sow it in the Spring in shallow pans, placed in a gentle hot-bed, or on a shelf close to the glass in a warm greenhouse or propagating house When the seedlings come up, prick them out in similar pans rather thinly.   This can scarcely be done too early, for if allowed to remain too long in the seed-pan there is great danger of their damping off.   When they have made three or four leaves put them singly into thumb-pots ; and, as soon as there is no fear of frosts injuring them, plant them out in a nursery-bed till they flower.

Soil.—Loam procured from the surface of a pasture is best.   Of this loam take one-half, add to it one-quarter leaf mould, one-eighth well decomposed hot-bed manure, one-eighth sandy peat, and as much sand as would give the compost a sandy character.

Spring and Summer Treatment.—The soil for repotting being moderately dry, let the plants be brought out of the greenhouse to the bench, and prepare the pots to receive them.   If old and dirty, let them be clean-washed, and do not use them till they are perfectly dry ; put in drainage in the usual way ; place some rough siftings over the drainage, and -upon them place as much soil as will raise the ball of earth the plants are growing in to the level of the rim of the new pots ; then turn the plants in succession out of the pots ; remove carefully the drainage that may be attached to each ball ; place the plant in the fresh pot, and fill round the ball the new compost till the pot is full ; then give a gentle stroke upon the bench and fill up the deficiency ; the old ball should then be covered about half an inch, and a small space left below the level of the rim ; then give a gentle watering and return them to the greenhouse or cold frame, placing them close to the glass. As they grow, take care to stop each shoot, thereby inducing a bushy habit. The tops, if required, may be made use of as cuttings. In this stage the plants will require constant attention to keep them duly supplied with water, and plenty of air when the weather is mild.

About the middle of October they will require a second shift into larger pots, using the same kind of compost, taking the same precautions as to drying the soil, draining the pots and so forth. Most probably the green fly will now make its appearance, and it must be instantly destroyed by frequent fumigations with tobacco. When the weather becomes warmer they will grow much stronger and more bushy in a cold frame or pit, upon a layer of coal ashes, than on the greenhouse stage.

A third and last shift will be necessary in December. The plants should then be put into pots nine inches in diameter, and in these they are to flower. As soon as the usual inhabitants of the greenhouse are removed into their Summer quarters the Petunias will be in a fit state to take their place. Plenty of air should be given, and the roof should be shaded whenever the sun shines brightly.

Out-door Culture.—Petunias may be planted out in beds or borders as soon as the frosts have gone. They require a rich, deep, loamy soil. They may be pegged down like verbenas ; but as the young branches are very brittle, they must be handled gently. They may also be staked ; either plan should be attended to, otherwise a whole season's beauty may be destroyed by one fitful blast of wind. The single varieties are the best for out-door culture.

Pink.—*Characteristics of a Show Pink.*—The flower
must be fully double; so much so, that it should form the
half of a ball, rising up to the centre, and should be perfectly circular in outline.   Each *petal* should be stout, broad,
and smooth at the edges.   This smoothness is called *rose-
edged*; that is, without any notches or teeth.   The lowest
tier of petals should be the widest, reaching in diameter at
least from two to two and a-half inches.   The next row
should be shorter, so much so as to show the lacing fully on
the lower petals; and the next shorter again, and so on up
to the centre, which should be well filled up without confusion.   The *ground colour* should be pure white.   The
lacing, or circular stripe, should leave an edge of white outside of it, and another inside; this lacing of colour should
be of the same width as the outside edging of white, and
should be smooth and even at the edges; in fact, laid on
as if it had been traced by a skilful hand with a fine camel-
hair pencil.   Then at the bottom of the petals, there should
be another body of colour, the same as the lacing, to form
a bold, rich eye.

Soil and Situation of the Bed.—The Pink requires a
generous soil, moderately manured with thoroughly-decayed
hotbed manure.   This, if the soil is good, may be laid upon
the bed intended for Pinks, two inches thick, about April,
and immediately dug in deep, and the soil well mixed with
it.   To accomplish this well it is of advantage to dig the
bed or piece of ground two or three times over.

Propagation by Seed.—As soon as the seed is judged
to be ripe, let it be gathered and separated from the pod,
dried moderately, packed in brown paper, and kept in a dry
place till the sowing season.

Sowing.—Sow in September in shallow pans, or boxes,
placed under a frame without heat.   Set the pans upon coal
ashes, and carefully close every crevice, to prevent slugs
from entering.   Give abundance of air during warm, sunny
days, and water very gently whenever the surface appears
dry.   The seeds, if good, will quickly germinate, and the
seedlings will require particular attention to prevent them
from damping off or being devoured by slugs.   Give air
every day, and on very warm, sunny days, pull off the light
entirely.   When the plants have attained a sufficient size to

be handled, let them be carefully pricked out, four inches apart, into a bed prepared according to the preceding directions. By the Autumn they will be strong plants, and will all flower the following season. If you have not a frame you may choose a warm border, sow your choice Pink seed upon it in October, transplant your seedlings in December, and have them tolerably strong before the Autumn.

By Cuttings, or, as they are called, *Pipings*.—The time for this work depends upon the growth of the plant. As soon as the side-shoots are long enough, they may be taken off and planted. This will be about the end of November, or beginning of December. The earlier it can be done, the better plants the pipings will make, and the finer they will flower the following season.

The pipings may be planted either in pots under a frame, or in a shaded border under handlights, or in the open border facing south. For an amateur the pot method will be the most certain. The materials necessary for this purpose are a good sharp knife, a few bell-glasses, and pots of a size to match them. The soil most suitable is good, light, sandy loam, without any admixture, and a portion of pure sharp sand to place on the surface. When the pipings are two or three inches long, proceed to cut, not pull them off. Cut them close to the old plant, but do not injure its stem. When as many pipings as one variety will afford, or as many as may be required of it, are cut off, put a number or name to them, and then dress off close to the lower leaves, plant the pipings, and place the tally to them at once. Do not cut off the ends of the leaves that are left; give a gentle watering to settle the sand close to each piping, and plant them so far within the rim of each pot as to leave room for the bell-glasses to rest upon the sand within the pot. As soon as the pipings are well rooted, they may be carefully taken out of the cutting pots, and planted where they are to bloom the following season. This propagating process must be performed every season. One-year-old plants only produce blooms fit for the exhibition table. Two-year-old plants will do to plant in the flower garden.

Pinks may be propagated by layers, exactly in the same way as directed for the Carnation, and when the layers are rooted, take them up and plant out at once in the blooming bed.

General Management: Planting.—The bed to receive the plants being duly prepared, and the pipings rooted, they may be planted out. The best time to do this is in the early part of March. By being planted in the blooming bed thus early, the plants become well established, firmly rooted, and even make some growth before Winter sets in. Plant across the bed in rows twelve inches apart, and twelve inches from plant to plant in the row. When planting take the pot of pipings to the bed, turn them out, and carefully divide them, retaining every root, and even a small portion of soil to each. Commence with No. 1 ; plant it with a trowel, taking out a small quantity of earth ; then put in the plant, and press the earth firmly to it. The first row may be planted from the walk at the end of the bed. The first row being finished, procure a board nearly as long as the bed is broad, lay this across it, and when planting the second row place the foot upon the board. After the second row is finished planting, and the tally or tallies correctly placed, remove the board backwards, stir up the soil where it has been laid, and proceed to plant the third row ; and so on till all are finished. The only point to attend to is not to have too many plants out of the soil at once, as, if that were the case, the young roots being tender would perish at the ends. The wire worm is a deadly enemy to Pinks, Carnations, and Picotees. A sharp look-out for them should be kept, and everyone destroyed. They frequent fresh loamy soil.

Mulching.—A little protection from frosts will be useful. That protection consists in laying upon the bed, between the rows, a thin covering of either very short, littery manure, or one-year-old leaf mould. This precaution is, however, rarely necessary in this climate.

Spring and Summer Culture.—The heavy Spring rains will make the soil hard, and when such is the case, stir the surface of the soil with a very short three-pronged fork, being careful not to disturb the roots of the plants. The mulching, if any has been used, may be mixed with the soil in the operation. This forking may be repeated as the plants advance in growth, and will be useful to keep down the weeds as well as keeping the surface of the soil loose and open. As the season advances, and the heat of the sun becomes powerful, a mulching will be desirable to shelter the roots from the heat and drought.

The Blooming Season.—As the flower-stems advance in height, sticks will be required. Place them to the plants for that purpose before the flowers open, because, if delayed till that takes place, a heavy fall of rain might break them off. Give the stakes a coat of lead-coloured paint, and when that is dry, a second coating of light green, approaching as nearly as possible to the colour of the stems of the plants. The best article to tie them with is shreds of soft new bass mats. This special attention is only necessary for show plants. When grown in tufts, a couple of stakes will suffice for the whole plant.

Thinning the Buds.—To produce extra fine flowers for exhibition it will be necessary to thin out the buds.

Polyanthus.—*Characteristics of a show Polyanthus.*— The *plant* should be healthy ; the *foliage* large and abundant; the *stem* stout enough to bear the truss well up above the leaves, which should cover the pot, and rise up in the centre ; from the centre of the leaves the stem should rise ; the *truss* should consist of at least five flowers, and the footstalks of each flower be able to support each bloom level with the rest. Each flower, or *pip*, should be round and flat, neither inclined to cup nor reflex. The pips should be divided, near the outermost edge, into segments ; each division, or *segment*, should be slightly indented or scolloped in the centre. Each flower should have a yellow centre, or *eye*; in the centre of that there should appear a *tube* containing the anthers, but the pistil should not be seen. This yellow centre including the tube, should be of the same width as the *ground* or *body colour*, which colour should either be a rich dark crimson or a bright red. Round this body colour the *margin*, or *lacing*, should appear of a uniform width surrounding each petal, and continuing down the centre of each to the yellow eye. The colour of this lacing, or margin, should be uniform, whether it is sulphur, lemon colour, or clear yellow.

Propagation : by Seed.—This should be saved only from flowers of good form and clear bright colours. As soon as the seed is ripe, gather it before the pods burst. The seed is generally ripe when the pods turn brown ; cleanse the seed and keep it dry till September. Then sow it in the soil hereafter described, and place it in a gentle-heated frame, or pit, close to the glass. As soon as the seedlings are large enough to take hold of, transplant them, six inches apart, into a prepared border, rather shaded from the mid-day sun. Keep them watered in dry weather, and let them remain there through the Winter. They ought to flower the following season. All the care they require is to keep them clear from weeds and slugs. As soon as they have done flowering, those worth keeping should be retained and the rest discarded.

By Division.—The Polyanthus generally sends out plenty of offsets. When these have made roots they may be taken off the parent plant, and planted in a nursery bed, or potted, if so required. Care must be taken in dividing them that the stem or root-stock of the old plant is not injured

Soil.—They do well in any open rich soil.

Spring Treatment.—If grown in pots for show purposes, top-dress the plants, and keep them well supplied with water. A gentle syringing over the leaves will be found beneficial, done early in the mornings of fine Spring days, and withheld when the weather is dull, cold, and gloomy. When the blooms appear they should be slightly shaded from bright sunshine ; but they will bear more sun than Auriculas, especially the dark-ground varieties. When the blooms are fully expanded, they will last much longer if the plants are placed where the sun cannot reach them during the middle of the day.

Summer Treatment.—After the bloom is over, they should be placed in their Summer quarters. The south side of a low wall or fence is the best situation for them ; and in order to prevent the attacks of the red spider, the great enemy to these plants, place the pots in saucers or garden pans. When watered, that portion that runs through the pots remains in the pans, and by keeping the air round them moist, prevents the red spider from attacking them. In this situation they may remain till February. In the early part of that month they should be repotted, and that is a proper time to take off the offsets ; strong plants should be potted into pots from six to seven inches in diameter. These should be moderately drained. If the plants are already in the full-sized pot, the balls should be reduced, and the roots partially pruned, so as to allow of a large quantity of fresh soil being added. Give a gentle watering to settle the soil, and keep them a fortnight longer under the shade of the fence.

Autumn Treatment—This commences in the last week in February. The plants should be removed into a more open place. If the weather is then moist, the pans should be dispensed with, and the pots set upon a bed of coal ashes, thick enough to keep worms from working in at the holes at the bottom of the pots.

Winter Treatment.—This commences about the end of April. The Polyanthus is more hardy than the Auricula, and will do better if kept in a separate frame, where it can have plenty of air, and rather less protection from frost. The care necessary is, to place them upon a bed of coal ashes, sufficiently thick to prevent worms entering the pots. At the time they are placed under the frame let each pot and plant be examined. If the pots are green and dirty they should be washed clean, the hole at the bottom of the pot should be examined to see that it is quite open, to allow the superfluous water to run off freely; the soil on the surface should be stirred, all weeds and moss cleared away, a thin top-dressing of fresh soil put on, and every decayed or decaying leaf removed. If the leaves project over the edge of the pots, let the latter stand in the frame so that the leaves of one plant do not touch the leaves of the others: In the Winter months they require only just enough water to prevent them from flagging.

Open Air Culture.—These delightful Spring flowers require a good soil free from superfluous moisture. If divided in Autumn or in Spring they will flower all the better.

Ranunculuses.—The Turban Ranunculuses are the hardiest, and may be planted in beds, lines, or patches, as hereafter described.

Soil.—The soil should be retentive of moisture rather than otherwise, water must not, however, stagnate in the subsoil. The soil must be deeply trenched, and receive a dressing of well-rotted manure ; old cow manure will be better dug in sometime previous to planting. Let it be thoroughly mixed with the lower soil.

K

Planting.—Planting may commence in May, while some
gardeners prefer planting in August—either season will
answer if the ground has become tolerably dry. Some
recommend steeping the roots for twelve hours in water
before planting, but we think this not necessary, except the
planting season has been put off till the middle of August,
and the soil at that season happens to be unusually dry;
then it may be useful : we do not, however, recommend this
plan, as the soil is generally moist enough in August. Sup-
posing, then, that the weather is propitious, and all things
prepared, commence by drawing with a hoe a drill across
the end of the bed, one inch and a-half deep ; if deeper the
roots will be weakened the succeeding year, by forming a
kind of stem nearer the surface ; and if shallower the plants
are more liable to be struck with drought. The drill being
drawn the right depth, press each bulb or tuber slightly
down into the ground ; plant them if large, six inches apart
in the row ; if small, four inches will be a sufficient distance.
Cover the crown of each tuber with fine sand. This will
cause the tubers, when they are taken up in January, to
come out of the ground quite clean for keeping. Then
with a short-toothed rake, draw the soil over the bulbs, and
when it is level, with the head of the rake gently press the
soil pretty closely upon them. Draw another drill, proceed
in the same way in planting and covering up, and so on till
the whole are planted.

Watering.—Should the Spring prove dry watering will
have to be resorted to. Previously to the first watering,
immediately after the plants have broken through the soil,
and when the surface is moderately dry, tread down the soil
between the rows pretty firmly with the feet. After the bed
is regularly pressed down, then press the soil close to the
neck of each plant, and between them, with the hand.
Then proceed to water the bed with a rather coarse-rosed
watering pot ; give it freely and liberally ; and to do this
well, go over the whole bed with a heavy shower, and as
soon as that has sunk in and disappeared, commence
again and repeat the shower. In most cases this
will be amply sufficient for a week's consumption. If
the weather still continue dry, at the end of the week
repeat the watering, and do so until heavy showers take

place. It is probable that the soil will, with such heavy waterings, become baked on the surface, and will crack. Whenever that is observed, let the surface be broken fine with a small three-pronged fork, or push hoe ; but the roots must not be disturbed nor the foliage injured by this operation. A gentle watering should be given immediately after the forking. Continue this abundant supply of water whenever the weather is dry, up to the bloom beginning to open, and then discontinue it, and more especially if the plants are shaded during the time the sun has its greatest power.

Shading.—This shade should be applied at the time the flowers begin to expand, and not before. A shelter formed like the one we shall describe for the Tulip would be the best, as it would allow all the blooms to be constantly seen, and would protect them from heavy rains and dews, which very soon tarnish the bright colours almost as much as the scorching rays of a December sun. Those who may not choose to erect such a Summer shelter may form one of the arched hoops and long rods, covered with coarse canvas, or scrim, to be taken off when the sun does not shine brightly, and in fair weather. The arches may be made of rods bent over a long stout rail, nailed to upright posts at each end of the bed, with a sufficient number of posts in the bed itself. Shading is not usually resorted to in colonial gardens, nor is it necessary, except where it is desired to prolong the pleasure of the blooming season of these gorgeous flowers.

Taking Up and Storing.—The right time to take up the roots is as soon as the leaves have withered. When the bloom is quite over, cut down all the flower stems. If the weather be hot and dry, the leaves will soon decay after the flower stems are removed. They may then be lifted, and left exposed to the air until they are thoroughly dried, then pack them up in paper, and keep them in a dry, airy place. Here they may remain till the season of planting returns, requiring only to be looked over occasionally, and all decaying roots or other injurious matter removed. Should mouldiness appear upon the tubers, you may be certain either that the room is too damp, or that they have been put away before they were properly dried.

Propagation by Division or Offsets.—Offsets may be taken from the old tubers before storing for the winter. These small tubers will probably not flower the following season, they should therefore be planted in a nursery bed by themselves.

Propagation by Seed.—The seeds must be saved from flowers likely to improve the breed; they must be looked for in semi-double flowers. Form is the first property to attend to. When the seed is ripe gather it immediately, or the wind will soon disperse it. Keep gathering it as it ripens; when it is perfectly dry, wrap it up in paper, and keep it in a dry, cool place till wanted.

Sowing.—Early in Spring mix a compost of strong loam and leaf mould, and fill some boxes or seed-pans, well-drained, very nearly full; sift a portion of it, and place a thin layer over the rough compost, and press it very gently down. Mix the seed with some fine soil, rubbing it and the soil well together till the seeds are separated from each other. Sow this mixture upon the soil in the boxes or shallow pans; press it down level, and with a fine sieve sift some of the compost evenly over it, the thickness of a shilling; then water gently with a fine-rose watering pot. Place the seed-pans under glass in a cold frame or pit, or in front of a fence facing the east, and cover with a sheet of glass to protect them from heavy showers. Whenever the soil appears dry, give water, and in strong sunshine place a shade over them till the seedlings appear above ground, and have attained a leaf or two to each plant. Search well about where the boxes or seed-pans stand, and even lift them up, and examine under them, to see if any slugs or wood-lice have crept there to hide themselves. Continue this attention till the leaves begin to decay, and then cease watering. When the leaves are all decayed, and Winter is approaching, place the pans or boxes of seedlings in some very cool place where no rain can fall upon them, and keep them there till Spring. About the middle of September bring them out, and give them a good watering. Sift over the soil a thin layer of fresh compost, and repeat the care and attention with regard to watering, looking after insects, and keeping clear of weeds as in the previous season. This second year, when the leaves fail, and the plants are at rest, the tubers will have attained some size. They should now be taken out of the soil, and the surest way to accomplish this without losing any roots is to sift the upper part of the soil through a fine sieve, fine enough to catch even the smallest roots. Store them away in a cool, dry room, and in the Spring plant them out, and manage them like the named varieties. The following are good varieties :—Turban black, crimson and gold ; Turban scarlet, spotted white and yellow.

Roses.—The Rose, the queen of flowers, should find a prominent place in every garden. There is no kind of shrub, however beautiful, that is used to ornament a garden scene, so well adapted to take various forms as the rose. It can be used as a dwarf, tiny plant to fill the smallest bed ; as a bush to plant amongst other shrubs ; as one to plant in beds of large dimensions in groups ; as a tall standard. Standards can also be planted in groups on a lawn. These, also, are planted in the centre of a large circular bed, with half standards around them and dwarfs in front, thus forming one of the finest sights in the garden when in bloom. The rose is also admirably adapted for covering old fences or banks ; but there is no form which shows off the glory of the rose to equal the effect produced by training up pillars or poles. Three poles placed as a triangle and tied firmly at the top with tarred rope or wire, will stand the strongest gales. Should this plan be adopted, three different varieties may be planted, one at the foot of each pole, and trained from pole to pole so as to completely hide them when in full foliage and flower, they will then form a beautiful pyramid of flowers. Previous to planting, the ground should be made rich, in order that the growth may be vigorous. The following are admirably adapted for training as pillar and climbing roses :—Devoniensis (climbing), Cloth of Gold, Marechal Neil, Cheshunt Hybrid, Triumphe de Rennes, Celine Forestier.

Pruning : Pillar Roses should receive a kind of temporary pruning about May. At that time shorten in the long, straggling branches only. In the beginning of September, prune in the side shoots to three or four eyes, and tie in the leading ones to nearly their full length ; take away all coarse, strong-growing shoots—those robbers of the strength which ought to be husbanded to nourish the flower-bearing branches. Remove all suckers from the roots, so that no growth of the stock may escape notice.

Roses for Bedding.—Roses for the open ground may be planted from the middle of April to the end of September. May is perhaps the best month of all, provided the season is mild and open. Roses are classed into two grand divisions —Summer-blooming and Autumn-blooming. By making proper selections the blooming may be kept up from November till May. The following is a list of a few of the best for general purposes :—

List of *Hybrid Perpetuals* : Abel Carriere, crimson carmine; Alfred Colomb, fiery red; A. K. Williams, carmine red ; Beauty of Waltham, cherry crimson ; Captain Christie, delicate flesh colour ; Charles Lefevre, bright crimson ; John Hopper, rosy crimson ; La France, silvery white ; Lord Raglan, crimson scarlet.

Tea Roses : Cheshunt Hybrid, cherry carmine, a good pillar rose ; Devoniensis, creamy white ; Devoniensis, climbing ; Glorie de Dijon, fawn ; Madame Falcot, yellow ; Marie Van Houtte, white, tinted with yellow.

Noisettes : Cloth of Gold, yellow, a good climber ; Celine Forestier, yellow ; Marechal Neil, deep golden colour, a good climber ; Marie Accary, creamy blush.

Moss Roses : Moss Cristata, pale rose ; White Bath.

Austrian Briar : Persian Yellow.

Bourbons : Souvenir de la Malmaison, blush ; Reine Victoria, rose, a good climber ; Model of Perfection, lively pink.

The best Soil for Roses is a strong loam ; but they may be grown in any soil by the introduction of fertilisers of various kinds. For clay soils take chalk, loam, peat, sand, and stable manure ; for chalky soils, loam, stable manure, and night-soil ; for gravelly, sandy, and peaty soils, loam, clay, and night-soil. All soils should be trenched two feet deep, and drained where necessary before planting.

Pegging Down.—To train Roses for this system the first year's growth must be pruned back to three buds of the previous year's growth. In the Autumn of the following year, fork the bed over and lay on a fresh supply of rotten manure ; then in the Spring, early in September, procure a few hooked pegs, and peg down a sufficient number of the strongest shoots to cover the bed completely, shortening to a few inches from the extremity of each shoot. Cut off the shoots that are not wanted, to the same length as was done the Spring previously. The shoots thus pruned, and those pegged down, will send up short shoots, and each will have a bunch of fine flowers. To prevent this bed being entirely bare of flowers in the Spring, some patches of Crocuses and Snowdrops might be planted among them without any injury to the Roses. Roses grown in beds as above suffer little from high winds.

The more general way is to grow them in beds and borders as bushes ; in all cases keep a look out for spurious root-suckers which should be at once removed, as they soon exhaust the plant if allowed to remain ; cut them close into the stem, otherwise they will again shoot.

Some Rose growers recommend pruning one half the Roses in August, and the other half in October, thus throwing the flowering back a full month and making a second season.

Budding.—As soon as the stocks have grown sufficiently, and the bark readily separates from the wood, budding should be commenced ; this will be in December and January. The operation is almost identical with that described for Peaches ; and, if possible, insert the bud on the side of the branch, or stock, shaded from the sun. As soon as the bud has completed a union with the stock, which may be indicated by the plumpness of the eye of the bud, the stock may be cut away a few inches above the bud ; it is not, however, absolutely necessary to cut away the stock as directed, as buds may be inserted in different parts of the stock, particularly on climbing Roses.

Rose Stocks for budding or grafting should be planted in May or June, in rows two feet apart, and eighteen inches in the rows.

Rose Cuttings.—Roses may be grown from cuttings—the prunings will answer. Plant in rows a foot apart, and six inches cutting from cutting. A moist shady border is best. A little sharp sand at the base of the cuttings will be of service. The best time for this operation is in March.

The Culture of Roses in Pots.—Roses grow to such perfection in the open air in New Zealand that little attention is paid to their culture in pots. The following instructions may, however, be of service to those who wish to make the attempt. Roses in pots may be successfully grown in pits or glazed frames. To have fine specimens of Roses in pots, to flower in October or November, there should be a house properly constructed, and a pit to shelter the tenderer kinds in from frosts and heavy rains, and to place the plants in after potting. The best kind of house is a span-roof, with aspects east and west, because then the plants have the benefit of the sun early in the morning and late in the afternoon. The house should be wide enough to allow room for a tolerable platform in the centre, and a narrow one round the sides. The centre platform will serve exceedingly well to hold large plants, and those round the sides will do to place the smaller ones on. It should be high enough to bring the tops of the plants within at least two feet of the glass. Covering the platform with coal ashes or sand, for the pots to stand upon is of great use. If it be thoroughly wetted now and then, it slowly gives out a moisture to the atmosphere of the house, which is very agreeable and healthful to the inmates.

Soil for Roses in Pots.—For the strong-growing varieties three parts strong turfy loam taken from some pasture not more than three inches deep, and one part good hot-bed manure. Chop the loam well up, and mix the manure thoroughly into every part of it ; a small quantity of quick-lime cast in amongst it at the time will be beneficial. For the slender growing varieties, three parts of the same kind of loam, two parts leaf mould, and one part sharp sand, with the lime added as before.

Potting Roses.—The potting season for them all, at whatever time they are to bloom, is early in April. At the time of potting, the stems below the ground should be examined, and every bud likely to produce a sucker rubbed off close to the stem, as well as the suckers already produced. Drain the pots moderately well, and proportion their size to that of the plants. In potting, prune off any roots that may have been broken or bruised ; then open the roots from each other, and spread them equally on every side amongst the soil, covering the highest layer about one inch, and leaving about half-an-inch below the rim of the pots. After the potting is finished, place the plants in the cold pit, syringe them frequently, and keep them close, shading from bright midday sun. As soon as new roots are formed, give them plenty of air, and draw off the lights every fine dry day. Water must be plentifully supplied during the growing season, saturating the pots at each watering. Use liquid manure once a week. The tea roses must, however, be watered less abundantly, as they are impatient of water at their roots. The tender kinds would pass the winter more securely in the pit, but the hardy ones should be removed out of it, and plunged in a bed of coal ashes, there to remain till the time arrives to start them into growth.

On the Pruning of Roses.—As regards the time for pruning, some recommend Autumn or Winter, while others advise its being done in August and September. We like the latter season best. By Winter pruning the buds break in the latter part of the Winter, and are almost sure to be cut off by frosts in September and October. Pruning effects two objects : it makes compact, handsome trees, free from weak shoots and dead wood, and it increases the amount or floral beauty throughout the Summer and Autumn It is susceptible of three divisions—first, long ; second, moderate; and third, close pruning.

Long Pruning is employed for all strong, vigorous, free-growing kinds. The consequence of a vigorous growing rose being closer pruned is that it will make a quantity of strong shoots, generally springing from the crown close to the stock, and very likely no flower during the whole year— at all events, not until late in Autumn. The proper plan is to leave from five to eight strong shoots, placed as regularly as possible, to cut them back, so as to leave four or five buds of last year's wood, and then carefully to prune away all weak and dead branches. Roses do not flower well in the centre of the bush, and, therefore, that part should be well thinned out, leaving the branches as free of each other as possible. As a general rule, it is not right to cut into the bush below the preceding year's wood ; but when the trees become old it is necessary now and then to cut away a portion of the old wood, which becomes clubbed, and this applies more or less to all rose trees. It should be removed with a saw, of small size and the wounds afterwards

smoothed over with the pruning knife.   These remarks
apply to most of the hybrid Chinas and hybrid Bourbons,
also to some of the hybrid Provence, hybrid perpetuals and
Bourbons.

Moderate Pruning consists in using the knife more freely
than in the former case, in leaving but two eyes of last year's
wood, and in carefully training the branches, so as to make
the head round and compact.   As roses that require
moderate pruning have a greater natural tendency to flower
than those in the last mentioned class, a little inattention is
not so injurious to them.   Under this head may be
enumerated the greater part of our newest and best roses,
including the moss, Gallica, damask, hybrid damask, perpetual, and a great portion of the best hybrid perpetuals and
Bourbons.

The third method, or close pruning system, is used for
those roses which are termed dwarf growers, or that make
but little wood.   This class is not numerous in comparison
with the others, but it contains many of the brightest gems
of the rosery.   They succeed better on dwarf stocks than on
those of four or five feet in height.   In some cases they are
shy growers, and apt to overflower their strength.   This is
obviated by close pruning : as the strongest shoots come
from the crown, and as it is the interest of the grower to get
wood in this class, the last year's shoots should be cut away
pretty freely.   Under this head may be classed a few of the
best moss roses and many hybrid perpetuals, damask perpetuals, and some of the Bourbon tribe.

Yellow Briar Roses.—Roses of this class are peculiar in
their flowering, and therefore require peculiar pruning ; they
are very early bloomers, and make no wood previous to
flowering.   They generally put forth the leaf and bud about
the same time ; it is, therefore, necessary that as much as
possible of last year's wood be retained, particularly the ends
of the branches, from whence most of the flowers proceed.
The method that must be pursued in order to get as much
flowering wood as possible is not to prune them when other
roses are pruned, but shortly after they have done flowering,
leaving three or four branches a little shortened.   The rest
must be cut well back, when they will make good flowering
wood the remainder of the season and ripen it well.

Tulips.—Florists call Tulips *seedlings* until they have bloomed; after this those preserved on account of their good form and habit, as well as the offsets they produce, are called *breeders*. After some years the petals of these become striped, and they are then said to be *broken*. If the striping is good, they are said to have a *good strain;* if it be inferior, they are described as having a *bad strain*. A *rectified* Tulip is synonymous with a Tulip having a good strain. A *feathered* Tulip has a dark coloured edge round its petals, gradually becoming lighter on the margin next the centre of the petal; the feathering is said to be *light*, if narrow; *heavy*, if broad; and *irregular*, if its inner edge has a broken outline. A *flamed* Tulip is one that has a dark-pointed spot, somewhat in shape like the flame of a candle, in the centre of each petal. Sometimes a Tulip is both *feathered* and *flamed*. A *Bizarre* Tulip has a yellow ground, and coloured marks on its petals. A *Babylœmen* is white, marked with black, or lilac, or purple. A *Rose* is white with marks of crimson, pink, or scarlet.

Characteristics of a Show Tulip.—1. The cup when fully expanded should form, as nearly as possible, half a hollow ball. The petals, six in number, must be broad at the ends, smooth at the edges, and the divisions where the petals meet scarcely showing an indentation. 2. The three inner petals should set close to the three outer ones, and the whole should be broad enough to allow of the fullest expansion without *quartering* (as it is called), that is, exhibiting any vacancy between the petals. 3. The petals should be thick, smooth, and stiff, and keep their form well. 4. The ground colour* should be clear and distinct, whether white or yellow. The least stain, even at the lower end of the petal, would render a Tulip comparatively valueless. 5. Whatever be the colours or marks upon a Tulip, all the petals should be marked alike, and be perfectly uniform. 6. The *feathered* flowers should have an even, close feathering all round, and whether the feathering be narrow or wide, light or heavy, it should reach far enough round the petals to form, when they are expanded, an unbroken edging all round. 7. If the flower have any marking besides the feathering at the edge,

---

Ground colour is that upon which the other colours are laid.

it should be a beam, or bold mark down the centre, but not to reach the bottom, or near the bottom of the cup ; the mark or beam must be similar in all the six petals.   8. Flowers not feathered, and with *a flame* only, must have no marks on the edges of the flower. None of the colour must break through to the edge. The colour may be in any form not in blotches, so that it may be perfectly uniform in all the petals, and does not go too near the bottom. 9. The colour, whatever it be, must be dense and decided. Whether it be delicate and light, or bright, or dark, it must be distinct in its outline, and not shaded or flushed, or broken.   10. The height of a Tulip should be from eighteen to thirty-six inches ; the shortest is proper for the outside row in a bed, and the tallest for the highest row. 11. The purity of the white, and the brightness of the yellow ground colours should be permanent, that is to say, should continue until the petals actually fall.

Early in March is a good time for preparing the Tulip bed.

Situation.—The aspect should be open to the north, but well sheltered from high winds. If hedges of laurel or Cupressus macrocarpa surround the garden, the beds must be sufficiently removed from them to allow of a free circulation of air and sunlight. A six-foot paling fence is perhaps preferable, although not so sightly.

Manure and Soil.—A rich deep soil is necessary, yet it must not be over rich. Procure some one-year-old cow manure and mix it well with the soil, adding some sharp sand and well-decomposed hotbed manure. Mix the top surface with a considerable quantity of sharp sand ; this will cause the bulbs to come out of the soil at taking-up time, clean, and of a bright brown colour.

Shelter for the Flower before and when in Bloom.—Where the collection is small, hoops, either of wood or iron, with scrim covers to be thrown over the hoops, which ought to be high enough to keep the covering clear of the flowers, will do. On all favourable occasions remove the coverings entirely, and let the Tulips have the benefit of fine weather and gentle rains. If the Spring is unusually forward and warm, so as to bring the flowers on too early, retard them by putting on the covers only on the side exposed to the heat of the sun. Of course shading is not absolutely necessary ; but we think it pays for the trouble by the prolonged period of blooming. The shades need only be kept on during the hottest portion of the day, and during rough weather.

The best planting season is about the second week in May. Offsets may be planted a little sooner or later, as may be convenient.

Planting.—The tallest should be in the centre of the bed. This renders it necessary to plant them in rows length-ways of the bed, and not across it. This being determined upon, let the soil be levelled ; then with a hoe draw a drill the length of the bed, as nearly two inches deep as possible. As soon as the drill is drawn, bring out all the tall growers, and plant them, five inches apart, at the bottom of the drill, giving each a gentle pressure. When the row is finished, thrust in at each end a strong stick, to mark where the row of bulbs is when covered up. Cover up the bulbs by the aid of a short-toothed rake. After that let the soil on each side of the planted row be stirred up with a three-pronged fork. Then set the line at the right distance from the centre (we mentioned that the beds should be four feet wide, which would allow nine inches between each of the five rows, and six inches next the edging) ; the line then must be set at such a distance from the centre that the next row of bulbs will be exactly nine inches apart from the centre one. Draw the drill the same depth as the first, and plant the next tallest flowers in it. Then mark the row with a stick at each end, and so proceed till the whole is finished ; the lowest growers will then be next the paths all round the bed. Each variety must be numbered.

Taking up and Storing.—As soon as the Tulips have done blooming cut down the flower-stems, but do not injure the leaves. When the leaves have turned yellow take up the bulbs. If delayed some time, and the weather should be wet, there is danger of their starting fresh roots, which would injure the bloom next year. When taken up, expose them to the sun until they turn brown ; and when perfectly dry, divide from the flowering bulbs all the offsets. They should be kept in a cool dry room till the planting season arrives again. Common varieties may be left in the ground all the year round, but they will require lifting every two or three years for the purpose of thinning out, and renewing the soil.

Tuberous-rooted Begonias.—This highly ornamental class of beautiful free-flowering plants, with their graceful pendulous and upright flowers forming an effective contrast to their glossy, marbled foliage, stand pre-eminent for conservatory or greenhouse decoration, and they are equally adapted too for out-door bedding in Summer.   In habit, the plants are dwarf, compact, and very free-blooming, the individual blooms being of large size and good substance. The colours of the flowers are very brilliant, and comprise many beautiful and rich shades of crimson, scarlet, orange yellow, pink and rose.

Propagation by Seed.—The best time for sowing is about the middle of August.   It is necessary to use more than ordinary care when sowing the seed, so that it is not buried too deep.   Care must also be taken that good drainage is secured, by putting two inches of broken pots in the bottom of the pots or pans, on this place a little rough-sifted mould or moss, filling up with compost composed of two-thirds good loam, one-third peat, and sharp sand, and a little well decomposed cow manure (this latter ingredient may be omitted when preparing compost for sowing).   Fill the pots to within an inch of the top, make the surface as smooth as possible by lightly pressing it with some smooth substance, water gently with a fine-rosed watering-pot before sowing the seed, then distribute the seed evenly ; after which, sift through a fine sieve just sufficient mould mixed with sharp sand to cover the seeds.   Cover with squares of glass and place the pots and pans in a frame or propagating box in a temperature of 60° to 70°, shading from the sun during the heat of the day.   When the plants have made two or three rough leaves they may be pricked off into boxes or pans and kept close for a few days ; in about a month they will be fit to pot off into three-inch pots, using the same compost as first recommended.   Shift again as soon as the roots have reached the edge of the pots, into five or six-inch pots, which will be large enough to bloom them in the first season. When the plants have done blooming they may be dried off gradually, and the pots placed under the stage on their edges.   They must be kept dry.   In the following Spring, if desired, the tubers may be repotted for indoor blooming or planted out in the borders, where they will make a grand display during the Summer months, and in the Autumn they may be treated in the same manner as Dahlias, or the tubers may be left in the ground all Winter, care being taken to mark with a stick or label where each plant grew, so that they may not be disturbed when digging the borders.

Verbena.—*Characteristics of a Show Flower.*—1st. The flower should be round, with scarcely any indenture, and no notch or serrature. 2nd. The petals should be thick and flat, and bright. 3rd. The plant should be compact, the joints short and strong, and distinctly of a shrubby habit or a close ground creeper; those which partake of all are bad. 4th. The trusses of bloom should be compact, and stand out from the foliage, the flowers touching each other, but not crowding. 5th. The foliage should be short, broad, and bright, and enough of it to hide the stalks.

The colours should be perfectly clear and distinct in selfs, no shade should prevail, and in stripes the line where the colours separate should be well defined. The form of the truss should be as nearly flat as possible, so as to show off every individual flower to advantage.

Soil.—The best is a mixture of old turfy loam, leaf mould, and peat in equal parts. If vegetable mould cannot be had, use the loam and sand, and about a sixth part of very rotten manure, but almost any kind of light friable soil will answer.

Situation.—Verbenas thrive best in an open, airy situation, provided they are sheltered from high winds. The bed or beds should be long, and not more than four feet wide. This sized bed would contain two rows, allowing them space to spread out a little every way.

Plants in Pots.—Verbenas grow so luxuriantly out of doors in this country with the most ordinary treatment, that few persons care to take the necessary trouble to grow them in pots. Still as some may be desirous of doing so for the purpose of exhibition, the following directions will be found useful:—The pots should be kept in a pit or frame deep enough to keep them at least nine inches from the glass when in bloom, standing in three or four inches of ashes.

Potting.—The plants must be healthy, clear of insects, well furnished with leaves, low, bushy, and with numerous branches close to the soil; and the kind such as produce good trusses of well-shaped, bright-coloured flowers. The best season for this operation is September. The potting soil or compost may be the same as recommended for out-door culture. As soon as the potting is finished give a gentle watering, and place them in the frame. Peg down such shoots as are long enough for the purpose, spread them out equally over the surface of the pot, and nip off the ends of every long shoot, which will cause them to break out more shoots, and the pinning down will also induce shoots to spring up from the centre of the plant.

The plants will grow rapidly, and will soon require a second shift. At this shift they will require at least an inch of drainage. There should be about an inch of space between the ball and the sides of the fresh pots. Turn the plants carefully out of the pots, pick out the greater part of the old drainage, place as much soil upon the new drainage as will raise the ball nearly level with the rim of the pot, avoid deep potting, press the earth down round the ball firmly, but gently, and give a smart stroke upon a firm part of the bench to settle the whole. This will leave sufficient space within the rim of the pot to hold a good watering. As potting is finished, return the plants to the pit, and water them moderately overhead. During the operation peg down the shoots when long enough, trim off the decayed leaves, stop the shoots, apply sticks, and clear off insects by fumi-gation if any appear.

Protecting Bloom.—As soon as the flowers begin to ex-pand they require to be sheltered from the bright rays of the sun, high or hot winds. Those in pots, in frames, are very easily protected from too bright sun by a covering of thin canvas. Shading will only be necessary for those blooms required for show purposes.

Planting in Beds.—The bed or beds to receive the plants should be in good order about the last week in October ; the plants should, by a little care in stopping, be nice little bushes. Plant in beds or borders eighteen inches plant from plant.

Propagation : *by Cuttings.*—There are two seasons for this operation—Spring and Autumn. The time for making the first batch of cuttings may be August and September. It will be necessary to place the stock plants in heat for the purpose of preventing young growth. This system of propagation is only necessary where large numbers of plants are required. When the plants are fairly established abundance of air must be given. In mild weather draw off the lights of the frame; and, in rainy weather, give air by tilting the lights.

Large quantities of strong, well-rooted plants may be obtained with very little trouble, if undertaken at the proper time. Shallow boxes, say four inches deep by one foot wide, will answer, having two or three auger holes in the bottom for drainage; put one inch of rough cinders, broken pots, or chopped sods, and fill up with compost, composed of fresh loam, decomposed leaf mould, and sharp sand—two parts of the former and one each of the latter. Any ordinary soil will answer if fresh loam cannot be had. Sprinkle the surface with sharp sand. Press the compost firmly in the boxes, and water well the day before planting the cuttings. The cuttings should be taken from the parent plant early in March. Select the young shoots which have no bloom upon them. Cut at a joint, trim off the lower leaves, and insert the cuttings in the soil about two inches deep, and two inches one from the other. Press the soil against each cutting with the planting stick (which should not be more than six inches long with a blunted point.) The cutting should not be more than three inches long. As each box is filled with cuttings as directed, it should receive a gentle watering, just enough to settle the soil about the stems; remove the boxes at once to the cold frame, where the sun cannot reach them. Sprinkle gently with a syringe every fine evening, and keep the frame closed until the cuttings begin to grow, when air may be admitted gradually. If Verbena cuttings are once allowed to flag, it is rarely that they can be revived (except placed in a gentle heat.) In this country Verbenas require very little protection from frosts. They will live through the Winter standing on a verandah facing north. Water only when absolutely necessary. An occasional soaking in fine open weather will be better than frequent sprinklings. The great point to aim at in preparing young stock to be kept through the Winter, is to have the plants well rooted before the cold weather sets in.

L

GRAFTING.

THIS operation is of high importance in practical gardening, for, although hundreds of subjects can be raised from cuttings, they cannot be rendered useful for years; while the same cutting grafted on a vigorous stock might form a tree the second year. The whole strength of the stock may be thrown into the small piece grafted on it, whereas if grown as a cutting it could not grow at all until it struck root, and even then but slowly, for a considerable time. The advantages of grafting are not limited to this nor any other, but are many. First, it enables us to multiply any new or distinct variety to a much greater extent than by any other means, because a piece with a single bud on it is sufficient for a graft. Secondly, it enables us, if desirable, to throw greater or lesser nourishment or vigour into the graft, according to the stock we place it on. Thirdly, it enables us to change the variety of any tree, or shrub, or plant already established, instead of removing the old tree or shrub, and placing a new one in its stead. The manner in which the operation is performed is adapted to the circumstances under which it is undertaken; for instance, if

Plate 1.

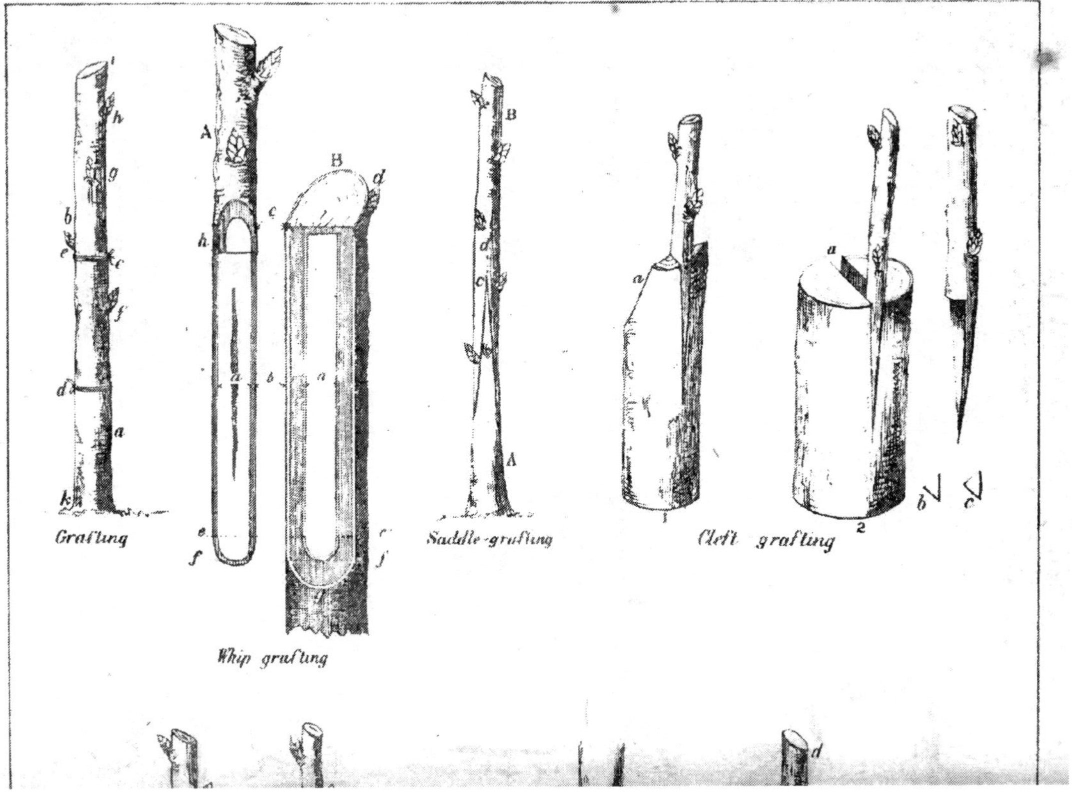

Grafting

Whip grafting

Saddle-grafting

Cleft grafting

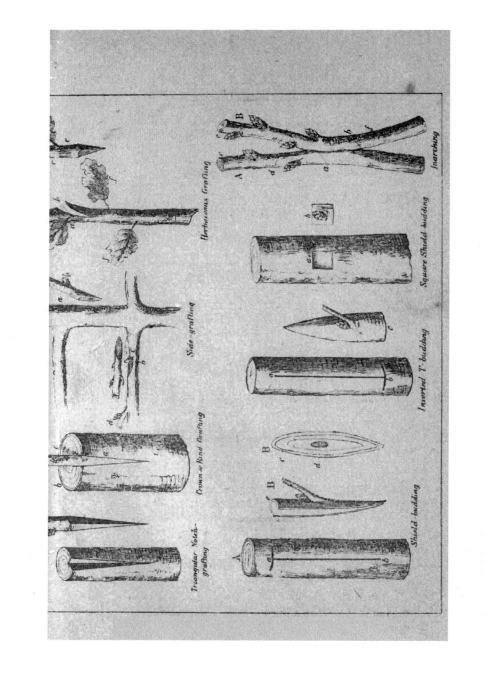

Triangular Notch-grafting

Crown or Rind Grafting

Side-grafting

Herbaceous Grafting

Shield-budding

Inverted T-budding

Square Shield-budding

Inarching

grafting is performed for the purpose of multiplying a variety, stocks of the proper kind are selected, for the purpose of conveniently removing when the graft has taken ; generally a year established in the ground if for fruit trees, or a year old in pots. The first is, because fruit trees and shrubs in the open ground ought not to be more than three years in a place undisturbed, and, therefore, as one year after planting a stock is strong enough to be grafted, it allows of one year to let the graft grow, and a second to form a sort of head or to grow into stuff, as gardeners call it.

EXPLANATION OF PLATE 1.

Grafting.—*A* and *B* sloping cut commencing at *a, c* and *d* ligatures, *f, g* and *h* buds, *k, d, e* stock, *a, b, i* scion.

Whip Grafting.—*A* the scion, *B* the stock, *a a* the cut surface showing the wood, the points marked < should touch the inner bark of both stock and scion, while the points at *b* touch the outer barks. In preparing the graft, cut the top of the stock in a sloping direction from *c* towards *b*, terminating, if possible, above a bud, as at *d*. Cut the scion sloping from *c* to *f*, then enter the knife at *h*, and cut a thin tongue upwards to *c*. The scion is then ready for inserting on the stock. To prepare the stock enter the knife at *g* and cut a slice upwards to *c*, taking care to make the surface as nearly as possible the same size as that of the scion. Enter the knife very little below *c*, and cut a notch to receive the tongue of the scion ; insert the tongue of the scion (made at *h* by cutting half-an-inch upwards). See that the barks meet as directed ; then tie with matting, and surround with clay or grafting wax—the whole secret of successful grafting lies in the coincidence of the inner bark of the stock and scion.

Saddle Grafting should only be attempted when the stock and scion are about the same size. The stock *A* is cut like a wedge, terminating at *c*; *B*, the scion is split up the centre, and placed over *A* the stock, taking care that the barks of both meet : tie and cover as directed above.

Cleft Grafting.—This mode of grafting derives its name from the mode in which it is performed, viz., a cleft is made in the stock with a chisel at *a*, keeping the cleft open till the scion is inserted. The section of the scion should be an oval *c*, and not a triangle *b*; care being always taken to make the barks meet. Tie and cover with clay or wax. Cleft grafting is not recommended.

Triangular Notch Grafting is sometimes adopted instead of cleft grafting. The illustration will explain itself.

Crown or Rind Grafting.—This mode of grafting is preferable to cleft grafting, for the reason that the wood of the stock is not interfered with. This form of grafting is adopted with old trees. The lower end of the scion is cut sloping, as in whip grafting. The head of the stock is cut over horizontally, and a slit *a* is made just through the inner bark. A piece of wood or bone, resembling the thinned end of the scion, is introduced at the top of the slit, and pushed gently down in order to raise the bark sufficient to introduce the thinned end of the scion without being bruised. The edges of the bark are then brought close to the scion, and the whole is bound with matting and clay. Other scions may be inserted in like manner at *b* and *c*.

Side Grafting is a modification of whip grafting, and is performed in the same manner, except that the stem or branch, instead of being cut completely off, is notched to a greater or less depth, as at *b*. It is also useful for supplying a branch where required, as at *a*. In supplying a branch, as at *a*, the scion must be placed with a head pointing outwards, and the shoot proceeding from it trained in a horizontal direction towards *e*. When required to substitute another branch, a notch is made, as at *b*, and a slice is taken off between the notch and the stem, as at *c*. The graft is placed there. As the shoot grows it must be trained horizontally, and spurs, as at *d*, cut away. When the new branch has made a considerable growth, the original branch may be clean cut away at *b*.

Herbaceous Grafting.—As its name implies, is applied to herbaceous plants, when in full growth. Make an oblique incision, *b*, as close as possible to the base of the petiole of the leaf *a*, merely saving the bud in the axil. Into this incision the scion *c*, of the same diameter, and in the same state of growth as the stock, is fitted. The graft is then tied with coarse worsted. The leaf *a* is intended to draw the sap toward that point; whilst the leaf *e*, in the scion, partly absorbs the sap thus obtained. The fifth day after the operation, the centre eye in the axil of the leaf *a* is removed.

Shield Budding.—*A* the stock, *B B* the bud in different positions, *a* and *b* transverse and longitudinal incision, *c* the wood to be removed from the bud; it is not absolutely necessary to remove this wood. *D* the eye, *e* the bud ready for insertion. For full instructions see page 67.

THE GREENHOUSE.

NOTHING adds so much to the pleasure of those who have a taste for gardening, as the possession of a glass house, however small it may be. Timber and glass are now cheap; and any amateur (at all handy with carpenters' tools) may, at a very little cost, erect a house suitable for his purpose.

The house represented in the frontespiece is a fac-simile of one built entirely by the author in his spare moments (with the exception of a few pounds paid for assistance while erecting the roof and putting in the glass). Length of house 18ft. by 11ft., height of sides 5ft., height to ridge 9ft. The structure is composed of wood and glass. The total cost has been £25, this is exclusive of the heating apparatus, which cost £5.

Every greenhouse should be supplied with a heating apparatus to be used during severe weather in Winter, lacking which, it will be difficult to save tender plants. For small houses a kerosene lamp or two will suffice to keep out frost. A cold frame is also indispensable for the successful working of a greenhouse. If built of brick, all the better, as there will be less trouble with vermin than if constructed of wood.

CALENDAR OF WORK TO BE DONE IN THE GREENHOUSE DURING THE YEAR.

Commencing with July.—Admit air on every favourable occasion, especially amongst Heaths, Epacris, and Azaleas, not required for early blooming. During dull, frosty, and foggy weather, such as is frequently experienced at this season, a little heat will be of service, as it promotes a circulation of the stagnant air, which is beneficial to growing plants. The most forward fuchsias may now be pruned and repotted. Pelargoniums and Cinerarias will, in like manner, require cleaning and fumigating. The first may now be repotted for late November and early December blooming ; and the latter must be shifted and kept growing, so as to prevent them throwing up flower stalks, if late bloom and late specimens are desired. Place a few Achimenes, Gesnera, and Gloxinia roots in heat, if available, for early blooming ; a medium temperature of 50° will answer for these plants.

August.—Admit air freely amongst hard-wooded plants, such as Camellias, Azaleas, Ericas, and Epacris, when the weather is fine. In damp, foggy, or frosty weather use a little firing to dry the air, and promote a free circulation. Water only when the plants are getting dry, and then do so copiously. Azaleas and Camellias will now be coming into bloom, and must be supplied rather liberally with water. Bulbs, Cinerarias, and Primulas in flower will be the better for a little weak manure water once a week. Calceolarias and Pelargoniums require plenty of light. Fuchsias should now be started in a gentle heat. Achimenes, Gesneras, and Gloxinias may be potted. Insects will now be troublesome, and the best antidotes are sulphur vapour and tobacco fumigation ; but above all, cleanliness and good cultivation. Old plants of Scarlet Geraniums stored in boxes, in sheds, or other temporary shelter, should be kept free from mould and damp by removing all dead or decaying leaves.

September.—Admit an abundance of air in fine weather. An occasional fire in damp or frosty weather will be required to dry the atmosphere. Camellias, Calceolarias,

and Cinerarias, now in bloom, will require a liberal supply
of water, with liquid manure once a week ; avoid giving
liquid manure to Heaths, Epacris, and Azaleas ; shade on
sunny days.   Heaths and Epacris require an abundance of
air when growing and flowering.   Continue the occasional
use of manure water for Primulas.   Train large plants of
Pelargoniums intended for early flowering ; stop those for late
Summer and Autumn flowering.   Shading must now be
attended to ; as the sun gains strength this will be all the
more necessary, particularly for such plants as Calceolarias,
Fuschias, &c., &c.   A sowing of Primula Sinensis may
now be made for early Winter blooming ; a sowing may also
be made of Balsams, Cockscombs, Thunbergias, &c.

October.—Admit air freely on all fine days.   All
flowering plants will require an abundance of water.   Growing plants will be greatly improved by the occasional use of
a fine syringe, avoiding those in full bloom.   Manure water
may now be given more freely to Pelargoniums that have set
their flower buds.

November.—Great attention must now be paid to
ventilation—leaving a little air all night—increasing it as the
month advances.   Balsams and Cockscombs should now be
sown or potted as they are ready.   Young shoots of Heaths,
Epacris, and Azaleas, &c., may now be struck.   Stir the
surface of pots.   Syringing and watering must now be carefully attended to ; plants with large leaves require most
water.   Syringing should only be done after sunset.

December.—Admit air freely.   Seeds, such as Ciner
arias, Calceolaris, and Primulas, may now be sown.   Many
Winter-flowering things, such as Daphnes, Heaths, &c., &c.,
may now be set out of doors, in a sheltered place, to make
room for other plants coming forward from the cold pits.
Plants placed at first in a sheltered place must in general be
fully exposed before Autumn, to perfect their wood.   Sudden
extremes must, however, be avoided ; the roots in the pots
suffer more from complete exposure than the branches.
Grafting may still be done in the case of Daphnes, &c.
Oranges and Lemons should have their blossoms thinned,
and impregnated where fruit is wanted.   Plants done
blooming, such as early Camellias and Azaleas, require a high
temperature and a moist atmosphere for a short period, to

enable them to make their wood and set their buds early. These conditions may be secured by shutting up the greenhouse early in the afternoon; syringing plants at the same time, and give but little air during the day. But this treatment would soon ruin the health and appearance of such things as Calceolarias, &c., in bloom; though it would answer well for bringing on large Fuchsias and Pelargoniums for succession. To grow these plants successfully, a separate house should be provided. Pick off yellow leaves as they appear. Cleanliness must be strictly attended to; this will obviate the necessity for too frequent fumigation, which is always more or less injurious to the plants. Manure water may be frequently applied, but it must be weak. Cut down Pelargoniums as they go out of flower. Give Fuchsias for late blooming a liberal shift, and water with manure water. Shade plants in flower if their beauty is required to be prolonged. Newly-potted plants also require to be shaded and kept rather close for a few days, till the roots lay hold of the fresh soil. Put in cuttings of Pelargoniums. Propagate Chrysanthemums, and shift and stop established plants. Afrer getting the final shift, stand, or far better still, plunge the pots in open, airy quarters, and take special care that they are well supplied with water. Green fly will now be troublesome in the greenhouse; the finger and thumb, aphis brush, and, above all, the syringe, must be constantly in requisition to keep this pest and the red spider in check.

January.—Admit air freely night and day, except during sudden changes. Water plentifully; syringe in the afternoon. Continue to shift, pot, and regulate the plants as necessity occurs. Graft Oranges, Camellias and Azaleas. Remove Azaleas and Camellias that have done growing to a dry, airy place, out of doors, to rest and harden their wood. Cinerarias which have finished blooming may be cut down and planted out of doors, or kept in pots if required to be grown for suckers, or merely by thinning out, or dividing the old plants.

Apply weak manure-water to late flowering Calceolarias. Cut down those finished blooming; thin the pods of those left for seed, as one pod will give hundreds of plants. Those which have finished flowering may be planted out on a border facing south. Sow seeds of these and Cinerarias for successful blooming plants. Cut down the most forward

Pelargoniums ; tie and train successions ; prepare for an early supply of cuttings ; they will strike better now in an open border, than two months hence in pits or frames. Choice varieties should be struck in thumb pots, they are less liable to damp off, and after they have struck can be shifted without the smallest injury to the roots. Cut down Heaths when done flowering ; shift those starting again, after being pruned ; propagate by seed and by cuttings in a pit under hand-glasses. Shifting must be attended to with all successions, such as Fuchsias, Pelargoniums, Balsams, Cockscombs, &c. Cuttings of Petunias and shrubby Calceolarias may be put in, as directed for Pelargoniums. Petunias put in now will make excellent stock plants to strike from, for bedding-out next year. Cuttings of all soft-wooded plants, for bedding-out, may be put in as they can be spared in the open border. Take off decayed blooms unless where seed is required, and keep plants clear of dead leaves. Chrysanthemums will now require stopping, that they may throw out laterals. If dwarf specimens be an object, top cuttings may be put in ; or single shoots, layered into pots, placed beside the parent, will make fine, short flowering plants.

February.—Give air night and day, especially during the former. In very hot weather, it is advisable to keep rather close with a moist atmosphere during the day, giving all the air possible during the evening and night. This treatment will apply to Heaths, Azaleas, and Camellias, &c., that are now making their growth. Those which have set their buds may be removed to a sheltered place, and have no glass protection for a time. Pelargoniums which have been cut down, and have started to grow, may now have the soil shaken from them, potted in light soil and placed in a close, moist pit to encourage free growth ; until that growth has taken place, give little water at the roots. In growing from cuttings, success will greatly depend in never allowing them to stand still, but keeping them constantly but slowly growing. Cut down successional plants as they finish blooming. If required to flower again before Winter, simply remove the old flowers and nip the points of the branches, this being more applicable to the fancy varieties. Zonale Geraniums for Winter flowering should be placed in an exposed sunny situation, and kept moderately dry, in order to harden their growth. All young stock, growing freely, should be hardened off by the end of the month. Potting should now be proceeded with in order that the roots may have time to establish themselves before Winter. Almost everything may now be successfully propagated. The whole of the soft-wooded Geranium family will do best in a south border ; gather seeds as they ripen. The propagation of half-hardy plants such as Calceolarias may be commenced by the end of this month. Sow seeds of herbaceous kinds in a cool pit. Use the syringe amongst growing plants freely on warm evenings. Dress, tie, and keep all plants neat and clean. Chrysanthemums should now be particularly attended to, and if the pots be well filled with roots, be liberally supplied with manure water. A mulching of manure, too, over the surface of the soil in the pots will benefit them much.

March.—Continue to give air freely night and day in fine weather. Pot bulbs for early blooming, such as Hyacinths, Narcissus, Tulips, &c. Camellias may still be exposed, but they should be sheltered from heavy rains. Cuttings may still be made, and budding proceeded with. Early sown Cinerarias may now receive their final shift for Winter blooming. Propagate Calceolarias by cuttings ; shift small plants already struck ; get Ericas and Azaleas under shelter, ready for housing by the end of the month. Pelargonium cuttings now rooted, may be potted off for flowering or specimen plants. Those planted in the open border may be taken up by the end of the month, and potted or placed closely together in boxes. Continue to propagate Pelargoniums, Fuchsias, Verbenas, Ageratums, Petunias, &c. ; the smallest pieces will do best (the tips of the shoots). Verbena cuttings must be carefully shaded after planting, and sprinkled freely with water ; but the soil must not be kept saturated. Plants still growing freely must be abundantly supplied with water, and those intended to bloom in Winter, such as Cinerarias, Primroses, and Chrysanthemums in pots should have manure water given freely. Water must now be sparingly applied to plants that are to be placed in a state of rest, such as Pelargoniums, Fuchsias, &c.

April.—Air must still be admitted freely during the day, but sparingly at night. Camellias and Azaleas should now be housed, as the least frost will discolour their leaves.

Continue to pot bulbs. Cinerarias should now be housed.
Prick off seedling Calceolarias, and pot forward plants.
Prune in climbers on rafters to admit the sun and light to
the plants beneath. Keep Azaleas, Camellias, Fuchsias,
&c., in the coolest part of the house. All kinds of cuttings
intended for outdoor work next season must be kept secure
from dampness, which is their greatest enemy. Be careful
how you apply any artificial heat, it generally does more
harm than good at this season of the year. Pelargoniums
must be kept clear from the fly ; and kept slowly growing.
This last condition is the best antidote against the former ;
avoid, however, letting them be chilled and soaked, as this
engenders spot. Fuchsias and Geraniums should now be
lifted from the beds and borders, and planted in boxes and
pots, to stand in an open shed, or on a verandah, or under
the stage, in fact, in any dry, airy place free from sharp frosts,
or their crowns may be covered over with a few inches of
coal ashes or litter ; lifting and storing is, however, the better
plan.

All plants should be thoroughly cleaned, as well as every
part of the house and glass washed. Water must be
sparingly given, and only when necessary.

May.—Continue to admit air freely in fine weather.
Azaleas required for blooming early should be kept in the
warmest part of the house. Those required for flowering in
Spring and early Summer must be kept as cool as possible.
Keep Calceolarias and Cinerarias growing slowly in a moist
and airy atmosphere ; those intended for late blooming must
be kept cool. Continue to pot off seedlings. The earliest
Camellias will now be swelling their flower buds, which
should be thinned if necessary. A little cow-manure water
clear and not too strong, will do them good. Water only
when necessary. Keep all plants clean by washing, and
fumigation when necessary. When a plant requires water,
water it thoroughly, never superficially, or the consequence
may be that plants with delicate, hair-like roots may have
the surface of the soil apparently wet, while the ball of earth
is really quite dry. Airing well on brisk, drying days is the
only means that should now be resorted to in the greenhouse
for the prevention of damp ; but should fire heat be
absolutely necessary to counteract it, have recourse to it

only on brisk, dry days, when the house can be at the same time freely aired and the temperature kept up. Chrysanthemums should have plenty of room and air, and also an almost daily dose of liquid manure.

Cold Pits and Frames.—Plants in these will require constant attention, both as to giving air and preventing damp. When, during bad weather, the sashes cannot be taken off, air should be given by tilting the front of one sash and the back of the other, alternately. See that no decayed leaves are allowed to remain on Calceolarias, Pelargoniums, Verbenas, or other soft-wooded plants wintered in frames or pits. Verbenas are very subject to mildew, and a sharp look-out for its appearance should be kept. Immediately on the first trace being observed, dust with sulphur.

June.—Whenever the weather is mild and dry, give plenty of air, but not in a way to create draughts or currents ; water cautiously, but at the same time thoroughly, but avoid wetting the leaves. Fires may be lighted occasionally, but only to expel damp, and this only on fine, dry, brisk days, when, at the same time, air can be given freely. Decayed leaves and flowers should be promptly removed. Remove Chrysanthemum blooms as they decay, and the plants themselves as they go out of flower, and place them out of doors ; encourage later blooming specimens with liquid manure, light, air, and water. Zonale Geraniums in flower should be kept well up to the light, and should be helped to occasional doses of soot-water, or other mild stimulant. Cinerarias and Chinese Primroses coming into flower should be brought forward to where they will have plenty of air and light, and have occasionally a little weak manure-water given them. Camellias in flower will require to be well supplied with water, provided the drainage is good, and the soil not sour or saturated. Clear soot-water agrees particularly well with Camellias, and forms a wholesome stimulant, provided the pots be full of roots. Herbaceous Calceolarias and Cinerarias may be shifted into their blooming pots. They like a liberal shift and rich feeding as soon as the pots get well filled with roots. It will not be amiss to remark that, before re-potting, care should be taken to see that there is no green fly on the foliage. If there be, its riddance should be effected in the first instance before re-potting. Pelargoniums for early blooming must have plenty of air, and a temperature not lower than 45°; they will also require tying out. Young plants in their cutting boxes in frames will require all the air they can get to prevent them from damping off. A little occasional heat for the next two months will be of great service.

Cold Pits and Frames.—Plants wintered in pots in frames should, in favourable weather, be often and carefully looked over, and every decayed leaf removed. On mild, dry days the sashes may with advantage be taken off for a few hours in the middle of the day. Auriculas in pots should be carefully attended to this month. Give them plenty of air whenever circumstances are favourable for it, and remove with the scissors dead or decaying leaves. The soil in the pots should be kept just barely damp throughout, but not more, and there should be no crowding of the plants. Keep a sharp look-out for green fly, and with the aphis brush or the finger and thumb, or by fumigation, promptly dispose of the pest. Thrip, too, is a great enemy of the Auricula, and any plant so placed as to be affected by it should be immediately removed to another position.

ORCHIDS.

⸺⸻✳⸻⸺

SINCE it has been discovered that some Orchids can be grown in cool greenhouses in this favoured clime with the greatest ease, a demand has arisen for this beautiful race of plants. A few degrees of frost do not seem to injure them, as they have been successfully grown in a fernery from which frost was not excluded. In the following remarks only those kinds which are called cool-house Orchids will be referred to, and which are known to succeed in a greenhouse without any extra amount of care or which require the skilful treatment of a professional gardener.

Orchids are grown in baskets suspended from the roof, in imitation of their natural condition as parasites on trees, but they can be equally well grown in pots on the stages. The latter system is to be recommended for the amateur who may not be able to give frequent attention to the plants, as treated in that way they do not dry up so quickly. When grown in pots there should be a shallow pan fixed under the stages to contain water, which will supply the necessary moisture by evaporation. When grown in baskets suspended from the roof the plants must be plunged in water for a few seconds every day during the Summer months, but in Winter once a fortnight will suffice to keep them in the necessary condition of moisture, the water being previously warmed. Shade is essential during the Summer and Autumn.

The materials for growing Orchids are good sweet fibrous peat in lumps, charcoal, broken brick, and sphagnum moss.

To Basket an Orchid—Place a layer of sphagnum on the bottom of the basket, then fill up with pieces of peat, brick, and charcoal in equal proportions until the basket is heaped up in the centre. Then place one or two stout stakes in the compost, put the base of the plant in the centre, spreading out the roots on the surface, and tie the principal shoots to the stakes to keep the Orchids in position. Cover the whole with sphagnum and the work is done. Some species, such as Phajus and Disa, are terrestrial orchids, and should be grown in pots in a compost of loam, leaf mould and rotten manure, well mixed together. Two inches of drainage should be put at the bottom of the pot, then a layer of moss, or rough peat, filling up with the compost so that the base of the plant is about level with the rim.

The following list includes both epiphytal and terrestrial species, the latter being marked with an asterisk :—

*Cypripedium, or Ladies' Slipper Orchids.—There are about a dozen sorts, which can be grown in a frame or cool house.

*Disa Grandiflora and its Varieties.—These are best grown in shallow pans in fibrous peat, sharp sand, and sphagnum moss. Water freely when growing, as the plant grows in boggy places on Table Mountain.

Dendrobium, Speciosum, and Nobile.—These Orchids are very hardy and free growers. They will succeed either in pots or in baskets.

*Goodyera Pubescens.—This is a beautiful foliage plant, suitable for a cold frame. It should never be allowed to get dry at the roots.

Lycaste Skinneri.—This species is easy to grow, and its blooms are both beautiful and durable.

*Orchis Foliosa.—This is a fine terrestrial species from Madeira, and makes a good exhibition plant when well grown.

*Satyrium.—A very interesting genus of Orchids from the Cape, which succeed well in a cold frame in the compost given above.

Odontoglossum.—There are many species in this large genus which can be successfully grown in a cool-house in which the temperature ranges from 45° to 55° in Autumn and Winter. They come from the South American Andes. Some are best grown in baskets, but most of the species do well in pots.

Oncidium.—A few of these decorative Orchids will thrive in a cool house, and, as they are good growers, they may be recommended for cultivation by the amateur.

*Phajus.—This is a handsome, strong-growing class of Orchids of easy culture. They require warmth in the growing season in Spring, but when at rest in the Winter months they do well in a cool house if kept dry.

NEW ZEALAND PLANTS.

 THE following list of plants suitable for borders, specimens, hedge plants, and rock-work, has been furnished by Messrs. Adams & Sons, Christchurch, who have made a speciality of this department of horticulture.

Few persons, except those who have visited the Alpine regions of New Zealand, have any idea of the beauty of the flora. It is therefore a matter for congratulation that the above-named firm have commenced making a collection of those little-known but lovely Alpine plants and shrubs, many of which could be grown with ease in our gardens, thereby adding greatly to their beauty. The following are a few of those which have been tested and have been found to thrive on the low lands :—

Aciphylla Colensoi and Lyalli, the bayonet plant flowers white.

Acæna adscendens, and microphylla, suitable for rock-work.

Astelia Nervosa, Bush Flax, resembling a Yucca, a good ornamental plant.

Carmichælia nana, a pretty dwarf flowering plant, suitable for edgings.

Cassinia fulgida, ornamental flowering shrub.

Celmisias: these are all fine foliage plants and easy of culture.

Clematis indivisa, and hexasepala, evergreen climbers, white flowers.

Coprosma acerosa, a dwarf shrub, bearing blue berries.

Coprosma lucida, dwarf, with beautiful red berries.

Cordyline australis, and indivisa, the Cabbage Palms.

Corokia cotoneaster, a small shrub with orange berries.

Fagus cliffortioides, the Mountain Beech.

Forstera scdifolia, a lovely little plant with pure white flowers.

Gaultheria Antipoda, the Snowberry, dwarf shrub with white berries.

Gaultheria rupestris, flowers like the Arbutus.

Gentiana pleurogynoides, the Mountain Gentian.

Gentiana saxosa, Mountain Snowdrop, free flowering herbaceous plant.

Gnaphalium bellidioides, the Mountain Daisy.

Gnaphalium grandiceps, the New Zealand Edelweiss.

Hoheria angustifolia, the Lacewood, ornamental flowering tree.

Ligusticum Haastii, a handsome, herbaceous, foliage plant.

Metrosideros lucida, the Rata, handsome evergreen shrub, with brilliant crimson flowers.

Olearia avicennæfolia, dentata, ilicifolia, and Colensoi, all tall-growing shrubs and free bloomers, suitable for hedge plants or shelter.

Ourisia macrophylla, a fine bloomer, with dwarf habit.

Ourisia macrocarpa, a fine foliage plant with splendid spikes of white blossoms.

Panax Colensoi, a beautiful berry-bearing shrub, suitable for hedges and shelter.

Pittosporum eugenioides, free growing evergreen shrub, good hedge plant.

Plagianthus betulinus and Lyalli, Alpine trees, beautiful in flower and foliage.

Panax longissimum, the Lancewood.

Ranunculus Lyalli, Mountain Lily, large white flowers and very handsome foliage.

Raoulia glabra and subcericea, handsome carpet plants, with
  lovely white flowers.   These plants will probably be
  useful for lawns instead of grass.
Raoulia grandiflora, a fine rock plant.
Senecio bellidioides, a herbaceous plant with yellow flowers.
Senecio Bidwillii, a shrub with fine wax-like foliage.
Senecio elæagnifolius, a shrub with bright green foliage.
Senecio laxifolia, a dwarf flowering shrub, free grower.
Sophora or Edwardsia grandiflora, New Zealand Laburnum.
Veronica Bidwillii, Lyalli, linifolia, Lavaudiana and pingui-
  folia.   These are all dwarf of habit, and are suitable
  for growing on rock-work.

The lowland plants in the above list are easy to grow in any
garden soil, and when once established their growth is rapid.
The Cabbage Palm is easily raised from the seed, and plants
eight feet high can be grown in as many years.   A fine
specimen in the Victoria Nursery, Christchurch, a foot
through in the stem and carrying eight heads, which have
broken again into sixteen crowns, has been grown from seed
in ten years.   The tree is fifteen feet high, and the head
measures twenty-four feet in circumference.   An avenue
of these Dracœnas planted twelve feet apart in deeply-
trenched soil would have a fine tropical appearance.
With the exception of the Pittosporums, very few of the
native trees and shrubs have been cultivated, but there are
few finer things for the back ground of a shrubbery than the
New Zealand Laburnum when covered with its large golden
flowers.   The alpine trees Plagianthus betulinus and Lyalli
both do well on the plains, and being deciduous, if they were
largely used, they would add a new character to our landscape
in the Autumn.   They grow rapidly in strong loams, and their
clusters of white flowers, like cherry blossoms, are very
charming.   The very distinct character of Panax longissimum renders it a suitable plant for gardens, and never fails
to attract the eye from its singular mode of growth.   The
Olearias are all worth growing, being evergreen and free in
bloom.   Olearia Haasti is very fragrant, whilst Olearia
ilicifolia, the New Zealand Holly, is a very desirable shrub.
Of the climbing plants we have several species of Clematis,
the Parsonsia and the Calystegia, an evergreen convolvulus,
which are worth a place in every garden.

The alpine plants are more difficult to grow, but it has been proved that when a suitable place is chosen for them that they soon establish themselves. These gems from the mountain, if shaded from the sun and sheltered from hot winds, grow freely among stones in a peaty soil. Those who wish to grow the fine Ranunculus Lyalli, Celmisias, Aciphyuas, and other alpine plants should make a rockery in a shady place, and if a small fountain could be arranged in the centre to keep the plants moist in hot weather, success would be certain. Small patches of the Raoulias, Pratias, and Wahlenbergias, which can be easily collected in the river beds, would soon cover the rockwork and help to keep the ground in that cool condition which all alpine plants love. In a rock-work of this description the spear grasses are at home, and the Celmisias soon grow into large specimens, which never fail to throw up their bold, aster-like bloom. In short, a collection of alpines is a never-ending source of interest; and looking forward to the time when the railway will pass through the heart of the ranges, the collection of the plants will be a great source of pleasure and relaxation.

THE FERNERY.

THE First Napoleon said that the drum
was the only instrument which was
never out of tune. In like manner it
may be said that Ferns are the only plants
which are never out of season.

The fernery, whether under cover or
out of doors, is usually the favourite spot
in the flower garden or pleasure grounds.
To retire from the full glare of noon and
the dazzling beauty of the flower garden,
into the cool retirement of the fernery,
situated as it should be in some secluded
spot, affords a most refreshing change to
both body and mind. The beautiful forms
and varied shades of green which the fern tribe present,
render them objects of perpetual beauty. To correspond
both with the requirements of ferns generally, and that
situation which the mind associates with these denizens of
shade and rock, the fernery should occupy some quiet and
shady, and if possible, romantic retreat. When the ground
presents none of these features they may to some extent be
created by mounds of earth and excavations with roots of
trees, rocks, and old bricks and slags tastefully arranged.
Shade and moisture must however be provided by planting
trees, such as cupressus macrocarpa on the outside, or a
few weeping willows and a profusion of tree ferns; with

these materials a natural looking fernery may soon be formed. Failing these, ferns may be successfully grown along a south wall or fence. The most successful fern growers are those who copy as nearly as possible the natural habitat of each fern in their collection. It is not reasonable to suppose that the little stunted fern which grows in the crevices of rocks, exposed to the sun, and every blast of wind will thrive when subjected to the treatment necessary for the denizens of damp and shady forests.

The secret of successful fern growing under cover is to protect them from the wind and sun. This may be done by placing them in an enclosure covered in with thin canvas (such as paper hangers use), stretched over a frame work ; or in a lean-to placed against a wall or fence with a south aspect. Most ferns will thrive if planted in peaty soil, or decomposed nigger-head roots mixed with a little sharp sand, bits of charcoal, and broken pots, and kept moist; but the drainage must be good. An artificial rockery may be formed by excavating the soil in the enclosure, and banking it up on each side of the walk. Rocks, or even clinkers from the brick kiln, will answer for forming the rockery, leaving sufficient space between them for planting the ferns ; the stems of fern trees should be largely used when procurable. Wood of any sort must, however, be avoided, as it harbours woodlice, and promotes fungoid growth, which will soon destroy the ferns if not eradicated. Otherwise, the old roots of trees could be used with great advantage in building the rockery. Roots may be used out of doors. Most ferns require constant moisture at their roots, which must not, however, be stagnant, and a moist atmosphere, particularly in Summer, when they should be syringed morning and evening.

Growing Ferns in Pots.—Where large collections of ferns are kept, it will be better to grow some of them in pots, as the same kind of soil will not suit all ferns. Such ferns as are found in moist, shady forests, require a mixture of peat mould and rotten leaves. Those that grow on mountains will thrive in gravelly loam, while those that flourish in peat bogs require peaty soil, and such as are natives of heaths, or crevices of rocks, do best if planted in sandy, fibrous mould. With these different soils most kinds of ferns may be successfully cultivated. The pots should be filled one-third with drainage, composed of broken pots and lumps of charcoal. A little of these materials broken rather finely and mixed with the soil will be an improvement. The pots should be plunged in tan, coal ashes, or sawdust, for the purpose of keeping the soil in the pots uniformly moist and cool.

Raising Ferns from Seed (or Spores).—Large numbers of ferns may be raised from seed by adopting the following method :—Take peat soil one part, sharp sand one part, loamy soil one part, and one part of finely broken potsherds (broken pots) and charcoal, well mixed together. Take boxes, pans, or pots, fill one-third with roughly broken potsherds, filling the remainder with the mixture to within an inch of the top. Before, however making the compost, it is a good plan to partially roast the soil and peat in an oven or over the fire, this will effectually destroy any seeds of weeds, and all insects or germs of life of any kind; this plan is strongly recommended. Having filled the pots or boxes, water with a fine rose watering pot, saturating the soil thoroughly, after which let them stand for a few hours, then take the spores and dust them thinly over the surface : they will not require any covering of soil. Cover the pots and boxes with sheets of glass, and place in a cool shady place, for at least a fortnight, be particular to place the pots or boxes on boards or slates, or on a thick coat of coal ashes to prevent the entry of worms into the pots which would destroy the young plants. Be careful not to let the surface get too dry ; the best way to administer water will be by placing the pots in a shallow vessel filled with water, but not more than will reach about half way up the pot. Let them stand in the water for a few hours, when the whole surface will be moistened by capillary attraction ; once a fortnight or three weeks will be often enough to repeat the moistening. The young plants should begin to appear in about two months (although some slow-growing ferns take a much longer time to germinate), and in another month they will have developed their perfect fronds when the young plants will be ready for transplanting. The glass may be removed from the pots as soon as the young plants have for the most part sent up one or two regular fronds.

Procuring Fern Spores.—In selecting spores for sowing, the aid of a pocket microscope is necessary to see that the seed vessels have not all opened, in which case the spores will have escaped. The spore cases should be plump, and brown in colour, portions of the frond secured in this condition and folded in paper till required for sowing, will be in the best possible condition for sowing for reproduction.

Filmy Ferns.—These exquisitely beautiful plants are considered by many persons difficult to cultivate An impression that no doubt originates in the failure to grow them in a warm, dry atmosphere ; but they are just as easy to manage as the generality of other ferns, when treated in accordance with their requirements. Exposure of the delicate pellucid fronds to the sun or dry air is certain destruction. Those who wish to grow these delicate ferns should devote a special house to them. The house must be entirely shaded from the sun, and, above all, protected from hot winds. The walls may be of brick, concrete, or wood—the two former are best—and the roof must be glass painted green ; canvas does not answer so well. A humid, still atmosphere is requisite. If these conditions are not regularly maintained, failure will follow. As we have just said, a house must be set apart for these gems of the fern world. Tricihomanes and Todeas will also thrive best under the same conditions.

Many of the filmy ferns will grow best on decomposing rocks, or on the stems of tree ferns, while others delight to grow in a mixture of fibrous peat and sphagnum moss. There are about fifteen species of filmy ferns in New Zealand. Hymenophyllum, dilatatum, pulcherrimum, and scabrum, with their delicate, transparent fronds, from twelve to eighteen inches long, are, perhaps, the finest of the genus ; while Hymenophyllum Armstrongii is the smallest. Any of the filmy ferns will grow. and thrive in pits, under bell glasses, or anywhere so long as the sun is not allowed to reach them.

Potting.—Ferns, like other plants, require to be repotted occasionally. The best time to do this will be in August, before new fronds make their appearance Moisture must be regularly supplied, but water must not be allowed to stagnate about the roots. A mistake often made by growers of ferns is keeping them in too high a temperature. New Zealand ferns simply require shade and moisture. Ferns

grown in a warm, dry atmosphere soon fall victims to thrip·
and scale.   Collectors of ferns should carefully note the
conditions surrounding ferns found growing in their native
haunts, and endeavour, as nearly as possible, to imitate
nature, as to aspect, soil, shade, or otherwise.   Those who
do so will be the most successful growers.

Insects injurious to Ferns.—Ferns are subject to·
the attacks of thrip, green fly, and brown scale, slugs and
woodlice.   In warm, dry atmospheres the thrip will be found
the most troublesome, and if not destroyed they soon make
havoc with the young fronds.   (For description see chapter·
on injurious insects.)

Fumigation.—The easiest and most certain method·
of destroying thrip is by fumigation with tobacco ; tobacco
paper, if strong, will answer as well.   Fumigation will also
rid the house of green fly.   Scale is not so easily got rid.
of.   It attacks the back of the fronds and in the midribs.
The only certain method of getting rid of this pest is by
carefully washing them off with a sponge or soft brush.
Great care must be used in this operation to avoid injuring the
fronds.   Some of the infested fronds may be cut away ; but
only a few of the fronds can be removed with safety at one
time, however infested they may be.   The best time to
fumigate will be in the evening.   It is safer to smoke the
house a little at a time and to repeat it often—say, twice
a week, when necessary   Thrip and green fly will only be
troublesome where ferns are grown under glass, and where
watering and syringing is not regularly attended to during
the hot weather.   An occasional syringing with Gishurst's
compound, 1 oz. to two gallons of water, will also be of
service.   They must be syringed next morning with clean
water.

Woodlice and Slugs.—Where woodlice abound, they
may be kept under by trapping them in the following manner :
Place a few small flower pots about the house inverted,
stuffed half full of dry moss.   Large quantities may be
caught in this way, as they resort to these hiding places·
during the day time.   They may also be caught by candle
light, by seeking for them quietly—the least noise causes·
them to drop off the fronds where they have just been·

feeding. A few slices of carrots, or potatoes or half withered cabbage leaves placed amongst the pots will attract slugs, where they can be gathered every morning and destroyed.

It is quite unnecessary to give a list of names of ferns suitable for house culture, as all native ferns are eligible, and may be successfully grown if the proper conditions are attended to, as briefly indicated in the foregoing remarks. We may, however, mention the following as being suitable for growing in rustic hanging baskets:—Asplenuim flabellifolium: its delicate trailing fronds and long tendril-like midribs, which hang in graceful festoons over the edge of the basket, render it an object of great beauty when grown in that manner; this common little fern is a denizen of the Port and other hills, near Christchurch, growing in the dry crevices of rocks. Adiantum affiney and Adiantum assimile, both beautiful maiden-hair ferns suitable for the purpose.

ORANGE CULTURE.

THE successful growing of oranges on a large scale in many parts of New Zealand is a problem yet to be solved. There is one point, however, which admits of no difference of opinion; and that is, that oranges will only thrive on certain classes of soil, the most suitable of all being the deep volcanic land with a dry subsoil. This latter feature is *indispensable.* A light sandy loam will also answer. The least suitable soils are the heavy clays. That oranges will thrive in New Zealand when planted in suitable localities and well sheltered is proved by the results achieved in some parts of the North Island. For instance, there is a tree at the Bay of Islands Road, Whangarei, which yields from one hundred and fifty to two hundred dozen of fruit annually; and at Waimate and Wanganui as much as seven pounds worth of fruit is frequently gathered from trees twenty years old.

Propagation.—Grafting and budding are the usual methods adopted; although many experienced orange growers in Australia prefer raising their trees from the pip, asserting that they are less liable to the attacks of blight, although they take much longer in coming to maturity. A grafted tree will be in good bearing in about ten years, continuing to increase each year. The method of grafting is that known as cleft grafting. This operation should be performed in September. Orange pips should be sown in July.

Planting.—About 70 trees per acre is the best number to plant; and it is estimated that one man can attend to ten acres, or, if on hilly land, five acres. Trees ten years old at

Parramatta, in New South Wales, are said to yield at least one hundred dozen oranges, the usual wholesale price being 6d. per dozen or £2 10s. per tree, showing a return of £175 per acre ; the only expense being a little well-rotted manure and one man's time attending to them, although some authorities discountenance the use of manure of any kind.

Diseases.—The most fertile of all causes of disease is a cold, wet subsoil. Hundreds of acres of trees have been lost in Australia from this cause, and it will be well to remember that it is only throwing away money to plant orange trees on land having a retentive subsoil.

Scales.—The kinds which infest orange trees most in New Zealand are the black scale, Lecanium oleæ, and Hesperidum. The latter is more injurious than the former. The best remedy for these pests is that adopted by the best orange growers in New South Wales, viz., to brush the infected trees with a hard brush or piece of sacking, and then wash well with Gishurst's compound, which has a beneficial effect on the bark of the trees. Icerya Purchasi— or cotton cushion scale—is without doubt the most destructive of all the pests which infest orange or lemon groves ; nor are its ravages confined to these trees ; it is said to be omnivorous. Every effort should be made to get rid of this terrible pest, failing which the infected trees should be cut down and burned.

Borers are also destructive to orange and lemon trees. As soon as the holes are observed, the twig or branch should either be cut out or the holes should be probed with a bit of pliant wire or whalebone, salad oil syringed into the holes, and the holes plugged with wax.

The Varieties to Plant.—This is a difficult point to settle. The best and most prolific oranges in Parramatta (New South Wales) are now known as Parramatta oranges.

For fuller information on this subject we would direct our readers' attention to a treatise on Orange Culture, by George E. Alderton, published by the New Zealand Government, 1884.

MISCELLANEOUS.

On the Culture of the Camellia.—The soil best adapted to the growth of camellias is a mixture of peat earth and loam, in nearly equal proportions. Where the loam is peculiarly light and sandy, a less quantity of peat is requisite. The earth should be well mixed and passed through a coarse sieve, reserving the detached portions of peat and loam that will not pass the sieve, to fill the bottom of the pots, thereby securing a free drainage—a circumstance indispensable to the success of the plants. The proper season for the general shifting is when the young growth has hardened, and the blossom buds for next year can be detected at the extremity of the shoots. After shifting all those that require it, they may be placed in a cold pit or frame, or retained in the greenhouse, according to the season they are wanted to flower; if kept in the greenhouse, as much air as possible should be admitted, and occasionally sprinkling the foliage will improve the appearance, as well as be beneficial to the health of the plants. At all times attention must be paid to watering them properly, the roots being apt to become matted in the pots, so as to render the ball of earth impervious to moisture; hence it is necessary to see that the ball of earth is moistened by the water poured upon it, instead of the web of fibres only. This renders an examination of the roots, or reducing and replanting them once a year, a measure indispensable.

The usual methods of propagation are by grafting and budding on the single red camellia, grown from seed or cuttings and layers. The cuttings are taken in February and March, or as soon as the young shoots are sufficiently ripe at the base. They are carefully prepared by being cut smoothly over with a sharp knife at a joint, and divested of one or two leaves at the bottom, and then planted firmly, about two inches deep, in pots half filled with the camellia compost before described, and the upper half with fine, sharp sand. They are then well watered and the pots plunged in a slight hotbed, and kept closely shaded for three or four months, by which time they will be rooted. When sufficiently rooted to bear removal, they are potted singly in small pots, the sand being then carefully removed; the pots should be well drained and filled with the same compost as above mentioned, with the addition of a little sharp sand. They are afterwards to be sprinkled with water, and placed in a close frame or pit until they begin to root afresh, and by degrees exposed to the air. The succeeding season they may be potted in the same soil as the other camellias and similarly treated, and many of the plants will then have attained sufficient size and strength for inarching or budding, and all of them by the following season. The best time for inarching is early in Spring, just before the plants begin to grow, and for budding as soon as the new wood is sufficiently ripened, but it may be done at almost any season of the year.

Rules for Watering Pot Plants.—Never giving water until it is actually required, and then enough should be given to reach every part of the ball. Watering by driblets is the worst of all practices. By such a system one portion of the roots is perishing with drought, while the other is surfeited with water. To determine, therefore, when a plant requires water is not so difficult as may at first appear. It is not always when the surface soil looks dry that the roots are in that condition, and to administer water on that evidence alone would be, to say the least of it, a bad practice, more especially as regards plants which require considerable care in their cultivation. The plant itself will frequently indicate its wants in this respect, but it is not always judicious to wait for such proofs, neither would it be prudent to turn the plant out of the pot, in order to ascertain its condition, although in nice cultivation, and in some especial cases, this is occasionally done. but in general practice it is to be avoided.   A little careful observation is, of course, necessary, especially with respect to plants grown in peat soil , and if any uncertainty exist as to whether or not the plant wants water, strike the pot with the knuckle on the side ; the ring produced will, with a little practice, prove an unerring guide. If this plan is followed for a short time, the ring of the wet pot will be readily distinguishable from that of the dry one ; this, therefore, taken in conjunction with the appearances which the plants exhibit, must determine when water is to be applied or not.

The above instructions are more particularly applicable to the Winter culture of pot plants.

Wireworms.—There is no plague in a garden more destructive than this little industrious, though slothful-looking insect.   Where they abound whole crops are destroyed in a very little time, and if a solitary specimen get into a bed of carnations it will soon destroy the lot.   One might almost think that a pair of carnations would feed a score of them for a month ; but it attacks the root, eats its way upwards to the pith, kills the plant, and makes off for another. When turned up or disturbed the wireworm seems half asleep, and very slow in its movements.   They are rarely seen to progress much, but they must be rapid travellers, or one could not do a tithe of the mischief it accomplishes.   The only way to destroy them is to catch them ; their shelly hides defy ordinary means of destruction.   Salt and lime water are of no use whatever.   By thrusting carrots into the ground many may be caught ; every time you pull up the carrot you will find some sticking to it, eating their way in. Heaps of rotted turfs, the most useful of all sorts for potted plants, are very much infested generally, and we have known several good plant growers to pass every particle of the mould in which they pot their plants through their hands before using it ; such is their natural and well-founded dread of the wireworm.   We have seen a whole crop of potatoes completely destroyed by these garden and farm pests.   An instance of this occurred at Opawa, near Christchurch, in 1886.

Air in Greenhouses.—The circulation of air is one of the most important provisions in all kinds of horticultural buildings. Nothing but that will fairly exclude damp, or in any damp weather counteract its effects. It is not enough to open every front window. It would be far better to open only one and let down a top light a little. In all cases there should be an outlet as well as an inlet, and for the want of this many houses do not answer well for plants. A circulation of air causes a more rapid evaporation, and it is a common thing among good gardeners to open a lower window even in wet, cloudy weather, let down one of the top lights a little, and light a fire. By this a free circulation is created and the house dried, although it were in the midst of rains and cloudy weather. It is too common a thing to see the top lights let down to give air to a house and no other part opened. This is all wrong; for there should be a draught. On the other hand, we see all the front windows and no top lights down. Many persons build pits three or four feet high at the back and half the height in the front, and no air but what can be obtained at the top. We would always provide air holes at the bottom, as without such there can be no draught, no free circulation. When pits are built without this provision the best mode of giving air is to pull up one light to let in air at the foot of it, and push down the next to open at the top, and so on alternately through the whole range of lights, however long the pit may be. It is the same in giving air to a hotbed; only that when the air is rarefied, as it is inside, tilting the light a little lets out the steam, and the cool air will get in somewhere; but sometimes when a frame is made too close and the glass is puttied at the joints, things damp off in spite of tilting, because there is no circulation.

Potted Plants.—All plants in pots, when exposed to the sun and wind, require frequent watering, and simply because the pots dry fast, when the fibres of the plants suffer directly. This would seem to demand that when pots are in the open air they should be plunged; but there is another mischief that awaits them if this be done—worms get into the pots, and the roots get out of the pots, and, striking into the earth, excite a growth which is not desirable while there, and receive an awful check when the pot is

N

removed and the roots that have struck through into the ground are broken off, because the plant has depended on them for all its extra growth. It has been found the best plan to place the pots on a hard bottom, paved, cemented, bricked, slated, tiled, or otherwise firm and waterproof; to place them as close together as they will stand, in breadths of six feet and any length, with the ends south and north, and the sides of course, east and west. If they are to remain in the same situation all the Summer it will be worth while to pack them, as it were, in ashes, gravel, or naturally dry material, because the watering of the pots will moisten whatever they are packed in, while the hard bottom will prevent the wet from lodging. The roots will even here strike through the bottom of the pot; but, in the first place, there is less disposition, because the hard bottom and the ashes or gravel will not be so inviting as the common earth, and they will greatly protect the sides of the pots from sun and wind, and thus keep up a moisture among the fibres that have reached them; but if the pots have no packing an occasional examination and constant watering, when the sun becomes weakened in the afternoon, will make all but the outside rows pretty safe—a row of turves, or a foot wall, or a piece of plank along the sunny side will always protect them enough.

Blooming Mignonette in Winter.—The blooming of this universal favourite may be continued throughout the year by a little management on the part of those who possess a cold frame or a greenhouse. To accomplish this the seed should be sown in the beginning of February, in pots of any convenient size. The soil should be good loam, moderately enriched with well-rotted farm-yard manure, and kept open by a pretty liberal intermixture of old mortar or lime rubbish. It is essential that the pots be thoroughly drained. After sowing the seed set the pots where they will not require frequent waterings, too much moisture being extremely injurious to mignonette; for this reason, therefore, it will be safer to place the pots in a frame or pit, where they may be covered by the lights in rainy weather. As the plants increase in size they should be gradually thinned, ultimately leaving three in each pot. Nip off every flower bud as it appears, give water only when the plants really require it, and then in sufficient quantity to moisten the whole of the soil—not dribbling a few drops over the plants to-day to prevent them from being dry to-morrow, a practice too much followed with plants in pots.

Continue to pinch off any premature flowers that may appear; keep the pots free from weeds, and far enough asunder to prevent the plants from being crowded, and when they are removed to Winter quarters set them near the glass in an airy situation. Plants treated in this manner will form nice bushy plants and will flower through the Winter months.

Advantages' of Budding.—Budding, when done properly, is not without its advantages to the propagator. For instance, there are some trees that propagate more readily by budding than by grafting, although budded trees may be later in producing fruit than those that are grafted. But when a tree is rare, every eye may produce a plant, which cannot be done by means of grafts; or when a graft may fail in Spring, a bud can be applied in Summer. Fruits may be improved by working one kind upon another; and it is a well known fact that the double yellow rose, which is so difficult to grow in many places, does well when budded upon the common China rose. Seedling fruit trees are often a long time in bearing, but by means of budding they will bear fruit much sooner than by any other method. Advantage should, then, be taken of this mode of improving our fruits and flowers.

The Drainage of Pots.—The successful cultivation of plants in pots depends in a great measure upon the proper placing of the materials employed in potting. The first condition essential to success is perfect drainage; if water-logged, no plant can continue long in a healthy state, whether it be in a pot or in the open ground. The first thing to observe in potting is to place two pieces of broken potsherds over the hole in the bottom of the pot. Arrange them so that they may lie side by side. These pieces should have a slightly concave form, and the concave sides should be placed downwards; this will enable the water to pass off freely. The next point is, the best kind of material to use above these pieces, and this is broken pots. For very small plants these may be reduced to the size of peas, but they should be increased in proportion to the size of the pots.

Four-inch and smaller pots would require the size mentioned,
but from that to eight-inch pots may be drained with a
coarser kind, say the size of Windsor beans, and for larger
pots two or three times these dimensions will answer.   The
depth of the drainage must also be guided by the size of the
pots.   Three-quarter inch will be enough for small pots, one
inch for medium sizes, and for larger sizes 1 ½ inch and even
two-inch will occasionally be required.   It is an error, however, to drain too much, as it must obviously be at the
expense of the material in which the plant has to feed.   A
proper and careful regulation of the drainage is, therefore,
necessarily required, in order that the object aimed at may
be perfectly secured.

Standard Geraniums.—It is an axiom in flower culture
that at least for the amateur one fine, well-grown specimen is
worth more than any number of spindling, over-crowded,
or sickly plants.   No plant responds more readily to careful
and generous treatment than a geranium.   A correspondent
of *Gardening* gives the following report of experience in
training a fine specimen:—"It takes two or three years, and
a great deal of patience, to train a geranium to 4 or 5 feet
high with a good head, but when achieved it thoroughly
repays itself.   A Vesuvius geranium grown by me some years
ago is now a standard 6 feet high, giving a profusion of bloom
eight months out of the year.   During the Summer months
last year it had forty to forty-five fair trusses of bloom
(outdoors), and continued giving a few trusses up to the
beginning of this year.   It has only been potted three times
during its growth, and always has plenty of liquid manure
while in flower.   A good subject to commence with is a
lanky geranium that has survived the Winter, such as is
generally to be found in most collections.   Carefully pinch
off any side shoots there may be, and repot in a fairly rich
compost ; the stem should be tied to a stout stick, and made
as straight as possible.   Now all that is necessary is to nip
off all side shoots and flower buds the moment they appear
and give twice a week liquid manure.   When sufficiently
tall, pinch off the top, which will at once induce laterals ; it
will then, with judicious training, form a good head, and
when this is achieved, it can be allowed to bloom.   The
growth will be greatly retarded if the plant is allowed to

flower before the training process is over; in fact, it will simply take twice as long to arrive at anything like a standard."

Striking Rose Cuttings.—An important element of success in striking rose cuttings in Summer is keeping them perfectly fresh—*i.e.*, they must be just as fresh when placed in the soil as when cut from the trees; in fact, the work cannot be done too quickly. If once the cuttings shrivel—and they shrivel rapidly—few will grow; but if quite fresh, well selected, and rightly inserted, few will fail. This essential of perfect freshness can be maintained when the number of cuttings is limited; but cannot, at any rate without some trouble and difficulty, when they amount to thousands, and those who have to be entrusted with the work cannot be depended on for exercising the care that is really requisite when they cannot see the necessity for it.

The Time to Prune.—Opinions differ as to the best time to prune trees. There is really no one best time for all purposes. If more wood is wished, prune when the tree is bare of leaves and before the sap starts. If the tree is making too much wood and fruitage is desired, prune while in full leaf. This checks growth and induces the formation of fruit buds. But it is always good policy to keep a close watch on trees and remove growth that will be in the way as soon as it starts. It has been said that the best implement for pruning was the thumb and finger, pinching off superfluous growth before it is large enough to require the knife.

Night Flowering Cacti.—These peculiar and lovely floral wonders are rarely met with outside botanical gardens; and yet there is no reason why they should not occupy a place in every glass house where heat is used. They require a dry atmosphere, so that they are not suited to orchid houses. They need little attention. The blooms commence to unfold their beauty at sunset, and are fully open by 8 or 9 p.m., commencing to fade away by sunrise. The finest varieties of these nocturnal beauties are Cereus Grandiflorus, Cereus Nycticalus, and Cereus McDonaldia, all of which have climbing or creeping stems. The two former bear blooms of ivory whiteness quite ten inches across—and deliciously fragrant. The blooms of the latter are tinged with orange red. They are as easy of cultivation as other plants of the same tribe usually are.

INSECT PESTS & DISEASES
OF PLANTS.

(See Plates Nos. 2 and 3 with Reference attached.)

GARDENING can afford but little enjoyment or profit unless good cultivation and cleanliness form its chief characteristics. Plants covered with green fly, mealy bug, or red spider are too frequently seen in neglected gardens. What possible enjoyment can such wretched gardening afford. Amateurs as well as experienced horticulturists should make themselves familiar with the life history of the numerous creatures which infest their trees, flowers, and vegetables. When this knowledge is attained, the fruit and flower grower can go to work intelligently to exterminate their insect enemies.

All garden plants are subject more or less to the attacks of insects of some kind or other. The best means at our disposal for the prevention of their attacks is to keep the plants in a vigorous state of health; this will not, however, always succeed. It is therefore necessary that other means should be taken whereby they may be kept in check.

Aphides, commonly called Green Fly or Plant Lice, are amongst the greatest enemies of the vegetable world, upwards of 300 species have been described—the powers of multiplication possessed by these little insects is almost incredible. Professor Huxley calculates that a single Aphis, in five generations, may be the progenitor of nearly six millions of descendants. It will therefore be seen that unless constant war is waged against these tiny foes, they would soon destroy every plant they attack. Fortunately they are easily destroyed. Plants growing in houses if attacked, as they frequently are, by green fly may be cleared of them by an application of Gishurst's compound, 1 ounce to each gallon of water. The liquid should be applied with a syringe. Fumigation with tobacco leaf or tobacco paper is also a certain remedy. The plants should be well syringed the following morning.

Mode of Application.—Get an old oil or nail can, punch holes in it for the purpose of ventilation ; then make a fire of sticks inside the can. Do this outside the house. When the sticks have been reduced to a red mass in the bottom of the can lift it inside the house. Take about ¼ lb. teased out tobacco leaf, slightly damped with water, place it on the red embers and leave the house, closing it up for the night. Syringe the plants next morning, and ventilate fully. Repeat the operation in a few days, syringing afterwards. ¼ lb. tobacco will fumigate a house 20ft. x 12ft.

Some of our small birds are of service in destroying Aphides, especially the native white-eye. The Ladybird beetles (so common in England) and their larvæ feed on them voraciously. Black Fly (or aphis). This pest is well-known in England, and is very troublesome on cherry trees. The following is also a good wash for destroying green, blue, or black Aphis :—To fifty-six gallons of soft water add six pints of sulphurous acid, mixing thoroughly. Syringe the trees in the evening.

Tetranychus Telarius, or Red Mite, commonly called Red Spider. This pest has become almost universal of late years in the garden and hothouse. It attacks vines, apples, pears, plums, cucumbers, and melons. It frequently destroys whole hop gardens. Fruit trees badly infested— the foliage and branches appear as though they were covered with iron rust. These signs denote the presence of myriads of these pests. The red colour is said to be caused by the myriads of ova covering the surface of the bark. The creature attacks the under surface of the leaves of all plants, and can only be plainly seen by the aid of a glass.

Remedies.—For the spider in glass houses and frames— to every gallon of tobacco-water add two pounds of flour of sulphur and as much quicklime as will make the mixture as thick as whitewash, and with this wash your pits, frames, or houses inside ; for the mixture, when the sun is on it, will create an atmosphere in which no insect can survive. Another method of destroying the spider is by laying flour of sulphur on slates or boards about the house, where the sun will play upon it. The fumes caused by the heat will destroy the insects. Fumes of burning sulphur will soon rid a house of these and other pests ; but the greatest caution is necessary in using sulphur in this way, or the remedy may prove far worse than the disease. We have seen a whole year's crop of vines destroyed by an overdose. Cucumbers and melons, in frames or out of doors, are frequently much injured by the spider. They may be got rid of by dusting the surface of the soil, which should be frequently stirred, with fresh slack lime and flour of sulphur.

In the case of fruit trees infested with red spider—the leaves as they fall in Autumn should be carefully raked together and burned, and all prunings should be treated in the same manner. The stem and branches should receive a dressing—composed of soft soap containing nine per cent. of potash. This soap mixed with twenty-five per cent. of its weight of flour of sulphur; one pound of this mixture to the gallon of water will be strong enough. Apply with a stiff brush and rub well in.

Summer Wash.—Trees infested with red spider may be syringed with the above solution without injury to the foliage. The success or otherwise of these dressings depends entirely on the manner in which the washing or syringing is carried out. The red spider, like all other parasitical insect pests, lives on the sap of the plant it attacks.

Pear Slug (*Selandria Cerasi*).—This pest is now common in most parts of New Zealand. It attacks not only pears, but cherries and plums, and white thorn, preventing their healthy growth by destroying the leaves (or the lungs of the tree) before the tree has had time to mature the year's growth. The female makes an incision in the leaf, and then deposits its eggs, in a few days the young larva is hatched, and immediately commences to eat the leaves. After a time the larva ceases to feed, and drops to the ground, where it buries itself and spins a cocoon, and remains for the Winter.

Remedies.—The best known is Hellebore ; two ounces to the gallon of water. Saturate the foliage with this mixture top and bottom. One application when the slug first makes its appearance will usually suffice. Finely slacked lime, or road dust, may be used with advantage, for scattering over the leaves—a little flour of sulphur added will be of service —in checking the progress of the pest.

Oyster-Shell Bark Louse (*Aspidiotus Conchiformis*)

or Common Apple Scale.—This pest is rapidly spreading all over the Colony, and may be found on almost all fruit trees. Many white thorn hedges which a few years ago were strong and vigorous have been rendered stunted, and, in some instances, have died out altogether from the attacks of these minute insects. With a little extra activity in applying the following remedies it may be kept under.

Remedies.—Two parts of soft soap, one part of sulphur, and one part of turpentine, thoroughly incorporated and applied with a stiff paint brush. Castor oil, such as is sold for machinery, brushed on has proved an excellent remedy. Fresh slacked lime and sulphur, equal parts, applied as thick whitewash to the trees in Autumn, at the time of pruning, is said to be an excellent remedy.

The Californian remedy is a solution of one pound of concentrated commercial lye, or one and one-third pounds of commercial potash, dissolved in boiling water—mixed with one and a half gallons of water. Wash the trees with this mixture, heated to a temperature of 130° Farenheit. All prunings should be burned.

The best time for destroying this pest will be in the Spring, when the eggs have hatched out and the young larvæ are in a state of activity. This is only for a few days. They may, by the aid of a glass, be seen running about previous to attaching themselves permanently to the bark, where they make their final home. This pest is most vulnerable during this stage of its existence ; but care must, how-

ever, be taken not to use washes composed of potash at this
season of the year, as the young foliage would certainly be
injured.   This is the great difficulty in dealing with this
pest. Any wash sufficiently strong to be decidedly efficacious
will probably injure the foliage and young buds.   Better use
a weaker wash and apply oftener.   Lime and sulphur, with
a little soft soap made into a thin wash, thin enough to be
applied with a syringe.

Black Scale (*Lecanuim Oleæ*).—This scale infests the
olive, peach, apricot, plum, and citrus trees.

Remedies.—The Californian remedy is to wash the trees
with whale-oil soap—one pound to the gallon of water : use
hot.   This dressing will also destroy the soft orange scale.
For Summer syringing, use the wash recommended for red
spider.   When the scale attacks soft-wooded plants the best
remedy is : two ounces of Gishurst's compound dissolved in
a gallon of water ; syringe the plants thoroughly, and wash
with clean water the following morning.   The dose may be
repeated in a few days, if found necessary, syringing next
morning with clean-water.

Codlin Moth (*Carpocapsa pomonella*).—This pest
attacks the apple, pear, and quince ; its ravages are principally confined to the apple, causing an annual loss of many
thousands of pounds sterling to the fruit-growers of America,
England, Tasmania and elsewhere.   The plan of attack is
as follows :—When the young apples are formed, the moth
deposits a single egg on each fruit, usually on the upper
end, puncturing the rind at the same time.   Each moth
deposits from 70 to 80 eggs.   The larva is hatched in from
seven to ten days, and begins at once to eat its way into the
apple.   The following description is from Ormerod's
" Injurious Insects " :—" The caterpillar is about half-an-
inch long and slightly hairy, whitish, with a brown or black
head and dark markings.   As it grows, it continues its
gallery towards the stem or the lower side of the apple,
avoiding the core, when it makes an opening in the rind,
and thus is able to throw out the pellets of dirt.   After this
opening is made, it turns back to the middle of the apple,
and when nearly full grown pierces the core and feeds only
on the pips, and as a result of this injury the apple falls."

As soon as the apple falls, the caterpillar leaves the fruit and finds its way to the stem of the tree and secrets itself in the cracks and fissures of the bark, where it assumes the chrysalis form. The true larva of the codlin moth always destroys the pips of the apple—this will be a guide to those who sometimes have their apples injured by other grubs.

Remedies.—During Winter, trees which have been infested should be thoroughly scraped, and all loose bark and prunings burned. Then apply a dressing such as recommended for Winter dressing in the case of red spider. American fruit-growers resort to the following simple method of trapping the caterpillars as they creep about looking for a resting-place. They tie bands of old sacking round the stems of the trees not far from the ground ; these bands should be examined once a week, when large numbers of caterpillars are usually found. During the Summer, while the moths are about, cans containing vinegar and sugar if hung from the trees in the orchard would trap numbers of moths.' Fowls do good service in an infested orchard. Paris green is strongly recommended : one tablespoonful to 50 gallons of water, sprayed over the trees as soon as the blossoms have passed maturity. A second syringing may be given just before the fruit begins to turn down from its increasing weight. The codlin moth has not yet found its way into the Canterbury orchards.

American Blight, or Woolly Aphis (*Schizoneura lanigera*).—This well-known pest is now common in most parts of the Colony. Many remedies for its prevention have been suggested with more or less success. The following mixtures are recommended :—Dissolve one pound of soft soap, one pound of sulphur, and one gallon of lime in enough water to make a thick wash ; apply with a stiff brush to all infected parts. A good scrubbing with Gishurst's compound, four or five ounces to the gallon of water, will be found servicable. The dressings should be applied whenever the blight makes its appearance. Remove all old bark, which should be burned, together with the prunings The soil should be removed from about the stems down to the main roots, and the exposed parts well painted with the mixture. This must only be done in Autumn or Winter. Syringing has little effect on these creatures, as they are furnished with a soft downy covering which resists water.

Diamond Back Turnip Moth *(Plutella Crucifu-arium).*—This destructive insect has made its appearance in our gardens within the last two years.   In 1886 the caterpillar of this moth destroyed at least ⅔ of the whole turnip and garden crops (of the cabbage tribe) in Canterbury.   The caterpillar, which is green, attacks the underside of the leaves, and soon eats its way through : completely riddling the leaf and destroying the plant.   Several remedies have been suggested, such as dusting with lime, soot, and sulphur, but we cannot say that we have much faith in any of the remedies.   Small birds are our best allies, especially the native white-eye.

Mealy Bug *(Dactylopius adonidum).*—This is a universal pest in hothouses; it is also found in the gardens and nurseries.   A fine mealy substance covers the body, hence the name. This pest is very prolific.   Gishurst's compound is one of the best means of getting rid of this troublesome pest; fumigation, as recommended for aphis, may also be resorted to.   Whatever remedies are used, they must be thoroughly carried out, otherwise the bug will soon destroy all before it.   Mealy bug also attacks the leaves and bunches of grapes, rendering the fruit almost unfit for use. It harbours under the loose bark of the vine, in the border about the roots, and in walls and crevices in Winter.   The only way to get rid of it is to clean all the loose bark off the vines in Winter, wash the rods, and afterwards paint them with a thick smearing, composed of clay, tobacco liquor, soft soap, and sulphur.   Wash all the woodwork and walls.   The leaves must also be watched, and washed with soap and water.   This pest can only be eradicated by constant vigilance.

Grass Grub *(Odontria Zealandia)* commonly known as the Grass Grub.—The female deposits her eggs in the ground, where in a short time they change into grubs; these, when full fed, are about an inch long. They are soft and white, with a reddish head and strong jaws.   In this state the insect remains four years, during which time it commits terrible ravages on the roots of grasses and other plants, such as strawberries, gnawing away at the roots, so that the turf becomes brown.   When full grown the larvæ burrow into the earth for several feet, spin a smooth case, and then change into the chrysalis state. In this inactive form they remain till the following Spring. The perfect beetles then come from the ground, and commence an immediate attack on the leaves of trees ; concealing themselves during the heat of the day under clods, in the ground, and amongst herbage, coming to feed as evening approaches. Everyone who has had to do with grass lawns has had experience of this pest.

Remedies.—There does not seem to be any very certain method of coping with these pests, as the damage to the grass is usually done before the presence of the grub is detected. Constant rolling with a heavy roller, especially after rain, will so consolidate the soil as to impede the motion of the grub. The weight of the roller crushes those near the surface. Flooding with water impregnated with gas lime, is also recommended. More reliance can, however, be placed in constant rolling during Summer, Autumn, and Spring. When lawns become badly infested with the grub, the only alternative is to fork over the surface and turn on the fowls ; they will soon devour all within reach. Then apply a heavy dressing of gas or ordinary lime, at the rate of 10lbs. to the square yard, with a couple of pounds of soot, and dig in. This should be done in Autumn and the land should be left turned over roughly until Spring, when it may be sown again with grass or cropped. Professor Kirk says that this grub attacks the roots of trees, even the strongest-growing, such as Pinus Insignis, Araucaria Imbricata, and a number of others.

Vine Louse *(Phylloxera Vastatrix).*—This is the most destructive plague the vine is subject to, as no means have yet been devised for preventing its ravages when once it gets into the vine border. Affected vines grow sickly and die. All that can be done to stay its progress is to root up the plants and destroy them ; and to allow the ground to remain fallow for a season. This terrible plague has not yet made its appearance in any part of New Zealand, although well-known in Australia. It attacks the leaves and roots ; it is transmitted from place to place with the soil as well as with the plants.

Thrip is one of the most troublesome of all garden pests, destructive alike to melons, cucumbers, and greenhouse plants. If once they are allowed to establish themselves in a house, they are with difficulty got rid of.

Wire Worms are sometimes very destructive amongst the Carnation, Picotee, and Pink plantations. They are, however, easily trapped by placing slices of carrot or potato an inch or so below the surface of the soil, close to the plants attacked by them. Their presence may be detected by the foliage turning yellow. They are easily seen when turning the ground over, and should be picked out and destroyed.

Earth Worms.—Ten pounds of slacked lime to thirty gallons of water stirred up well together, and allowed to stand for two or three days, will, when free from sediment, form a liquid destructive to worms. Earth worms may be banished from flower pots by plugging the drainage hole with a cork, and then flood with lime water for a few hours, this will drive them to the surface, when they should be gathered and destroyed. Lime water must not be applied to Rhododendrons, Azaleas, or Heaths.

Slugs may be captured by laying slices of apples, potatoes, or carrots amongst the pots : these should be examined each morning, and the slugs found destroyed. Cabbage leaves will also answer the same purpose. A dusting of fresh-slacked lime applied late in the evening to young growing crops once a week, will effectually destroy these pests. Slugs deposit their eggs by hundreds below the surface of the soil. A dressing of gas lime dug into the soil early in the Spring, a month before it is required for cropping, will destroy the larva.

Woodlice.—These vermin, in frames, may be destroyed in the following manner.—Press the soil all round the frame, and then pour boiling water where you have pressed. The same pest in a greenhouse or conservatory, may be got rid of by taking a boiled potato, and wrap it up in dry hay, and put it in a flower-pot. Place this in one corner of your frame, or wherever woodlice abound, and they will congregate in it in great numbers. It should be examined every morning, and the vermin shaken out into boiling water or the fowl yard. Another way is to keep some dry hay between two ordinary paving tiles ; examine every day, and destroy those trapped. By so doing, their numbers will very soon be materially decreased.

Earwig.—This is the great enemy of the Dahlia grower (in the old country). They also feed upon other plants. They are shy creatures, and only feed at night. They devour the petals of Dahlias. They may be trapped by half filling thumb pots with dry moss, placed on the top of the Dahlia stakes A better plan is to place some small tiles half full of moss near the plants they feed upon. Pieces of bamboo will answer equally well. They should be examined every morning the first thing, and the vermin destroyed.

Mildew on Vines (*Oidium Tuckeri*).—This vegetable pest is caused by sudden chills, cold damp, and badly-ventilated atmospheres Mildew first made its appearance in England in 1845 and 1847. It appeared on the Continent, and laid waste hundreds of acres of vineyards. In 1851 the disease appeared in Italy, and in 1871 it appeared in the colony of Victoria. The first notice of it appeared in the *Australasian* of the 16th December, 1871. At last it was discovered that the fumes of sulphur had the effect of completely destroying the pest if properly applied, and at the right time. The action of sulphur in the cure of oidium (mildew), is due to the formation of sulphurous acid gas by the action of the oxygen of the atmosphere on the finely subdivided particles ; and as dryness and heat are essential to the oxidation of sulphur, it may be readily understood how it is that sulphur will not act curatively in wet, cold weather. After pruning, every bit of refuse should be collected and burned. The stems should then be washed with a solution of sulphur and lime ; this will stay the development of any germs which may be present. The addition of cow-manure and yellow clay will render the application more efficacious. By painting the hot-water pipes with this mixture an atmosphere will be created which will destroy mildew or red spider. Dusting with flour of sulphur, applied with a fumigating bellows, is also efficacious. When mildew attacks melons, cucumbers in frames or elsewhere, a little flour of sulphur dusted over the plants and on the soil under the leaves during hot weather will drive off noxious insects, and destroy the mildew. This remedy will also answer for all kinds of plants attacked by red spider or mildew.

Rust.—Rusty grapes are caused by sudden draughts of cold air against the berries when they are just set. Excessively hot pipes will produce rust sooner than anything else. Handling the grapes should be avoided as much as possible. Ordinary care will prevent this disease.

Warty Leaves in vines are the result of a close, damp atmosphere and insufficient ventilation; they never appear under any other conditions. The leaves become cupped and crumpled. The growth of the plant is greatly retarded —in bad cases completely arrested. The only preventives are a dry atmosphere and plenty of air.

Shanking in vines. This disease is the result of bad culture and unsuitable soil, although it sometimes attacks vines which have every attention. The disease attacks the foot-stalk of the berries at or after the stoning period, when the berries are changing colour. They lose their fleshiness, have a disagreeable acid taste, and soon shrivel and drop off if the bunch is shaken. There seems to be no certain remedy against this troublesome disease.

Spot in Pelargoniums is caused by the plants being overcrowded and over-watered, but a remedy will be found in the following mixture, if applied through a syringe :—One teaspoonful of Condy's disinfecting fluid to a quart of water. After doing this a few times the disease invariably leaves the plant.

Canker.—Fruit trees are subject to several different diseases, and each of them often goes by the name of canker. Practical cultivators, however, know well enough what canker is. A portion of the bark becomes diseased and dies, the dead portion falls off, leaving the wood exposed, which also decays, and when the trees are badly attacked whole branches die off. Of course wherever there is decay, insects or fungoid growths appear; and it is not unreasonable to assume that insects may be the cause of canker, which some have averred, but in reality they are only the result of the disease. At all events, it has been proved over and over again that the roots getting into wet, sour subsoil is the cause of canker, and that lifting them up nearer to the surface and giving them suitable soil to work into will cure it, or at least arrest the decay.

Root Fungus (*Lycoperden Gemmatum*).—This pest is becoming a terrible scourge in many parts of the North Island, destroying all kinds of fruit trees, forest trees, herbaceous plants and grasses. It is particularly destructive in the Waikato district; it is also very destructive in the Thames district, where it has destroyed many chains of thorn hedges. It has already killed many thousands of pounds worth of orchard trees in the Hamilton and Cambridge districts. Its ravages are principally confined to warm sandy lands, especially fern lands. It rarely, if ever, attacks trees planted in strong moist soils. Several remedies have been suggested for the destruction of the fungoid growth, such as applications of tar water, gas lime, soot. The most successful method we have heard of is to saturate the soil before planting with tar water. · Root fungus has not so far as we know been observed in the South Island of New Zealand.

White or Cotton Cushion Scale (*Icerya purahasi*).— This is one of the most dangerous pests which the lemon and orange grower has to contend against. It is common in many parts of the North Island, and as far south as Nelson. Badly-affected branches, or even trees, should be cut down and burned at once. Syringing the trees with a solution of caustic potash, two ounces to the gallon of water, has been found most effectual.

In addition to the above, Scale Citraceous trees are subject to other scale insects all more or less injurious, such as leaf scale, olive scale, orange scale, and sandalwood scale. All of which may be destroyed in the same manner as recommended for the white scale.

Canker Worm (*Clenopseustis Obliguana*). — The caterpillar of this moth feeds upon the leaves principally of the apricot; fastening them together it attaches them to the ripening fruit, feeding upon the epidermis. The cater-

o

pillars of several moths having similar habits—attacking apples and other fruits —are confused by fruit growers under the general term of canker worm.   Hand picking where practicable is the best remedy.

Currant and Gooseberry Borer.—This pest is becoming troublesome.   As soon as observed the affected branches should be cut out.   The creatures bore into the pith and feed upon it.   Stopping the holes up with wax, or probing with wire will sometimes answer, where the borers are not too numerous.   They frequently occur in such numbers as to kill the trees affected.

Lichen or Moss frequently attacks the stems and branches of neglected trees whose roots have got into a hard and impervious subsoil.   The only remedy is to encourage the trees to make surface roots by softening the surface soil and topdressing with manure ; scrape the trees and apply a dressing of lime wash in the Autumn.   If the trees are not too old they will be greatly benefited by transplanting as recommended under that heading.

***

EXPLANATION OF PLATE 2.

No. 1. Red Spider greatly magnified.   Natural size, half as large as a small pin-head.

No. 2 to 13, Scale Insects (*Hemiptera Homoptera : fam. Coccidæ*).—For practical purposes it will be sufficient to divide the Coccidæ into three great sections, viz.—(1) Diaspidæ—Flat scales adhering to the part of the plant on which they are fixed, without a slit or division at the posterior end of the scale.   (2) Lecanidæ—Also fixed, but having a notch or slit at the posterior end of the scale. Many of them having a cottony excretion.   This is never found in the Diaspidæ ; but may or may not be present in the (3) Coccidæ ; these being distinguished from the others by not being fixed, and by their walking about in all their stages.   It must however be remarked that the species of all the three sections move about the first day or two after being hatched.   After that time the Diaspidæ and Lecanidæ fix themselves to the plant by suckers, and never afterwards move.

Plate 2.

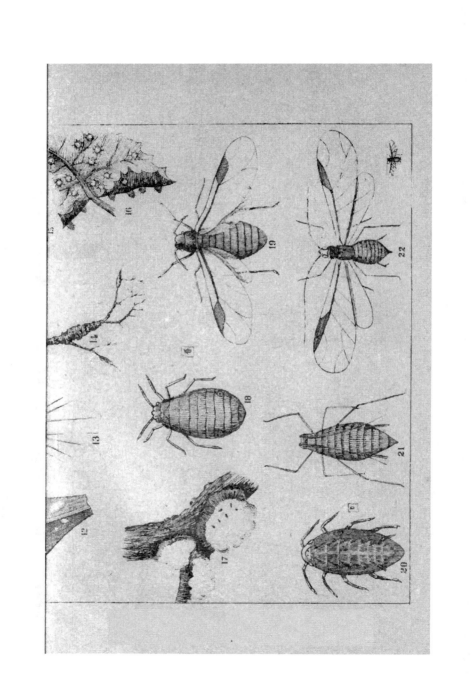

No. 2. Diaspis Ostræformis.—Branch with scales upon it. Natural size. Fig. 3, scale seen from above magnified. Common on the bark of pear trees.

No. 4, 5 and 6. MytilapsisPomonum.—Apple-tree scale, natural size and magnified.

No. 7, 8. Pulvinaria Vitis.—Vine scale. 7. Sketch of adult female scale on vine scale, natural size. Fig. 8. Adult female, magnified.

No. 9, 10. Lecanium Hibernaculorum.—Brown scale. No. 9. Twig with scale upon it, natural size. Fig. 10. Adult female scale, magnified. This scale is the pest of hot-houses. Lecanium filicum is found on ferns, L'hemisphæricum on dracaenas, L'rotundum on the peach, &c.

No. 11. Lecanium Hesperidum.—Magnified and natural size. Known in France as the orange-tree bug, or orange-tree louse.

No. 12, 13. Dactylopius Adonidum (Coccidæ proper) Mealy Bug. 12. Part of leaf with Mealy Bug upon it, natural size. 13. Sketch of adult female magnified and natural size. The mealy secretion which is excreted by this insect, and to which it owes its name, is exuded all over the body.

No. 14 to 16. Phylloxera Vastatrix (*Phylloxeridæ*). —Fig. 14. Vine root attacked by Phylloxera, natural size. Fig. 15. Subterranean form of female, magnified and natural size. Fig. 16. Part of leaf of vine, showing the galls formed on the leaf by the Phylloxera, as seen on upper and under surface of leaf.

No. 17 to 19. Eriosoma Lanigera (*Aphides*).— Apple-tree or American Blight. Fig. 17. Apple branch attacked by the blight, natural size. Fig. 18. Wingless larva, natural size and magnified. Fig. 19. Winged females, magnified.

No. 20 to 22. Siphonophora Rosæ (*Aphides*).— Rose Blight. Fig. 20. Young larva newly hatched and magnified; natural size and magnified. Fig. 21. Larva, more advanced stage, magnified. Fig. 22. Winged male, natural size and magnified. Aphis rosarum, A. dirhoda, A. trihoda, &c., also attack rose trees.

EXPLANATION OF PLATE 3.

No. 1, 2. **Thrip Larva** magnified.   Fig. 2. Perfect insect magnified.

No. 3. **Selandria Cerasi**—Pear Slug.   *a* Pupa, *b* leaf with larva feeding, *c* female fly.

No. 4. **Wireworms, Grubs of Click Beetles.**— Fig. *a*, Elater Obscurus.   Fig. *b*, Elater Spulator, natural size. Fig. *c*, *d*, larva of Elater Agriotes, natural size and magnified.

· No. 5ᴬ. **Coccinella Maculata**—Spotted Ladybird. These well-known little creatures are good friends to the horticulturists, as they feed voraciously on the Aphides, especially in the larvæ stage.   They often deposit their eggs in the midst of a group of plant lice, which the newly-hatched larvæ greedily devour.   *A* perfect beetle, *b* larva, *c* pupa.

No. 5, 6. **Carpocapsa Pomonella**—Codlin Moth.—*a* Nest of larva as it appears on inside of bark when taken off the tree, colour drab.   *b* Pupa or chrysalis; colour dark amber.   *c* Appearance of larva when cover is removed off Winter nest , colour, body yellowish white, head dark brown. *d* Winter nest when larva is removed following Spring.   *e* Larva looking for a tree or place to make its nest, when ready to assume the pupa or chrysalis forms; colour of full grown larvæ light pink.   *f* First appearance of moth.   *g* Moth with wings spread, length of body $\frac{7}{16}$ of an inch; spread of wing ¾ of an inch; colour, body and legs rich bronze, light drab; four wings, mottled grey and drab, with dark copper bar across hinder margin, in which is a golden ocellated patch near inner angle; hind wings plain drab, a little darker than body.   *h* Head of larva as seen through a glass magnifying nine times.   *i* Pupa or chrysalis case, prior to moth leaving it.

No. 6. *a* Blossom end or calyx of apple.   *b* Represents an empty space where ovarium or shell containing the seeds were before the entrance of the larva.   *c* Represents the

Plate 3.

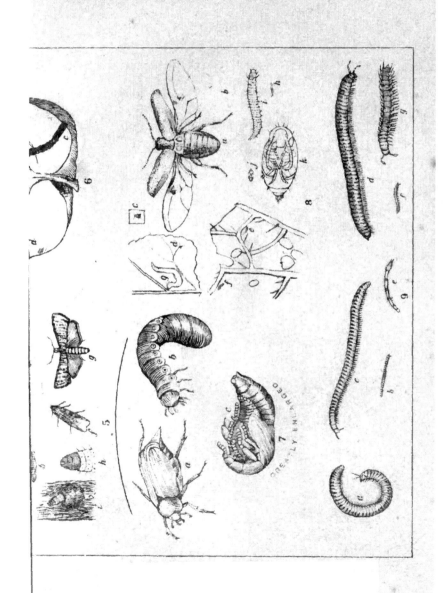

GREATLY ENLARGED

burrow made by the larva, by which it escapes from the fruit when it is ready to assume the chrysalis form. *d* Appearance of larva in burrow when six days old. *e* Appearance of larva in burrow when ten days old.

No. 7. Odontria Zelandia—Grass Grub, greatly magnified.—Fig. *a* the female, *b* the grub, *c* the pupa or inactive form.

No. 8. Haltica Nemorum—Turnip Beetle (or fly).—Fig. *a* and *c* beetle, *d* and *e* eggs, *f*, *g*, *h*, *i* maggot, *j*, *k* pupa. All natural size and magnified.

No. 9. False Wireworms, or Snake Millipedes.—*a* Julus londinensis, *b*, *c*, *J*. guttatus, natural size and magnified, *d*, *J*. terrestris, *e* horn, *f*, *g* flattened Millipede.

USEFUL HINTS.

Asphalt Garden Walks.—Excellent walks may be made in the following manner :—Remove the surface soil for four inches, make the bottom perfectly level and roll ; then spread a coating of tar, and sift coal ashes over—say one inch thick. When this is dry give another coat of tar and ashes, and repeat until you have four coats of tar and as many of ashes. Such a path will always be dry and hard, and will resist weeds and wear for years.

Guano.—This is a most excellent manure for top-dressing grass plots, or for growing all the cabbage and onion tribe. The best guano is the genuine Peruvian ; but any of the other kinds will answer, only they must be used in much larger quantities. Three pounds of Peruvian guano will suffice for a square rod of ground (five and a half by five and a half yards); before spreading, the guano should be mixed with twice its own bulk of dry earth or sand. The other guanos may be applied as purchased, and in double the quantity. Guano is an excellent manure for onions also. Apply Guano to grass plots, if possible, immediately before rain. Guano is an excellent dressing for flowers in pots, a pinch of Peruvian between the finger and thumb will suffice.

Liquid Manure.—Half-an-ounce of Peruvian guano to the gallon of water will suffice for pot plants, such as Pelargoniums, Calceolarias, Cinerarias, Achmens, &c., and one ounce per gallon to plants out of doors. Growing plants in pots will be greatly benefited by a watering of the weaker mixture once a week.

Liquid Manure Suitable for any Plant.—Put a bushel of horse-droppings into ten or twelve gallons of water, well stirred and allowed to stand for a couple of days. The clear liquid only must be used ; twice a week to growing plants.

Night-soil for Garden Use.—Ten parts of earth to one of night-soil is the proportion to be used ; mix well, and turn frequently. A small quantity of lime will act as a deodoriser. The compost should lie in a heap for at least three months before being used.

Poultry-manure as a Liquid Manure.—Twenty pounds dissolved in ten gallons of water will be strong enough. This should not be used more than once a week.

Poultry-manure as a dry Compost.—This should be mixed with ten times its bulk of light soil or sand, and laid by for a few weeks. This manure should never be used in a raw state.

Transparent Covering for Frames, &c., may be made of cheap, thin calico, covered with a composition made of three parts pale linseed oil, one ounce of sugar of lead, and four ounces of white resin. The sugar of lead to be ground with a small portion of the oil, then add the remainder of the oil ; the resin should then be put with it, the whole mixed, gently warmed, and stirred till the ingredients are thoroughly incorporated with each other. The material to be covered is to be stretched and tacked to a frame or to a floor, and the mixture laid on with a large paint brush. The next day it will be dry, and may be rolled up or applied to its use as a covering for frames. The best way is to put it on a roller.

Wood, how to Preserve.—Mix at the rate of five pounds of chloride of zinc to twenty-five gallons of water. This is the very best solution to steep wood in to prevent the dry rot.

To Preserve Timber in the Ground.—Take boiled linseed oil and stir in pulverised coal to the consistency of paint. Put a coat of this over the timber. This will preserve the timber sound for many years. See that the timber is well seasoned before applying the mixture.

Cats are sometimes very destructive to young trees, by tearing the young bark with their claws ; protect the stems by tying a thin layer of gorse round the stem for two feet high ; wire-netting will also answer.

Hares and Rabbits, especially the former, are very destructive to all kinds of deciduous trees while young. Scores of trees, especially fruit trees, may be destroyed in one night by hares stripping the stems of their bark. It will pay to enclose the whole orchard with wire netting, which may be had at from 4d. to 6d per yard. Where there are only a few trees they may be protected by tying gorse round the stems for a couple of feet from the ground upwards.

Fowls and Pigs in the Orchard.—Fowls do a large amount of good during the Winter and Spring and early Summer, scratching about the trees and feeding on insects and grubs. If pigs are turned in in Autumn, after the crop has been gathered, they will pick up the waste fruit.

How to know the Edible Mushroom.—When any doubt exists, put a little table-salt over the gills, which, if the mushroom be genuine, will turn black in a short time. Salt has no effect on poisonous fungi.

A Compost Heap.—What is it ? A heap of manure properly made ; a repository of all kinds of otherwise obnoxious matter, converting the same into harmless yet most valuable plant food. I say properly made, for there are heaps and heaps, and it is almost rare to find one so built as to rot well, and not to be either surrounded by valuable liquid which is too often allowed to run waste, or else the heap is thrown up anyhow to dry instead of rot, and much of its value is lost in that way.

To make a proper compost heap there must be a fair proportion of stable manure. Having that at command, first dig out an oblong trench in a convenient situation ; say eight feet or twelve feet for a garden : twice or three times the size for a field ; throw out all the black soil down to the clay on one side, leaving the other side clear for wheeling or carting alongside. Commence with, say, a layer of coarse stable manure about six inches thick, spread evenly over the bottom, then build up layer by layer evenly and flat with the clearings of hedge rows, ditches, grass walks,

weeds of all kinds (unless with ripe seeds, when they should
be burnt), lawn mowings, leaves, and pea or bean stalks,
&c., in fact anything which will rot, always shaking out the
stable manure or green stuff into an even layer, never so much
as a barrowful being left in one spot, building up the sides
as plumb, as the walls of a house.   Between every three or
four layers throw a sprinkling of the earth taken out to
prevent it heating too much, or a dressing of ashes if at
hand, also all the kitchen or house waste (old boots or tin
cans excepted), and don't forget to add the droppings from
the fowl-house, breaking up any lumps, or better still, throw
dry earth under the roosts, and clean out oftener and so
prevent lumps.   After every layer of stable manure or green
stuff, tread it down well, and so on, layer by layer, never
more than four or five inches of any one kind ; or if there
should be rather more stable manure than other materials,
throw over more soil, which will absorb the moisture and
assist in the decomposition ; scratch the sides down with
the fork, leaving it as neat as a stack, but with a flat top,
and when about four feet high cover over all with a layer of
three or four inches of soil to keep in the ammonia ; then if
at hand, after it has been allowed to heat for a week or so,
throw over it liquid waste from the house, &c., and if any
liquid should run from the heap, dig a hole at the lowest
corner to catch it, and throw it back over the top. Of course
if pigs and cows are kept the mixture will be all the better ;
and in about three or four months the whole will be found in
prime condition for any kind of crop.   A heap of this kind
should, always be under weigh, so as to dispose of all waste
or decaying matter, and the garden, &c., may be kept in
much better order ; and whenever the heap gets about four
feet high, top up and start another.

How to make a Mushroom Bed.—Get half-a-
dozen loads of stable manure ; shake out the long straw,
and put the short manure in heaps to ferment.   This it soon
does, when it should be turned to let out the fiery gases, and
moderate the heat, when it is ready for putting together.
The way to make the bed is to place the manure ridge
fashion, say three feet or four feet through at the bottom,
and about the same in height, making it narrow at the ridge,
and treading it down quite firm as the work proceeds, placing

the long litter in the centre. The treading prevents over-heating, and retains the heat longer, saving all the ammonia. When thus made up and the heat has subsided to 75 deg. or 80 deg., it is ready for spawning. This should be done by making holes in the sides of the bed a foot or so apart. In these put pieces of spawn about the size of small apples, and cover the bed thickly with long straw to ward off wet and maintain an equable temperature. In a couple of weeks or so the spawn will have run sufficiently for the bed to be earthed up, which should be done by placing an inch thick of soil over it and patting it down firm and smooth. Then replace the straw as a protection to the mushrooms, which will make their appearance in eight or ten weeks. In gathering mushrooms never cut them, only twist them gently off; if cut, the remaining stems soon rot, and injure the succeeding spawn. To be successful the site for the bed · must be a high and dry one, for if low, and water lies or soaks into the manure, it will drown and perish the spawn, and failure will be the result. If the object is to have mush-rooms during Summer, the position chosen for the bed should be a cool, shaded one, a good place being in an orchard under trees, or at the back of a south wall or build-ing where the sun does not shine, as mushrooms cannot en-dure hot air, and must have plenty of atmospheric moisture, in imitation of what they get naturally when they come up in pastures and other places during the Autumn. The thick covering helps to give them this, as it arrests evaporation, and the vapour escaping from the soil is held in suspension under the straw. Even in some mushroom houses it is necessary to cover the beds, as when the houses are lofty or not closely sealed, the atmosphere becomes arid, and the mushrooms die off as soon as they show themselves through the bed. Spawn may be had from most seedsmen.

· **How to Fumigate.**—Fumigating cans may be had at any seedsman's shop. The following plan is, however, simple and efficient. Take an empty nail can or oil drum, perforate it with holes in the bottom and half-way up the sides. In this light a fire of sticks (two or three handfuls); while this is burning, prepare the leaf, which may be damaged tobacco from the stores, local grown leaf, or tobacco paper. If the former, take a quarter-of-a-pound, tease it up, slightly damping it with water; by this time the fire will be a red mass of charcoal; lift the can into the house, placing it on a couple of bricks on the floor, then drop the leaves into the red embers; leave the house and close the door and all ventilators. If the other materials are used, a larger quantity will be required, about three-quarters of a pound of either. Evening is the best time to fumigate. Next morning syringe all the plants in the house. It will be necessary to repeat the process in three or four days afterwards.

How to Make Mushroom Spawn.—Lay a foundation of horse-droppings, say a square yard, let the first layer be four inches deep; have some artificial spawn ready crumbled into dust, of which scatter a handful over the first layer, and tread it down hard; then put another layer of horse-droppings, and then more spawn, and so on till the heap is about two feet high. The heat should not attain to more than 80 deg. Cover the heap slightly over with straw, and in about five or six weeks there will be a fine heap of pure spawn to scatter over newly-made beds. If kept dry the spawn will keep good for five or six months.

Trees required to Plant an Acre of Land.

Distance apart. Ft.	In.	No. required.	Distance apart. Ft.	In.	No. required.
3	0	4,840	9	0	538
3	6	3,556	10	0	436
4	0	2,722	12	0	302
4	6	2,151	14	0	223
5	0	1,742	15	0	194
6	0	1,210	16	0	171
7	0	889	18	0	135
8	0	680	20	0	109

Curative Powers of Lemon.—Lemons are one of the most useful fruits in our domestic economy. The juice of half a lemon in a glass of water, without sugar, will generally cure a sick headache. If the hand be stained, there is nothing to remove the stain better than a lemon, or a lemon and salt. After the juice has been squeezed from the lemon the refuse can be used for this purpose. Lemon juice is also a very good remedy for rheumatism and the so-called biliousness of Spring. In the latter case the juice should be taken before breakfast. The pulp may also be eaten, avoiding every particle of skin. Lemon juice and sugar mixed very thick is useful to relieve coughs and sore throats. It must be very acid as well as sweet. As a drink, lemonade is not only a luxury, but exceedingly wholesome. It is a good temperance drink. Hot lemonade in the Winter will break up a cold if taken at the start. Cool lemonade in Summer will refresh one who is tired and thirsty. As a harvest drink it has no equal. There is no danger in taking too much, and it never produces drunkenness or disease.

Medicinal Properties of Vegetables. — Spinach has a direct effect upon complaints of the kidneys.

The common dandelion, used as greens, is excellent for the same trouble.

Asparagus purges the blood. Celery acts admirably upon the nervous system, and is a cure for rheumatism and neuralgia.

Tomatoes act upon the liver.

Beet and turnips are excellent appetisers.

Lettuce and cucumbers are cooling in their effects upon the system.

Onions, garlic, leeks, olives, and shalots, all of which are similiar, possess medicinal virtues of a marked character, stimulating the circulatory system and the consequent increase of the saliva and the gastric juice, promoting digestion.

Red onions are an excellent diuretic, and the white ones are recommended to be eaten raw as a remedy for insomnia. They are a tonic and nutritious.

A soup made from onions is regarded by the French as an excellent restorative in debility of the digestive organs.

Number of Plants in a Rod of Land.

(160 Rods to the Acre.)

Distance apart. ches.	No. of Plants.	Distance apart. Inches.	No. of Plants.
4 x 4	2,450	12 x 12	272
5 x 4	1,960	15 x 10	261
6 x 4	1,633	30 x 12	109
6 x 6	1,069	30 x 18	72
8 x 6	816	30 x 24	55
8 x 8	612	30 x 30	43
10 x 8	490	30 x 36	36
10 x 10	392	30 x 42	25

Seeds Required to Sow Garden Plots.

Asparagus, bed of 15 square yards ... ... ¾ pt.
Beans, broad, per row of 80 feet... ... ... 1¼ qt.
Beet, row of 50 feet ... ... 1 oz.
Broccoli, per 4 square yards ... . ½ ,,
Brussels sprouts, per 4 square yards ... ... ½ ,,
Cabbage, bed of 8 square yards ... ... ½ ,,
Carrots, drill of 120 feet ... . 1½ ,,
Cauliflour, 4 square yards ... . ½ ,,
Celery, 4 square yards ... ... ½ ,,
Endive, 4 square yards ... ... ½ ,,
Kale, 4 square yards ... ... ½ ,,
Kidney beans, row 80 feet ... ... ½ pt.
Leek, 2 square yards ... ... ½ oz.
Lettuce, 4 square yards ... ... ¼ ,,
Onions, 9 square yards ... ... 1 ,,
Parsley, row of 100 feet ... ... 1 ,,
Parsnips, drill of 100 feet ... ... 1 ,,
Peas, row of 60 feet .. .. 1 pt.
Potatoes, row of 80 feet ... ... ½ pk.
Radishes, 4 square yards ... ... 1 oz.
Savoy, 4 square yards ... ... ½ ,,
Spinach ,, ,, ... 1 ,,
Turnip, 6 yards square ... ... 1 ,,

Table showing the number of yards over which 1lb. of Artificial Manure is required to be sown to equal 1cwt. to the statute acre.

Distance of drills in in. apart.	No. of Lineal yards in the statute acre.	Lengths of yards for 1lb. of Manure, to equal 1cwt. per statute acre.	Distance of drills in in. apart.	No. of Lineal yards in the statute acre.	Lengths of yards for 1lb. of Manure, to equal 1cwt. per statute acre.
36	4,840	43	28	6,222	55
35	4,978	44	27	6,453	57
34	5,124	45	26	6,701	59
33	5,280	47	25	6,969	62
32	5,445	48	24	7,260	64
31	5,620	50	23	7,575	67
30	5,808	51	22	7,920	70
29	6,008	54			

EXAMPLE.—Suppose the drills to be 36 inches apart—1lb. of manure to 43 yards is equal to 1 cwt. per acre ; 2lbs. to 43 yards is equal to 2 cwt. per acre ; and so on, every pound for 43 yards being equal to 1cwt. per acre.

Wholesale Current Prices of Flower Pots in Christchurch.

Size.	Price per Doz.		Size.	Price per Doz.	
Inches.	s.	d.	Inches.	s.	d.
2 x 2		10	8 x 8	5	6
2½ x 2½		10	9 x 9	8	0
3 x 3	1	0	10 x 10	10	0
4 x 4	1	6	12 x 12	16	0
5 x 5	2	3	14 x 14	36	0
6 x 6	3	0	16 x 16	48	0
7 x 7	4	0	18 x 18	72	0

THE POULTRY YARD

SYSTEMATIC FOWL FARMING has not as yet received much attention in New Zealand. Attempts, it is true, have been made with varying success. To succeed with a fowl farm every detail must be attended to with persevering industry and attention. The leading parts to be attended to are regularity in feeding, scrupulous cleanliness, and pure water. If these conditions be neglected, disease is sure to attack the flock. Fowl cholera is occasionally prevalent in this country; we have known it to sweep away 90% of the whole stock of fowls on a farm in the course of eight or ten days. There is little doubt but that neglect in some of the above particulars is the main cause of such mortality.

Soil for a Fowl Farm.——In selecting a site for a fowl farm choose a dry warm soil, not too poor or too gravelly, as a portion of the land will have to be cropped to produce green and corn food. In America, where fowl

farming is carried on on a large scale, the houses are made
moveable, the runs are fenced in with wire so that the whole
can be removed each year, and the lately-occupied portions
are cropped. Those who are desirous of going in for the
business of fowl farming will do well to procure a standard
work on the subject, and work to it always, taking surrounding
circumstances into consideration.

No homestead should be without a few fowls, which if
well managed should be a considerable source of profit.   A
dozen or fifteen well-selected and well-fed young fowls will
supply eggs for a family of twelve persons throughout the
year.   It is a difficult thing to advise as to the best breed of
fowls to keep, combining excellence as layers, and as table
birds.   For general purposes most authorities agree that the
Gray Dorkings and Shanghaes will give quite as good a
return for the care bestowed upon them as any other breed.
The Dorkings are fine Summer layers, while the Shanghaes
excel as Winter layers.   The Dorkings are best as early
Spring sitters, mothering the chickens for a much longer
period than most fowls.

The following crosses have been proved to answer
admirably for producing ordinary fowls :—A cross between
the Dorking and Game hen produces a plump table fowl
and a good layer ; the cross with a Brahma cock and Leghorn
hen are unsurpassed as layers, and fairly good table fowls ;
the cross between the Dorking and Brahma are better table
fowls, but not so good for laying. The Langshans are also
grand fowls for table and Winter eggs, but are not so early
ready for table as Wyandottes or Dorkings.

Breeds.—There has been a vast improvement in the
breeds of fowls during the last few years.   The various
breeds may be classed as follows :—

British breeds, viz. :—Dorking, Game, Cornish Game, Red-
caps, Scotch Greys and Hamburghs.

French breeds, viz. :—Houdans, Crevecœur, La Fleche, &c.

Mediterranean breeds, viz. :—Spanish, Minorca, Andalusians,
and Leghorns.

Asiatic breeds, viz. :—Brahmas, Cochins, Malay, and Langshans.

American breeds, viz. :— Dominique and Wyandotte,
Plymouth Rock, and other varieties, as Polish, Shino-
warapas and Japanese Bantams.

The merits or otherwise of any of the above breeds is a matter which must largely be regulated by circumstances.

The following experiment recently tried in England with a view to determine the consumption and profit of different breeds of poultry is suggestive; the following is the result :—

Dorkings	...	...	6 ounces	391	grains.
Games ...	...	...	4 do.	275	do.
Buff Cochins	...'	...	17 do.	296	do.
Langshans	...	...	7 do.	31	do.
Dominiques	...	...	4 do.	336	do.
Brown Leghorns		...	4 do.	398	do.
Hamburghs	...	...	4 do.	120	do.
Polish ...	...	...	4 do.	28	do.
Guinea Fowls ...	...		4 do.	182	do.

It will be seen that the Buff Cochins ate much more than any other breeds ; and to show the increase of weight in proportion to food consumed, it may be stated that each gained daily as follows for twenty days :—

Dorkings	...	138 grains and laid	130	eggs per year.
Games	...	92 do.	100	do.
Buff Cochins	...	77 do.	115	do.
Langshans	...	123 do.	115	do.
Dominiques	...	92 do.	110	do.
Brown Leghorns		107 do.	190	do.
Hamburghs	...	92 do.	239	do.
Polish	...	46 do.	98	do.
Guineas	...		75	do.

It will be noticed that the Hamburghs gave the largest number of eggs, and the brown Leghorns next, but the Dorkings and Langshans made the largest daily gain in growth ; while the Cochins, though consuming enormously of food, did not show its effects either in eggs or the first twenty days' growth. Taking the three highest for weight at six months, the following was the result :—

Dorkings weighed 10 lb. 1 oz. and 685 grs.
Buff Cochins weighed 9 lb. 13½ oz.
Langshans weighed 10 lb. 5 oz. and 437 grs.

The greatest gain was made by the Langshans, but for the food allowed the Dorkings are entitled to the honour.

Feeding.—Fowls confined to runs must have a regular supply of soft food once a day, consisting of scalded meal and refuse meat, boiled and chopped fine. This should be fed in troughs constructed so that the fowls cannot get their feet into them. They should have a daily supply of cabbage leaves, turnip tops or grass. The other feeding may consist of wheat, which will produce more eggs and of better quality than any other kind of grain. The grain, at least some of it, should be scattered about the enclosure, which will give the fowls employment seeking for it. The quantity of food required for each fowl is what each one will consume at a meal without waste.

Eggs.—The production of eggs must be the main object in keeping fowls, to keep up a regular supply of which young hens must be constantly coming forward, the hatching of which produces a large percentage of cocks; and the hens which have passed their prime will furnish a regular supply of birds for fattening for the market.

To fatten Fowls. — Prepare a coop. A box three feet high two feet wide, and four feet long, will hold half-a-dozen good-sized fowls, which should not be more than six months old. The front of the box must be constructed of bars three inches apart; the bottom should be of bars two inches apart. A shelf must be placed outside the front to hold the food boxes and water. Crushed barley, wheat, or oats, with scraps of cooked meat and a little dripping, will be the best food for fattening. A little and often is the best system. The coop must be well sheltered, and the fowls should be kept in partial darkness between the meals. If well attended to, they will be ready for the table in ten or twelve days. A constant supply can be kept up by putting in a pair for every pair killed.

The possible profits from Fowl Raising.—The following particulars of twelve months' work have been furnished by a party residing at Christchurch who keeps a few fowls in a systematic manner :—Commenced September, 1887, with 10 hens and 1 cock, a cross between a pure Dorking and game hens.

	£	s.	d.
Sept. 1—Dec. 31, Food	0	15	0
Jan. 1—July 31 ,, ...	4	2	5
	£4	17	5
Fowls and eggs sold from Jan. 1—July 31	5	12	4
On hand { 26 Pullets, value	2	12	0
7 Roosters	0	14	0
12 Bushels wheat @ 2s. ...	1	4	0
	10	2	4
Less food	4	17	5
	5	4	11
13 Chickens	0	3	0
4lb. Feathers	0	8	0
Profit on eggs, August, say	1	0	0
Eggs on hand	0	5	0
	£7	0	11

" P.S.—I reared 58 chickens and have the old stock still on hand. I may also add that results such as I have achieved are only to be obtained by the utmost attention to the following points :—Scrupulous cleanliness, regularity in feeding, and a supply of pure water and daily exercise in a paddock or grass plot. Fowls will not produce such results if kept constantly in their runs."

A FEW RULES FOR NOVICES GLEANED FROM THE BEST AUTHORS.

If you begin by purchasing eggs for hatching, order them from some reliable breeder in your own locality, and thus save the perils incident to their transportation a long distance.

Before hazarding your (it may be) valuable eggs, be certain that the hen is really broody. You may give her one or two worthless eggs as a trial, or if you are anxious not to lose time divide your setting between two or more hens, and if one prove truant at the end of a few days, give all to another.

By setting several hens at the same time you have the great advantage of being able to put all the chickens, as soon as they are hatched, under one, and of adding new comers to her flock. Eggs sometimes hatch irregularly, and unless some such system were established, the earliest hatched chicken would die of starvation before the whole were brought out.

In selecting eggs for setting choose the freshest, of moderate size, well-shaped, and having the air vessel distinctly marked, either in the centre of the top of the egg or slightly to the side.

Sitting hens brought from a distance should be carried in a basket, covered over with a cloth, never with the head downwards, as is too often seen, at the risk of suffocation, and the certain dissipation of their maternal dreams.

Brahmas and Cochins are excellent sitters, but Dorkings occasionally rebel and refuse to sit, unless in their own way. When they are very reliable, they are excellent mothers. You must be very gentle with them, and try by kindness to induce them to take to the nest selected.

Pullets are less to be trusted as sitters than more mature hens, and (being rather erratic in their dispositions) are not very careful mothers. Artificial incubators are now extensively used, and where there is a command of gas they are easily managed. The natural mother is, however, preferable where only a limited number of fowls are kept, as should some prove faithless, others will be found to take their place.

Always set your hens in the evening, and not in daylight. They will be more sure to stick to the nest; and for two or three days at first be careful that they are undisturbed.

If you can make your nest on the ground, do so; if not, place a fresh-cut grass sod at the bottom of your box, and sprinkle sulphur or coarse snuff into it to keep off vermin.

Scatter powdered sulphur through the hen's underfeathers, also during the period of setting. She must be kept free from lice. This is good for her comfort as well as the chickens.

Remove your hen daily, let her roll in the dust-box near by; feed and water regularly, see that she goes back before the eggs chill, and cover her sitting-box with coarse bagging if she seems half inclined to give up her work.

On the twenty-first day, when the chickens are coming out, leave her to herself until all are released. Then wait twenty-four hours for the little ones to get on their feet. Then clear the nest out nicely.

Apply a little sulphur upon the down and under each wing of the chicks as soon as they emerge from the nest. Keep mother and brood thus free from vermin. Give them food when a day old, and keep them dry and warm.

Commence feeding with soaked bread, crumbs, rice, and hard-boiled eggs. Follow this up for a week, then cooked soft food and broken wheat ; then chopped meat, or scraps, and plenty of green food.

Give the young ones sunshine—all you can command. If cold when hatched, look out for the harsh winds. Give dry shelter till weather is warm, and save them from rain and storms.

The growing fowls should have ample range over the pastures. Fowls will not thrive so well, no matter what attention they may receive, if kept constantly confined in their runs. If you have no grass-plots, let your runs be of a dry gravelly bottom, and give them cabbage leaves, turnip tops, &c., and cooked meat daily with their dry grain food.

Always supply young and old fowls with plenty of fresh clean water. Into this drop a little cayenne pepper tea, a prime tonic, as well as a preventive of gapes in chickens.

To " cure roup," look out that it doesn't get started in your flocks. It is helped by colds, dampness, exposure to rough weather, and neglect. Prevent its presence by constant care, good shelter, and dry, clean hen-houses.

Wash your roosts occasionally with spirits of turpentine or kerosene. This prevents the accumulation of lice in the poultry-houses, and the fumes of this pungent oil permeate the feathers of your fowls at night, and drive the vermin from their bodies.

Permit all your hens so inclined to sit and hatch one brood in the year. It is better for the fowls, and you will thus get just as many eggs from them in twelve months as if you bothered your brains " to break them up."

If you commence with fowls (instead of eggs), buy of reliable men, who know what you want, and who will deal honourably with you. Pay such a man his price—get good stock, of whatever variety it may be, and take care of it after you get it.

Keep but one kind at first, of whatever kind you may fancy. When you can breed that well, try something else if you get tired of this; but don't venture upon too much in the " variety line " at the commencement, or you will fail with all.

Don't attempt to raise five hundred birds within limits fitting the needs of five dozen or less. Crowding fowls into close quarters will breed thousands of lice, but precious few chickens, remember.

Select the best of your progeny for breeds. Sell your patrons what you have to·sell, honestly. If you dispose of eggs, send off fresh ones, and pack them carefully.

DUCKS.

THERÉ are several varieties of ducks, but the two breeds best adapted for general purposes are the Rouen and the Aylesbury. The former is a dark plumaged bird, while the latter is generally pure white. The average weight of these birds should be six pounds for the drakes, and five pounds for the ducks. Rouen ducks are grand table birds : they will thrive with less water to swim in than any of the other breeds. They are fairly good layers, beginning to lay early in Spring, and continuing to do so for a couple or three months. Ducklings hatched out in October, will, if well cared for, commence to lay in March, and lay on till May ; the eggs weigh 3¼ ozs. The Aylesbury Duck is a good layer, and is a better setter than the Rouen ; they have been known to lay 150 eggs in the year, averaging 3 ozs. each.

The Duck-house.—Ducks should never be housed with poultry, but should have a house to themselves. The floor of which should be of brick, in order that it may be frequently washed out. The crowding of ducks in their sleeping department is as objectionable as it is in the case of fowls, being productive of vermin and disease. The duck-house should be washed out at least once a week.

Feed.—Boiled potatoes and turnips mixed with a little barleymeal or pollard is the most suitable food for ducks, together with what they can pick up when liberated, as they should be for a few hours each day.

Sitting Ducks.—The nest should be made on the ground, in a cool retired spot. A dozen eggs will not be too many to place under a large duck. The duck while sitting must be supplied with fresh food twice a day, morning and evening, placed within her reach. Duck eggs may also be set under hens. The ducklings will thrive best on oatmeal porridge for the first eight or ten days, when they may have barley-meal, pollard, and crushed wheat, with a plentiful supply of chopped green food. If well attended to, the young ducks should be ready for the table in about ten weeks. They will thrive without the old duck when a fortnight old, provided they are kept in a warm house at night.

The ordinary farm-yard duck is a nondescript, so far as breeding is concerned. They are; however, excellent layers, good sitters, and make nice plump birds for the table. They require access to water more than either of the above described breeds do.

TURKEYS.

THE Cambridge, the Norfolk and the American are the hardiest breeds. Four hens to one cock are the best proportions. The hens, if well fed, will commence to lay in August, producing from fifteen to twenty eggs. It is a good practice to place the first seven eggs under a Shanghae hen, and to allow the turkey to sit on the balance if she wants to. The turkey hen must be kept perfectly quiet while sitting, as they are timid. October is the best time for setting turkeys. The young birds are very delicate, and require a large amount of attention until they are quite two months old, and must be protected from cold rains during that period; in other respects they require the same attention as ordinary chickens. Hens should not exceed four years old. The cocks should be changed every two years, and should not exceed that age.

Incubators.—This artificial and expeditious method of hatching chickens is only adapted to those who have made fowl farming a business. There are many varieties of incubators, each maker claiming for his particular machine superiority over all others. They are worked by kerosene, gas, or hot water. The successful use of these machines entails unremitting attention, not only while the eggs are being hatched, but during the time the chicks are being reared. Except where fowls are required to be raised on a very large scale, the natural system (the hen) will be found to answer best.

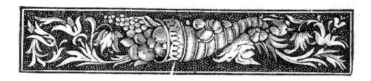

HINTS FOR BEE-KEEPING

(Collected from the best authors.)

BEE-KEEPING should be a profitable investment in New Zealand. We do not know of any country where there are so few drawbacks to bee-keeping. In America, where the industry is largely pursued, the drawbacks are numerous, especially in the northern territories, where the stocks have to be stored away for the Winter and the bees have to be fed. We are not troubled with ants, as in Australia and elsewhere. We have a mild and open Winter, the country abounds with clover and other honey-producing plants. In fact we have all the conditions naturally which have to be provided by artificial means in other countries; so that if bee-keeping pays as it assuredly does in such countries, how much better should it pay in New Zealand?

History informs us that the ancient Egyptians of the Nile had floating bee-houses, designed to take advantage of the honey harvest. They were warned when it was time to return home by the depth to which the boat sank in the water under the weight of the cargo of honey. That the bees might not be lost, they were obliged to journey during the night-time. Bee-houses, instead of single stands, may become popular; but many use inferior structures, which prevent the bees from being properly handled. You must for want of room operate in front of the hives, and thus obstruct the bees and make them irritable and hard to be managed. With the strides bee-culture is making there is a growing desire to house all hives, as it lessens labour and preserves them longer than when kept in the open air. People commencing with small capital must adopt the outdoor system. They cannot indulge in dear hives, much less costly houses, until such times as the sales of honey and bees will furnish needful capital for this necessary outlay. In erecting any form of bee-house we should have good room at the back of all hives to feed, examine and overhaul the apiary. It should be provided with a hinged shutter to allow bees to escape by. The room thus left will hold the necessary appliances when not in use.

Moving Hives.—No branch of bee culture is fraught with so many mishaps as moving bees unwisely. Bees fly for their stores a mile or two, and in times of scarcity three miles may be reckoned as within the limits of their pasturage. After a bee has fixed his locality, he starts out in the morning and never stops to take the points. If you have moved his hive about a yard or so it makes no difference, as he'll soon find it out; but if you have moved it a mile, half a mile, or quarter-mile, all of a sudden, he will never find it out, as he invariably returns for his old locality. On reaching there, and finding his hive gone, he is lost and helpless, and will never find it again. People imagine that they can move their hives anywhere and everywhere, and new hands move their hives together at the approach of Winter that they may better protect them. All goes very well until we have a fine, warm day. Then the bees start out for a fly, and return to their home just as they had been doing all the Summer. They fly about, get into the wrong hives, get stung, the whole apiary becomes mixed up, a general melée ensues, which ends in almost total destruction. Moving hives during the working season will cause a loss of more or less bees as well as honey. Natural swarms will remain where put up, as they depend very much on the surrounding objects in taking their points. Several hives can be moved successfully if we maintain their position in the apiary, and carefully preserve their respective positions with reference to each other. Where the new position is outside the radius of flight —that is, about two miles, they can be moved at any time.

If bees are sent long distances, they must be furnished with old, tough combs, otherwise no combs at all, as newly made combs on foundation are nice to look at, but surely break down in transit, and combs and bees at the end of the journey will be found to consist of one smothered mass of moving insects that survive but a few hours after arrival. Skeps will be found most convenient for sending swarms in. They should be covered over with sacking of coarse, open texture, and carried with mouth upwards.

Adding Supers.—Surplus comb-honey in all its attractive forms occupies a portion of the bee-keeper's fancy. He now finds to his cost that hives without some arrangement for securing pure honey, whether in large glasses placed on the top or in supers consisting of a crate of sections, is quite worthless. He must, therefore, provide some means of supering in advance, otherwise, his bees for want of additional space will swarm off. In placing crates over the frames we must be careful not to crush the bees. Carefully note that the quilt may be turned back, beginning at either end of the frame, but not parallel with them. As soon as we have a few inches of the quilt free, slide on the crate, making sure to turn back the quilt as we slide the crate; thus, when the quilt is removed, the crate or super is in exact position, without a single bee hurt or crushed; but before you are about to perform the operation give the hive a few puffs of smoke. This will prevent their flying about during the operation, which must be as near noonday as possible ; for then the bees will be abroad, foraging in the fields, and you have a less number to deal with than if you went to work at sundown. You can super your hives by placing a new hive over the old one. If you have a hole in the old one, give it a few puffs of smoke and commence a gentle tapping, when all will ascend and work with vigour instead of hanging out idly for weeks. If you have not already a hole in the old skep, make one with a sharp knife. The affair requires to be cased round and made air-tight to conserve the heat. People can super their bees when their hives are full of comb, and bees adhering to both sides of the frames.

Transferring Bees.—The bee-keeper's great friend is smoke, as by its use the bees may at any time be terrified into submission ; and for this purpose we procure an instrument called a smoker, which consists of a miniature bellows, fire box to hold the fuel, and a nozzle through which the smoke issues to terrify the bees by its introduction into their hive. This can be purchased complete for a few shillings, and when filled with pieces of courdroy or carpet it will smoulder without blazing, and thus produce the desired effect. The hive or hives from which the bees are to be driven for the purpose of uniting and transferring, must first of all be given a few puffs of smoke and tapped gently for the space of five minutes ; after which time the hive may be lifted off its floor board, replaced with an empty skep, and carried away about ten perches, inverted in a bucket or small barrel, with an empty hive over it. The two hives are now mouth to mouth, but to make the enclosures more complete and prevent the escape of a single bee, tie a cloth or piece of calico round the junction. Commence tapping the lower or full hive with two sticks ; the bees will be completely confounded, rushing about the combs, eagerly seeking some means of escape, then ascend into the upper or empty hive, making a roaring noise, which aids the operation very much. In about ten minutes the bees will have left their former dwelling and taken possession of the upper hive.

Having proceeded thus far, we carry the hive full of combs into an outhouse with an open window, in order that the few stragglers may have a means of exit. We now place the bees on their former stand, and proceed in like manner until we have gone over the lots to be saved, united, and transferred. Open driving is another method, but as we want to get over the job quickly, close driving is best. Whenever the bees threaten to get angry during the operation, administer a little more smoke. It will quiet without harming them.

Mistakes in Bee-keeping.—P.. C. Dempsey, an experienced Canadian bee-keeper, writes on mistakes in bee-keeping :—

1. It is a mistake to invest very largely in any business that you are not acquainted with. Better to post yourself thoroughly before commencing.

2. It is a mistake to invest in bees that are in a box or old log hives.

3. It is a mistake to reject a good moveable frame-hive because it costs a little more cash.

4. It is a mistake to take them direct from their Winter quarters and remove them long distances.

5. It is a mistake not to let them have an excursion on the wing before moving to another place.

6. It is a mistake not to examine them immediately, and ascertain if the supply of rations is about exhausted, and, if so, to supply them at once with honey or a substitute.

7. It is a mistake, if there is no brood found in the hive, not to unite them with another that is weak, but having brood, if a queen cannot be produced.

8. It is a mistake not to have your colonies strong at all seasons of the year.

9. It is a mistake to use up all the pots, kettles, pans, spoons, stove hooks, and other things, upon which to play the dead march when a swarm has started on an excursion to the groves.

10. It is a mistake to neglect to put on supers early enough in the Spring, if comb honey is required. The bees sometimes fill the cells with honey that is required for breeding purposes.

11. It is a mistake not to use foundation comb. By its use we can always depend upon straight combs and greater convenience for handling.

12 It is a mistake to neglect to remove all full boxes or sections as soon as properly sealed. Bees sometimes soil them by travelling over with dirty feet.

13. It is a mistake not to supply an abundance of space for them to store their surplus when honey is plentiful. Bees often remain idle for want of space to store their treasure.

14. It is a mistake to extract or take honey from the bees too late in the season without supplying them with more. It looks cruel to rob and then leave them to starve.

15. It is a mistake not to examine all the colonies early in March. Those that are queenless should be supplied at once, and those that have not honey enough to carry them through the Winter should be fed without delay.

15. It is a mistake to put off feeding until the nights become cold. Better to be done too early than too late. In New Zealand bees rarely require feeding.

17. It is a mistake to visit the bees too often during the Winter. It is apt to disturb them ; they become restless, and sometimes discharge their fæces, and by this means produce a stench that is enough to destroy them. Better have their Winter quarters so constructed that we can ascertain their condition without disturbing them.

Things to Know.—Every beginner at bee-keeping should know and remember :—

1. That the life of a worker bee during the working season is only from six to eight weeks duration, and that a majority of them never live to see seven weeks.

2. That a worker is from five to six days old before it comes out of the hive for the first time to take an airing ; and that it is from fourteen to sixteen days old before it begins to gather either pollen or honey.

3. That all swarms engaged in building comb, when they have not a fertile queen, build only drone comb, and that all the comb in the lower or breeding apartment should be worker or brood comb, except a very small quantity of drone comb, four inches square being amply sufficient.

4. That the more prolific the queen is the more young bees you have, and the more surplus honey will be gathered, other things being equal.

5. That you ought never to cut mouldy combs out of the hives, for the reason that you should never allow it to become mouldy.

6. That you ought never to double swarms or stocks of bees in the Autumn, because you ought to attend to that and make them strong during the Summer, by taking brood from the strong stock and giving it to the weaker.

Bee Veil.—If you are afraid of bees, you must use a veil, made as follows :—A piece of mosquito netting a yard and one-quarter by three-quarters or five-eighths of a yard, should be sewn together, with an elastic on one end to be adjusted over the hat crown. At a suitable distance from the bottom attach a narrow tape to tie about the neck.

Diseases and Pests of Bees.—Of all the diseases which attack bees Foul-brood is, perhaps, the most destructive. It is, unfortunately, rather prevalent in some parts of the colony. For a long time it baffled bee-keepers, who were at a loss to detect its real character, until the researches of modern German investigators determined it to be the result of fungoid growth, propagated by means of the spores, or seed-vessels.

Indication of Foul-brood.—The disease only affects the immature brood before it reaches the chrysalis state. The cappings of the infected cells are found to be somewhat sunken, with a small hole in the centre. By examining the brood cells it will be easy to ascertain if any of the larvæ be dead and putrid. Healthy larvæ are always white, until sometime after they assume the chrysalis form ; hence, if they are dark coloured, it indicates something wrong. Where the malady has made much headway, the unpleasant odour is simple evidence of its presence.

Foul-brood was much more prevalent in America a few years ago than it is now. The cause assigned for this is that the disease itself falls a prey to other parasites; perhaps one of the many which are known to infest hives.

Remedy for Foul-brood.—It is said that salicylic acid, dissolved in alcohol, or in a solution of borax in water —one hundred and twenty grains of salicylic acid, the same of soda borax, and sixteen ounces of distilled water. This fluid is thrown in a fine spray over the combs, the brood being previously uncapped. This is said to be harmless to the bees, but fatal to the fungi. The bees should be driven into an empty hive box and kept for twenty-four hours in a dark place, till they have consumed all the honey they had with them ; as there is no doubt but that honey from an infected hive will carry the contagion to a new stock of brood. Some authors advocate cutting out the combs having diseased brood and burying it, and making wax of the remainder; and if honey remain, it may be rendered harmless and fit for feeding purposes by boiling and skimming. The bees, after their long fast, are put into hives filled with healthy combs and foundation. The infected hive may then be cleaned by scalding with boiling water.

Mice and Ants.—Mice can easily be kept out of the hive by making the entrance in the form of a long slit, but too small for mice to enter. It is not so easy to cope with ants and other small pests. This may best be done by hanging the hive stands from the roof of a shed. We have seen this plan answer admirably in Australia. In New Zealand we are not troubled with ants; little care being taken of the hives except, perhaps, by throwing an old sack over them during Winter.

Whitcombe & Tombs Limited, Stationers and Printers, Christchurch.   9651

Thos. TURNER

IMPORTER OF

VEGETABLE, FLOWER AND FARM SEEDS

Horticultural Sundries, &c.

159, Colombo Street, CHRISTCHURCH

A CHOICE ASSORTMENT OF FLOWERING BULBS IN THE AUTUMN.

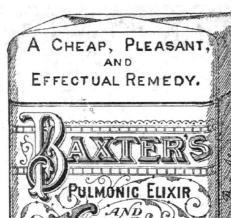